How Dating Apps Destroy Dating

The Challenge of Finding a Partner

A.A. CASTOR

Table of Contents

How Dating Apps Destroy Dating - The Challenge of Finding a Partner

A.A. Castor

A.A. Castor

Dedication

To my beloved family,

Your unconditional love, unwavering support, and endless encouragement have been my greatest blessings. From the earliest days of dreaming to the challenging moments of writing, you have stood by me with patience and belief. This book is as much yours as it is mine, a reflection of the values you've instilled and the faith you've shown in me. Thank you for being my rock and my inspiration.

To my dear friends,

Your friendship has illuminated my path with laughter, shared moments, and invaluable support. You've cheered me on through every triumph and lifted me up through every challenge. Your belief in my endeavors has been a source of strength and motivation. This book is a testament to the power of friendship, and I am grateful for each of you who has walked this journey by my side.

To God,

Your grace and guidance have been my constant companions. In moments of doubt, you've shown me the way; in moments of joy, you've multiplied my gratitude. This book is a testament to your faithfulness and the blessings you've bestowed upon me. May it serve as a reflection of your love and the lessons you continue to teach me.

With heartfelt gratitude and love,

A.A. Castor

Why I Am Writing This Book

In today's fast-paced digital age, the landscape of dating and relationships has undergone a profound transformation. Dating apps, once a novel concept, have become an integral part of how we seek and form romantic connections. While these platforms offer unprecedented convenience and access to potential partners, they also introduce a myriad of challenges and complexities that can undermine the depth and authenticity of our relationships.

Motivation and Inspiration:

I embarked on this writing journey to delve deeply into the intricate dynamics of modern dating. As a keen observer of societal trends and a passionate advocate for meaningful relationships, I have witnessed firsthand the profound impact of dating apps on individuals and society at large. Conversations with friends, personal experiences, and extensive research have revealed a common thread: the promise of connection offered by dating apps often comes with unintended consequences that can disrupt the very essence of human connection.

Addressing the Challenges:

This book aims to shed light on the multifaceted effects of dating apps, from psychological impacts to shifts in societal norms. By exploring these themes, I hope to provide readers with a comprehensive understanding of the benefits and pitfalls of digital dating. It's essential to recognize that while dating apps have their advantages, they also pose significant challenges that can hinder the development of genuine, lasting relationships.

Encouraging a Balanced Perspective:

One of my primary goals in writing this book is to encourage a balanced perspective on dating apps. Rather than adopting a wholly negative or overly optimistic stance, I strive to present a nuanced view that acknowledges both the opportunities and the challenges inherent in digital dating. By doing so, I aim to equip readers with the insights and strategies needed to navigate this complex landscape effectively.

Fostering Meaningful Connections:

At its core, this book is about fostering meaningful connections in an increasingly digital world. It is a call to action for individuals to approach dating with mindfulness, intentionality, and a commitment to authenticity. Whether you are a seasoned app user, a skeptic of digital dating, or someone seeking deeper connections, this book offers valuable perspectives and practical advice to enhance your dating experience.

A Personal Journey:

Writing this book has also been a personal journey of reflection and growth. It has allowed me to explore my own beliefs and experiences regarding love and relationships. Through this process, I have come to appreciate the enduring value of traditional dating methods and the importance of balancing digital interactions with real-life connections.

Conclusion:

Ultimately, I am writing this book to empower readers to navigate the digital dating landscape with confidence and clarity. By understanding the broader implications of dating apps and embracing a more mindful approach to dating, we can create a more fulfilling and authentic path to finding love. This book is a guide, a reflection, and an invitation to rethink how we connect in the modern world, with the hope that it will inspire readers to cultivate deeper, more meaningful relationships.

Warning and Disclaimer

Purpose of the Book:

The purpose of this book is to provide an in-depth exploration of the impact of dating apps on modern relationships. The discussions, analyses, and opinions presented herein are based on extensive research, personal observations, and anecdotal evidence. This book is intended to offer insights, provoke thought, and foster a deeper understanding of the dynamics of digital dating. It is not a definitive guide or a substitute for professional advice.

General Information Only:

The content of this book is for general informational purposes only. While efforts have been made to ensure the accuracy and reliability of the information provided, the author makes no representations or warranties of any kind, express or implied, about the completeness, accuracy, reliability, suitability, or availability of the information contained herein. Any reliance you place on such information is strictly at your own risk.

Not a Substitute for Professional Advice:

This book is not intended to replace or substitute for professional advice, whether psychological, medical, legal, or otherwise. Readers are encouraged to seek the guidance of qualified professionals regarding any concerns or issues related to their mental health, relationships, or personal well-being. The author does not assume any liability for any loss or damage incurred as a result of the use of information provided in this book.

Subjective Opinions:

The views and opinions expressed in this book are those of the author and do not necessarily reflect the official policy or position of any other individual, organization, or institution. The author acknowledges that dating experiences are highly subjective and that individual experiences with dating apps may vary widely.

Cultural Sensitivity:

Discussions in this book may touch upon cultural and societal norms related to dating and relationships. The author respects all cultural perspectives and does not intend to offend or marginalize any group. Readers are encouraged to consider cultural context and personal values when reflecting on the content of this book.

Evolving Nature of Technology:

The digital dating landscape is continually evolving. As such, the information and perspectives provided in this book may become outdated as new technologies and trends emerge. Readers are advised to stay informed about current developments in the field of digital dating and to approach new technologies with critical thinking and caution.

Personal Responsibility:

Readers are encouraged to exercise personal responsibility and judgment when using dating apps or engaging in online interactions. The author does not assume any responsibility for the actions or behaviors of individuals encountered through dating apps or other digital platforms.

Final Note:

This book is intended to spark meaningful conversations and encourage thoughtful consideration of the complex nature of modern dating. It is the hope of the author that readers will find value in the insights presented and will use this information to enhance their personal understanding and experiences in the realm of dating and relationships.

Thank you for reading, and may your journey towards meaningful connections be both fulfilling and enriching.

Thank you for your understanding.

Mr. A.A. Castor

About the Author

A.A. Castor

A.A. Castor is a dedicated writer and social commentator with a keen interest in exploring the intricate dynamics of human relationships in the modern world. With a background in sociology and psychology, Castor brings a unique blend of academic insight and real-world observation to the discussion of dating and relationships.

Professional Background:

Castor holds a degree in Sociology with a specialization in Human Relationships and Communication from a prestigious university. This academic foundation has equipped Castor with a deep understanding of the social constructs and psychological factors that influence human behavior and interactions. Throughout a diverse career, Castor has worked in various roles, including relationship counseling, social research, and freelance writing, all of which have enriched the perspectives shared in this book.

Writing Career:

As an author, A.A. Castor has written extensively on topics related to relationships, dating, and social trends. Castor's work often delves into the impact of technology on personal connections, offering a critical yet balanced viewpoint. The writing style is characterized by clarity, thoughtfulness, and a commitment to uncovering the truths that lie beneath the surface of contemporary social practices.

Personal Journey:

The inspiration for "How Dating Apps Destroy Dating - The Challenge of Finding a Partner" stems from Castor's personal observations and experiences in the dating world. Witnessing the profound changes brought about by digital platforms, Castor felt compelled to investigate and document these shifts, aiming to provide readers with a comprehensive understanding of the modern dating landscape.

Philosophy and Beliefs:

Castor is a firm believer in the value of traditional relationship principles while remaining open to the possibilities that modern innovations can bring. Acknowledging the benefits and drawbacks of both perspectives, Castor advocates for a balanced approach to dating and relationships, one that honors authenticity, mutual respect, and meaningful connection.

Commitment to Readers:

In writing this book, A.A. Castor aims to offer readers a thoughtful and engaging exploration of dating apps and their impact on finding a partner. The goal is to equip readers with the knowledge and insights needed to navigate the complexities of modern dating with confidence and clarity.

Personal Interests:

Outside of writing, A.A. Castor enjoys exploring diverse cultures, engaging in outdoor activities, and participating in community events. These interests not only enrich Castor's life but also provide a broader perspective that informs the writing and themes presented in this book.

Connect with the Author:

Readers are encouraged to connect with A.A. Castor through social media and the author's website, where they can find additional resources, articles, and updates on future projects. Castor values feedback and looks forward to engaging with readers to continue the conversation about dating, relationships, and the ever-evolving social landscape.

Closing Note:

A.A. Castor hopes that "How Dating Apps Destroy Dating - The Challenge of Finding a Partner" will inspire readers to reflect on their own dating experiences, consider alternative approaches, and ultimately find fulfilling and authentic connections in their personal lives.

Purpose of the Book: Introducing the Impact of Dating Apps on Modern Dating Culture

The purpose of this book, **"How Dating Apps Destroy Dating: The Challenge of Finding a Partner,"** is to critically examine the profound impact that dating apps have had on contemporary dating practices and relationships. Dating apps, ubiquitous in today's digital landscape, promise convenience, accessibility, and a seemingly endless array of potential partners. However, beneath this facade of connectivity lies a complex web of implications that reshape how individuals perceive, engage in, and sustain relationships.

Introduction to the Topic

In the introductory chapters, the book sets the stage by defining dating apps and tracing their evolution from niche platforms to global phenomena. It highlights how these apps have fundamentally altered the landscape of modern romance, influencing societal norms, expectations, and personal interactions. The introduction aims to provoke thought and reflection on how digital technologies have redefined the pursuit of romantic connection.

Exploring the Impact

The book delves into the multifaceted impacts of dating apps on contemporary dating culture. It examines both the positive and negative aspects, starting with the initial allure of enhanced accessibility and efficiency in meeting potential partners. It then transitions into a critical analysis of the superficiality, shallowness, and commodification of relationships facilitated by these platforms.

Unpacking Societal and Psychological Implications

Beyond surface-level interactions, the book explores deeper societal implications, such as the casualization of relationships, changes in communication dynamics, and the erosion of traditional relationship values. It also delves into the psychological toll on users, including heightened anxiety, decreased self-esteem, and the paradoxical increase in loneliness despite digital connectivity.

Challenging Assumptions and Exploring Alternatives

Throughout its exploration, the book challenges assumptions about the efficacy and sustainability of dating apps in fostering genuine connections. It advocates for a nuanced understanding of how these platforms influence personal agency, identity formation, and the pursuit of long-term compatibility.

Setting the Stage for Reflection and Action

By the conclusion, the book aims to prompt readers to reflect on their own experiences with dating apps and to consider the broader societal implications. It offers insights into navigating the complexities of modern dating while advocating for mindful technology use and a balanced approach to seeking meaningful connections.

In essence, **"How Dating Apps Destroy Dating: The Challenge of Finding a Partner"** serves as a critical examination of the digital age's impact on romance, aiming to foster deeper understanding and provoke dialogue on the evolving nature of relationships in an increasingly digital world.

Scope and Objectives

Introduction

In recent years, dating apps have fundamentally altered the landscape of modern romance. What began as a convenient tool for meeting potential partners has evolved into a cultural phenomenon with far-reaching implications. From Tinder to Bumble, Grindr to Hinge, these platforms promise a digital gateway to love, offering unprecedented access to a vast pool of potential matches at the swipe of a finger. Yet, beneath their glossy interfaces lie complex dynamics that reshape how we initiate, cultivate, and experience relationships.

Key Themes Explored

1. **Impact on Dating Dynamics:**

  ○ Dating apps have revolutionized how individuals connect, shifting the focus from traditional face-to-face interactions to digital engagements mediated by algorithms. This transformation raises questions about the authenticity and depth of modern relationships.

2. **Psychological and Emotional Effects:**

  ○ The ubiquitous nature of dating apps introduces new psychological challenges, such as anxiety over presentation, fear of rejection, and the psychological impact of constant validation-seeking behavior.

3. **Societal Implications:**

  ○ Beyond individual experiences, dating apps influence broader societal norms and values regarding relationships, intimacy, and gender dynamics. They reflect and amplify cultural shifts while challenging established social constructs.

4. **Ethical Considerations:**

  ○ As dating platforms amass vast amounts of user data, ethical concerns arise regarding privacy, security, and the responsible use of personal information. Questions about algorithmic biases and the monetization of user data prompt discussions on transparency and accountability.

5. **Alternative Perspectives:**

  ○ While dating apps dominate the dating landscape, alternative approaches like traditional matchmaking, social clubs, and meet-up groups offer contrasting paradigms. Exploring these alternatives illuminates diverse paths to meaningful connections beyond digital interfaces.

Key Questions and Discussions

- **How have dating apps reshaped the process of finding and forming relationships?**
- **What are the psychological implications of digital dating on individuals, and how can these be mitigated?**
- **In what ways do dating apps reflect and influence societal attitudes towards relationships and intimacy?**
- **What ethical responsibilities do dating app developers bear in safeguarding user privacy and fostering healthy digital interactions?**
- **What are the advantages and disadvantages of traditional and modern alternatives to dating apps?**

Objectives

The book aims to:

● **Educate and Inform:** By providing a comprehensive analysis of dating apps, it seeks to empower readers with a deeper understanding of their impact on contemporary dating culture.

● **Prompt Critical Reflection:** Through thought-provoking discussions, it encourages readers to critically examine the role of technology in their dating lives and societal interactions.

● **Offer Practical Insights:** Practical strategies and insights are provided for navigating digital dating environments with mindfulness and responsibility.

● **Stimulate Dialogue:** The book aims to stimulate constructive dialogue on the future of dating in an increasingly digital world, addressing ethical concerns, privacy issues, and emotional well-being.

Conclusion

"**How Dating Apps Destroy Dating: The Challenge of Finding a Partner**" endeavors to uncover the complexities behind the swipe culture and digital dating phenomena. By exploring its psychological, societal, and ethical dimensions, the book seeks to foster a deeper understanding of how technology shapes modern relationships and to guide readers towards more fulfilling and authentic connections in an evolving digital landscape.

Chapter 1: The Rise of Dating Apps

History and Evolution

The journey of dating apps can be traced back to the early days of online dating services in the 1990s. These initial platforms, such as Match.com (founded in 1995) and eHarmony (founded in 2000), aimed to connect individuals through detailed profiles and personality matching. These services laid the groundwork for the digital dating landscape by creating structured environments for people to meet potential partners.

As technology advanced, so did the concept of online dating. The early 2000s saw a proliferation of niche dating sites catering to specific interests and demographics. However, the true revolution in dating came with the advent of smartphones and the launch of Tinder in 2012. Tinder's swipe-based interface, which allowed users to quickly browse through profiles and make instant decisions, revolutionized the dating scene by making it more accessible and immediate.

Following Tinder's success, numerous other dating apps emerged, each offering unique features and targeting various audiences. Apps like Bumble, where women make the first move, and Hinge, which focuses on fostering meaningful connections, diversified the market. The evolution of dating apps reflects a shift towards convenience and immediacy, with technology increasingly mediating human connections.

Popularity and Appeal: The popularity and appeal of dating apps can be attributed to several key factors:

1. **Convenience and Accessibility:** Dating apps provide an easy and convenient way for people to meet potential partners. The ability to browse through profiles and chat with matches from the comfort of one's home or on the go has made dating more accessible than ever before.
2. **Efficiency:** The swipe-based interfaces of many dating apps allow users to quickly filter through a large number of potential matches. This efficiency appeals to those with busy lifestyles who may not have the time for traditional dating methods.
3. **Broad Reach:** Dating apps open up a wider pool of potential partners beyond one's immediate social circle. This expanded reach increases the chances of finding a compatible match.
4. **Personalization:** Many dating apps use algorithms to match users based on their preferences, interests, and behaviors. This personalized approach makes users feel more confident that they will find someone who meets their criteria.
5. **Social Acceptance:** The stigma associated with online dating has significantly decreased over the years. Today, using dating apps is widely accepted and even encouraged as a legitimate way to meet potential partners.
6. **Cultural Shifts:** Modern values and societal changes have also played a role in the rise of dating apps. As traditional dating rituals evolve, people are more open to exploring new ways of meeting partners.

While dating apps offer numerous benefits, it's essential to recognize that they also come with drawbacks. Critics argue that the superficial nature of swipe-based apps fosters a culture of disposability and instant gratification, undermining the potential for deep, meaningful connections. Additionally, the commodification of dating can lead to unrealistic expectations and a focus on quantity over quality in relationships.

The rise of dating apps reflects broader societal trends towards digitalization and instant access. While they have transformed the dating landscape, it's crucial to approach them with a critical eye, understanding both their potential benefits and inherent limitations.

Convenience and Accessibility

Dating Apps: A New Era of Accessibility

The convenience and accessibility of dating apps have revolutionized how people meet and form romantic connections. Here's a detailed look at how these platforms have transformed dating:

1. Ease of Use: Dating apps are designed with user-friendly interfaces that make it simple for individuals to create profiles, browse potential matches, and initiate conversations. This ease of use has lowered the barrier to entry, allowing even those who are less tech-savvy to engage with online dating. Traditional dating methods, like going to social events or relying on introductions from friends, can be time-consuming and stressful. Dating apps streamline this process, allowing users to connect with others quickly and efficiently.

2. Immediate Access: One of the most significant advantages of dating apps is their accessibility. Users can access dating platforms anytime and anywhere through their smartphones. Whether on a lunch break, commuting, or relaxing at home, individuals can browse profiles and communicate with potential matches at their convenience. This level of accessibility is unparalleled compared to traditional dating, which often requires coordinating schedules and attending events to meet new people.

3. Expanded Reach: Dating apps break down geographical barriers, enabling users to connect with individuals they might never encounter in their daily lives. This expanded reach increases the chances of finding a compatible partner by exposing users to a diverse pool of potential matches. For people living in rural or less populated areas, dating apps provide an invaluable opportunity to connect with others beyond their immediate vicinity.

4. Time Efficiency: The structured environment of dating apps saves users time by allowing them to filter potential matches based on specific criteria such as age, interests, and values. This targeted approach reduces the time spent on unproductive interactions, making the dating process more efficient. Unlike traditional dating, where finding a suitable partner can be a lengthy and uncertain process, dating apps provide a streamlined and goal-oriented experience.

5. Safety and Control: Dating apps offer features that enhance user safety and control over their dating experience. Users can choose to share personal information at their discretion, and many apps include privacy settings and reporting mechanisms to protect against harassment or inappropriate behavior. This level of control is often lacking in traditional dating scenarios, where individuals might feel pressured to share personal details or meet in uncomfortable settings.

6. Enhanced Communication: Dating apps facilitate communication through in-app messaging systems, allowing users to get to know each other before meeting in person. This initial online interaction helps individuals gauge compatibility and build a rapport, potentially leading to more successful and enjoyable first dates. The ability to communicate and establish a connection beforehand can also alleviate some of the anxiety associated with meeting new people in traditional dating contexts.

7. Inclusivity: Dating apps cater to a wide range of preferences and orientations, providing platforms for various demographics, including LGBTQ+ communities, seniors, and people with specific interests or cultural backgrounds. This inclusivity ensures that everyone has the opportunity to find a partner who shares their values and interests. Traditional dating methods often lack this level of inclusivity, making it challenging for individuals from diverse backgrounds to find compatible partners.

Challenges and Criticisms

While the convenience and accessibility of dating apps offer numerous benefits, there are also challenges and criticisms to consider:

- **Superficiality:** The swipe-based nature of many dating apps can lead to a focus on physical appearance rather than deeper qualities, fostering a culture of superficiality.
- **Paradox of Choice:** The abundance of options can sometimes lead to decision fatigue, where users feel overwhelmed by the number of potential matches and struggle to make meaningful connections.
- **Dependency on Technology:** Over-reliance on dating apps can diminish face-to-face social skills and reduce opportunities for organic, spontaneous interactions.

Conclusion

The convenience and accessibility of dating apps have made dating more manageable and less intimidating for many people. By offering immediate access, expanded reach, and enhanced communication, these platforms have transformed how individuals approach finding romantic partners. However, it is essential to be mindful of the potential downsides and strive to balance online interactions with real-world connections for a fulfilling dating experience.

Efficiency: The Impact of Swipe-Based Interfaces

Efficiency in Dating Apps

Dating apps have revolutionized the dating landscape with their swipe-based interfaces, offering users unprecedented efficiency in finding potential partners. Here's an in-depth exploration of how this functionality has reshaped modern dating:

1. Rapid Decision-Making: Swipe-based interfaces, popularized by apps like Tinder, enable users to make quick decisions about potential matches by swiping right to like or left to pass. This intuitive process condenses the initial stages of dating into a matter of seconds, allowing individuals to assess numerous profiles efficiently. This rapid decision-making is particularly appealing to busy professionals and individuals with demanding schedules who may not have the time for prolonged browsing or traditional dating methods.

2. Filtered Matchmaking: Dating apps use algorithms to present users with matches based on specified criteria such as location, age, interests, and preferences. This targeted matchmaking streamlines the search for compatible partners, reducing the uncertainty and guesswork associated with traditional dating. By filtering potential matches through predefined parameters, users can focus their attention on individuals who align with their preferences, increasing the likelihood of meaningful connections.

3. Time Optimization: Efficiency in dating apps translates into time optimization for users. Instead of investing time and energy in offline activities like attending social events or blind dates, individuals can engage with dating platforms during idle moments throughout the day. Whether commuting, waiting in line, or taking a break at work, users can efficiently browse profiles and engage in conversations, maximizing their dating prospects without disrupting their daily routines.

4. Accessibility and Availability: The accessibility of swipe-based dating interfaces extends beyond geographical limitations, allowing users to connect with potential matches globally. This broad reach expands the pool of available partners, offering individuals a diverse selection of profiles to explore. For users residing in remote or less populated areas, dating apps provide unparalleled access to a wider network of singles, overcoming traditional barriers to meeting new people.

5. Feedback Mechanisms: Dating apps incorporate feedback mechanisms such as mutual matches and messaging features that facilitate communication between interested parties. This interactive approach fosters engagement and encourages users to initiate conversations based on mutual interest. By receiving immediate feedback on their profile and interactions, individuals can adjust their approach and preferences to enhance their dating experience, contributing to overall efficiency in finding compatible partners.

Challenges and Considerations:

While swipe-based interfaces enhance efficiency in the dating process, they are not without challenges:

- **Superficiality:** The emphasis on rapid decision-making and visual impressions can prioritize superficial attributes over deeper compatibility factors.
- **Limited Information:** Profiles on dating apps may provide limited information about individuals' personalities, values, and intentions, potentially leading to miscommunication or misunderstandings.
- **Algorithm Dependency:** Users may become overly reliant on algorithms to make dating decisions, overlooking potential matches who do not fit within predefined criteria.

Conclusion

The efficiency of swipe-based interfaces in dating apps has redefined how individuals approach finding romantic partners, offering a streamlined and accessible platform for connecting with others. By simplifying the matchmaking process and optimizing time management, these interfaces cater to the needs of busy lifestyles while broadening the scope of dating possibilities. However, it is essential for users to balance efficiency with mindfulness, ensuring that they prioritize genuine connections and meaningful interactions in their quest for romance.

Broad Reach: Expanding Horizons in Dating Apps

Dating Apps: Breaking Social Boundaries

Dating apps have significantly expanded the reach of individuals seeking romantic connections by transcending geographical and social barriers. Here's a detailed exploration of how these platforms enhance the diversity and potential for finding compatible partners:

1. Geographical Accessibility: Dating apps eliminate the limitations of traditional dating by connecting users with potential matches regardless of their geographical location. Whether individuals reside in urban centers, rural areas, or even different countries, these platforms facilitate interactions that would otherwise be unlikely through conventional means. This geographical accessibility broadens the pool of available partners, increasing the likelihood of finding someone who shares similar interests, values, and goals.

2. Diverse User Base: The user base of dating apps encompasses a diverse range of demographics, including age groups, cultural backgrounds, professions, and interests. This diversity enriches the dating experience by exposing users to individuals with varied perspectives and lifestyles. Unlike traditional social circles that may be limited in scope, dating apps offer a melting pot of potential matches, enabling users to explore connections beyond their immediate social environment.

3. Niche Communities and Interests: Many dating apps cater to specific interests, lifestyles, or communities, further enhancing their appeal and effectiveness in connecting like-minded individuals. Whether users are seeking partners who share niche hobbies, cultural values, or professional backgrounds, these platforms provide tailored matchmaking services that align with specific preferences. This specialization fosters deeper connections based on mutual interests and compatibility, facilitating meaningful relationships that may not have flourished through traditional social networks.

4. Cross-Cultural Exchanges: Dating apps facilitate cross-cultural exchanges by enabling users to interact with individuals from different cultural and ethnic backgrounds. This cultural diversity enriches the dating experience by promoting intercultural understanding, appreciation, and learning. It allows users to broaden their perspectives, challenge stereotypes, and explore relationships beyond familiar cultural boundaries, fostering a more inclusive and globalized approach to dating.

5. Enhanced Compatibility: The expanded reach of dating apps increases the chances of finding compatible matches by presenting users with a diverse array of profiles that align with their preferences and relationship goals. By broadening the scope of potential partners, these platforms facilitate meaningful connections based on shared values, interests, and aspirations. Users have the opportunity to explore relationships with individuals who possess qualities and attributes that complement their own, thereby enhancing the likelihood of long-term compatibility and relationship satisfaction.

Challenges and Considerations:

While dating apps offer broad reach and diverse opportunities, there are considerations to keep in mind:

- **Communication Barriers:** Interacting with individuals from different cultural backgrounds or languages may present challenges in communication and understanding.
- **Cultural Sensitivity:** Respecting and navigating cultural differences is crucial to building respectful and harmonious relationships.
- **Authenticity:** Users should be mindful of presenting themselves authentically and transparently to foster genuine connections, regardless of geographical or cultural differences.

Conclusion

Dating apps revolutionize the dating landscape by expanding the reach of potential partners beyond traditional social circles and geographical boundaries. By embracing diversity, niche interests, and cross-cultural interactions, these platforms empower individuals to explore meaningful connections that transcend conventional limitations. However, maintaining open-mindedness, cultural sensitivity, and authenticity is essential in leveraging the broad reach of dating apps to foster genuine and fulfilling relationships.

Personalization in Dating Apps: Tailoring Matches to Individual Preferences

Customized Matching: Enhancing User Experience

Dating apps employ sophisticated algorithms to personalize the matchmaking process, aligning potential matches with users' specific preferences, interests, and behaviors. Here's a detailed exploration of how this personalized approach enhances user confidence and satisfaction:

1. Algorithmic Precision: Dating apps utilize algorithms that analyze users' profiles, preferences, and interaction patterns to generate tailored match suggestions. These algorithms consider factors such as age, location, hobbies, lifestyle choices, and relationship goals to identify potential partners who align closely with each user's criteria. By leveraging data-driven insights, dating apps optimize the likelihood of meaningful connections based on shared interests and compatibility indicators.

2. Enhanced User Confidence: The personalized matchmaking offered by dating apps enhances user confidence in the platform's ability to facilitate successful matches. Users feel reassured knowing that their preferences are considered in the selection process, increasing their trust and engagement with the app. This confidence encourages active participation in exploring potential matches and initiating conversations, fostering a proactive approach to finding compatible partners.

3. Tailored Recommendations: Dating apps provide users with personalized recommendations and notifications based on their activity and preferences. These proactive features keep users informed about new matches, mutual interests, and potential conversation starters, facilitating seamless engagement and interaction. By delivering relevant and timely updates, dating apps enhance user satisfaction and retention, ensuring a personalized and responsive user experience.

4. Adaptive Learning: Some dating apps incorporate machine learning and adaptive technologies that continuously refine their algorithms based on user feedback and behavior. This adaptive learning process enhances the accuracy of match suggestions over time, adapting to evolving preferences and relationship dynamics. By learning from user interactions and outcomes, dating apps optimize their matchmaking capabilities to better meet the diverse needs and expectations of their user base.

5. Transparency and Control: While algorithms drive personalized matchmaking, dating apps prioritize transparency and user control over their dating experience. Users have the flexibility to adjust their preferences, refine search criteria, and filter match suggestions based on specific attributes or characteristics. This level of customization empowers users to actively shape their dating journey and prioritize qualities that are most important to them in a potential partner.

Challenges and Considerations:

Despite the benefits of personalized matchmaking, there are considerations to bear in mind:

- **Overreliance on Algorithms:** Users should balance algorithmic recommendations with personal judgment and intuition to ensure compatibility beyond surface-level criteria.
- **Privacy Concerns:** Data privacy and security are critical considerations in the use of algorithms, requiring robust measures to protect users' personal information and preferences.
- **Human Element:** While algorithms optimize match suggestions, genuine connections often rely on emotional resonance, shared values, and interpersonal chemistry that may not be fully captured by data-driven algorithms alone.

Conclusion

Personalization in dating apps enhances the user experience by tailoring match suggestions to individual preferences, interests, and behaviors. By leveraging algorithms to optimize compatibility and user engagement, dating apps empower individuals to navigate the complexities of modern dating with confidence and efficiency. However, maintaining a balanced approach that values both algorithmic precision and authentic human connection is essential in fostering meaningful relationships and sustainable dating experiences.

Social Acceptance of Dating Apps: Shifting Perceptions and Cultural Norms

Changing Attitudes Towards Online Dating

Dating apps have witnessed a remarkable shift in social acceptance, evolving from a stigmatized practice to a widely embraced method for meeting potential partners. Here's an in-depth exploration of how perceptions have changed over time and why using dating apps is now considered a legitimate and acceptable approach:

1. Evolution of Cultural Norms: The stigma surrounding online dating can be traced back to its early days when it was perceived as unconventional and reserved for individuals who couldn't find partners through traditional means. However, as digital technology became more integrated into everyday life, attitudes towards online interactions evolved. Dating apps gained popularity among a diverse demographic, ranging from young adults to professionals and older adults seeking companionship.

2. Accessibility and Convenience: The widespread adoption of smartphones and the internet facilitated easier access to dating apps, making them accessible to a broader audience. This increased accessibility contributed to normalization as more people embraced the convenience of finding potential partners from the comfort of their homes or on the go. The ability to browse profiles, initiate conversations, and arrange dates through a few taps on a screen became not only accepted but also preferred by many individuals with busy lifestyles.

3. Success Stories and Positive Experiences: As more people found meaningful relationships and even marriages through dating apps, success stories became common anecdotes, challenging previous negative stereotypes. These success stories highlighted the efficacy of dating apps in fostering genuine connections and validating their role in modern relationship formation. Positive user experiences shared through social media and word of mouth further contributed to shifting perceptions towards acceptance and encouragement.

4. Cultural and Generational Shifts: Cultural shifts towards individualism, digital communication, and acceptance of diverse lifestyles have influenced attitudes towards dating apps. Younger generations, in particular, view technology as an integral part of social interaction and relationship building. The normalization of online platforms for various social activities, including dating, reflects broader societal changes where digital connectivity is valued as a legitimate means of expanding social circles and meeting romantic partners.

5. Media and Celebrity Endorsements: Public endorsements from celebrities, influencers, and media outlets have also contributed to the mainstream acceptance of dating apps. High-profile individuals openly discussing their use of dating apps and sharing positive experiences have helped normalize the practice and reduce any lingering stigma. These endorsements have portrayed dating apps as modern tools for relationship-seeking individuals rather than alternatives of last resort.

6. Research and Academic Validation: Research studies and academic publications have explored the efficacy and impact of dating apps on relationship formation and social interaction. Findings that highlight the positive outcomes and psychological benefits of using dating apps have contributed to their legitimacy in both academic circles and public discourse. These studies underscore the role of technology in modern romance and validate dating apps as viable platforms for meeting potential partners.

Challenges and Considerations:

Despite the growing acceptance of dating apps, challenges remain:

- **Safety and Security Concerns:** Ensuring user safety, privacy protection, and mitigating risks of harassment or fraudulent activities remain ongoing challenges for dating app developers.

- **Representation and Diversity:** Ensuring inclusivity and representation of diverse demographics, including LGBTQ+ communities and individuals from different cultural backgrounds, is essential for fostering a welcoming and equitable environment.
- **Balancing Technology with Authenticity:** Encouraging users to maintain authenticity and genuine connections amidst the convenience and efficiency of digital platforms remains a critical consideration for promoting meaningful relationships.

Conclusion

The increasing social acceptance of dating apps reflects broader cultural shifts towards digital connectivity and individual empowerment in relationship-seeking behaviors. From overcoming initial stigma to becoming mainstream tools for meeting potential partners, dating apps have reshaped how people perceive and engage in modern dating. As attitudes continue to evolve, maintaining a balance between technological convenience and genuine human connection remains paramount for ensuring positive and fulfilling dating experiences in the digital age.

Cultural Shifts and the Rise of Dating Apps

Adapting to Changing Relationship Norms

The ascent of dating apps is intricately linked to cultural shifts and evolving societal values, which have transformed how individuals approach romantic relationships. Here's a detailed exploration of how modern values and societal changes have contributed to the popularity and acceptance of dating apps:

1. Embrace of Digital Connectivity: In the digital age, connectivity and instant access to information have become integral aspects of daily life. This cultural shift towards digital communication has naturally extended to dating, where individuals seek convenient and efficient ways to meet potential partners. Dating apps capitalize on this cultural trend by offering streamlined platforms that facilitate introductions and interactions in a digital environment.

2. Individualism and Autonomy: Modern values emphasize individual autonomy and personal fulfillment, encouraging individuals to prioritize their own needs and desires in various aspects of life, including relationships. Dating apps align with these values by empowering users to take an active role in their dating journey, allowing them to set preferences, initiate conversations, and explore relationships at their own pace. This shift towards individualism contrasts with traditional dating norms that often emphasize social expectations and collective decision-making.

3. Changing Views on Relationships: Societal attitudes towards relationships have evolved to embrace diversity, flexibility, and non-traditional arrangements. Dating apps accommodate a spectrum of relationship preferences, from casual dating to long-term commitments, catering to individuals seeking varied experiences and connections. This inclusivity reflects a broader acceptance of diverse relationship dynamics and challenges traditional notions of monogamy and exclusivity.

4. Urbanization and Mobility: Urbanization and increased mobility have reshaped social landscapes, altering how people form and maintain social connections. In urban centers where traditional social networks may be less cohesive, dating apps provide a valuable tool for expanding one's social circle and meeting new people. This geographic flexibility enhances opportunities for interpersonal exploration and relationship-building beyond local constraints.

5. Digital Literacy and Accessibility: Advancements in digital literacy and widespread smartphone adoption have democratized access to dating apps across diverse demographics. Users of all ages and backgrounds can navigate these platforms with relative ease, fostering a more inclusive and accessible approach to dating. This accessibility transcends traditional barriers such as age, socioeconomic status, or geographical location, broadening the pool of potential partners and enhancing social connectivity.

6. Reshaping Traditional Dating Rituals: Dating apps challenge traditional dating rituals by introducing new norms and behaviors associated with online interactions. From profile creation and photo selection to messaging etiquette and virtual dates, these platforms redefine how individuals initiate and sustain romantic connections. This evolution reflects a broader cultural shift towards integrating technology into interpersonal relationships and adapting to modern lifestyles.

Challenges and Considerations:

Despite the benefits of cultural shifts towards dating apps, challenges remain:

- **Digital Disconnect:** Over-reliance on digital interactions may diminish face-to-face social skills and hinder authentic connection-building.

- **Ethical and Privacy Concerns:** Addressing issues of data privacy, algorithmic bias, and ethical use of user information is crucial for maintaining trust and integrity within dating app ecosystems.
- **Navigating Diversity:** Ensuring inclusivity and sensitivity to diverse cultural norms and values is essential for fostering a welcoming and respectful dating environment.

Conclusion

The rise of dating apps reflects profound cultural shifts towards digital connectivity, individual autonomy, and evolving relationship norms. As society embraces new ways of meeting partners and navigating relationships, dating apps continue to evolve as essential tools for connecting individuals in the digital age. By understanding and adapting to these cultural changes, dating apps play a pivotal role in reshaping how people find love and companionship in contemporary society.

Chapter 2: The Mechanics of Dating Apps

Dating apps have revolutionized the way people meet potential partners, employing a combination of intuitive interfaces and sophisticated algorithms to facilitate connections. Here's a detailed exploration of how dating apps work, from profile creation to matchmaking algorithms:

1. Profile Creation: Users begin by creating a profile on the dating app, typically providing information such as their age, gender, location, and a brief bio. Profiles may also include photos and additional details about interests, hobbies, and preferences. This information forms the foundation for matchmaking algorithms to suggest potential matches.

2. Swiping Mechanism: Many dating apps utilize a swipe-based mechanism for browsing profiles. Users are presented with profiles one at a time, accompanied by photos and basic information. To indicate interest, users swipe right; to decline, they swipe left. This intuitive interface simplifies the initial selection process, allowing users to quickly evaluate potential matches based on visual impressions and profile details.

3. Matching Process: When two users swipe right on each other's profiles, indicating mutual interest, a match is formed. This mutual match unlocks the ability for both users to initiate a conversation through the app's messaging feature. Matches are typically stored in a separate section of the app for easy reference and communication.

4. Messaging Features: Once a match is established, users can communicate through the app's messaging platform. This feature allows for text-based conversations, often supplemented with emojis, photos, and links. Messaging facilitates initial interactions and serves as a crucial step in getting to know potential partners before deciding to meet in person.

Algorithm Influence: How Algorithms Shape the Experience

1. Matching Algorithms: Dating apps employ sophisticated algorithms to suggest potential matches based on various criteria, including user preferences, location, age, interests, and past behavior on the app. These algorithms analyze user data to generate personalized recommendations that are likely to result in successful matches. For example, algorithms may prioritize profiles with similar interests or geographical proximity to enhance compatibility.

2. Machine Learning and Adaptation: Some dating apps use machine learning techniques to continuously improve their algorithms. These algorithms learn from user interactions and feedback, adjusting match suggestions over time to better reflect individual preferences and relationship outcomes. Machine learning enables dating apps to evolve and adapt to changing user behaviors, enhancing the accuracy and relevance of match recommendations.

3. Factors Influencing Matchmaking: Algorithms consider a variety of factors when making match suggestions, including:

- **Profile Information:** Details provided in user profiles, such as interests, hobbies, and relationship preferences.
- **Behavioral Data:** User activity on the app, including swiping patterns, messaging frequency, and response rates.
- **Location:** Proximity to potential matches, with algorithms often prioritizing users who are geographically closer to each other.
- **Compatibility Scores:** Some apps assign compatibility scores or percentages based on shared interests and demographics, helping users gauge the likelihood of a successful match.

4. Ethical Considerations: While algorithms enhance the efficiency and effectiveness of dating apps, ethical considerations include:

- **Transparency:** Providing clear explanations of how algorithms work and the data they use to make match suggestions.

- **User Control:** Allowing users to adjust preferences, filter criteria, and control their visibility on the platform.
- **Privacy Protection:** Safeguarding user data and maintaining confidentiality in accordance with privacy laws and regulations.

Conclusion

Dating apps streamline the process of finding romantic connections by combining user-friendly interfaces with powerful matchmaking algorithms. From profile creation and swiping through to messaging and algorithm-driven matching, these platforms offer a convenient and personalized approach to modern dating. By leveraging data-driven insights and continuous innovation, dating apps enhance user experiences while adapting to cultural shifts and evolving relationship norms in contemporary society.

Matching Algorithms in Dating Apps: Enhancing Compatibility and User Experience

Dating apps leverage advanced matching algorithms to facilitate meaningful connections between users based on a range of criteria and user behaviors. Here's an in-depth exploration of how these algorithms work and their impact on user experience:

1. Criteria Considered in Matching Algorithms:

Dating apps analyze a variety of factors to generate personalized match suggestions:

- **User Preferences:** Algorithms consider preferences specified by users in their profiles, such as desired age range, gender identity, relationship goals (e.g., casual dating, long-term relationship), and lifestyle choices (e.g., smoking habits, pets).

- **Location:** Geographical proximity is a crucial factor in many matching algorithms. Apps prioritize potential matches who are physically closer to each other to facilitate real-life meetings and increase the likelihood of successful relationships.

- **Interests and Hobbies:** Matching algorithms may weigh profiles that share similar interests, hobbies, or cultural backgrounds more heavily. This approach enhances compatibility by aligning users with common interests and values, which can foster deeper connections.

- **Past Behavior on the App:** Algorithms analyze user interactions within the app, including swiping patterns, messaging frequency, response rates, and engagement levels. Patterns of behavior help algorithms refine match suggestions over time, learning from user preferences and interactions to improve accuracy.

2. Personalized Recommendations:

Matching algorithms generate personalized recommendations by synthesizing the above criteria. For example:

- **Compatibility Scores:** Some apps assign compatibility scores or percentages based on the alignment of user profiles. These scores reflect the likelihood of a successful match based on shared interests, values, and demographics.

- **Machine Learning and Adaptation:** Advanced dating apps employ machine learning techniques to adapt their algorithms based on user feedback and success rates of previous matches. Machine learning allows algorithms to continuously refine match suggestions, adapting to evolving user preferences and relationship dynamics.

3. Enhancing User Experience:

Matching algorithms play a pivotal role in enhancing the user experience on dating apps in several ways:

- **Efficiency:** By automating the process of match suggestions, algorithms save users time and effort in finding potential partners who align with their preferences.

- **Accuracy:** Algorithms improve the accuracy of match suggestions by considering multiple dimensions of compatibility, such as demographic factors, lifestyle choices, and shared interests.

- **Increased Engagement:** Personalized recommendations encourage users to engage more actively with the app, leading to higher retention rates and increased user satisfaction.

4. Ethical and Privacy Considerations:

While matching algorithms offer significant benefits, dating apps must navigate ethical considerations:

- **Transparency:** Providing clear explanations of how algorithms work and the data they use to make match suggestions ensures transparency and builds trust among users.

- **User Control:** Allowing users to adjust their preferences, filter criteria, and control their visibility on the platform empowers them to curate their dating experience according to their comfort levels.

- **Data Privacy:** Safeguarding user data and adhering to privacy regulations are essential to protect users' personal information and maintain confidentiality.

Conclusion

Matching algorithms in dating apps are instrumental in facilitating meaningful connections by analyzing user preferences, behaviors, and demographics to generate personalized match suggestions. By enhancing efficiency, accuracy, and user engagement, these algorithms contribute to a positive and dynamic dating experience. Ethical considerations, including transparency and privacy protection, are crucial in ensuring that algorithms operate responsibly and ethically within the digital dating landscape. As technology advances and user expectations evolve, the evolution of matching algorithms will continue to shape the future of online dating, catering to diverse preferences and fostering genuine relationships in modern society.

Machine Learning and Adaptation in Dating Apps

Machine learning plays a pivotal role in modern dating apps, enabling them to evolve and improve their algorithms based on user interactions and feedback. Here's an in-depth exploration of how machine learning enhances the accuracy and relevance of match recommendations over time:

1. Understanding Machine Learning in Dating Apps:

Machine learning refers to algorithms that learn from data and iteratively improve their performance without being explicitly programmed. In the context of dating apps, machine learning algorithms analyze vast amounts of user data to understand patterns, preferences, and behaviors. This data-driven approach allows apps to make informed predictions and decisions regarding match suggestions.

2. Continuous Learning and Adaptation:

Dating apps leverage machine learning to continuously refine their algorithms by:

- **User Interactions:** Machine learning algorithms analyze how users interact with the app, including swiping behavior (likes and dislikes), messaging patterns, response rates, and engagement levels. These interactions provide valuable insights into user preferences, relationship goals, and the factors that contribute to successful matches.

- **Feedback Mechanisms:** Apps often incorporate feedback loops where users can rate their matches or provide feedback on suggested profiles. Machine learning algorithms utilize this feedback to adjust future match suggestions, prioritizing profiles that align more closely with user preferences and improving the overall user experience.

3. Enhancing Accuracy and Relevance:

Machine learning enhances the accuracy and relevance of match recommendations in several ways:

- **Personalization:** By analyzing individual behaviors and preferences, machine learning algorithms tailor match suggestions to each user's unique profile. This personalized approach increases the likelihood of connecting users with compatible partners who share similar interests, values, and relationship expectations.

- **Adaptability:** Machine learning algorithms adapt to changing user behaviors and preferences over time. As users engage with the app and their preferences evolve, algorithms dynamically adjust match criteria to reflect these changes, ensuring that recommendations remain relevant and aligned with current user expectations.

4. Predictive Modeling and Optimization:

Advanced dating apps use predictive modeling techniques within machine learning to forecast user behaviors and outcomes. For example:

- **Predicting Relationship Outcomes:** Algorithms may analyze historical data to predict the likelihood of a match leading to a successful relationship based on similar user profiles and interactions.

- **Optimizing Match Criteria:** Machine learning algorithms optimize match criteria based on user feedback and success rates, fine-tuning parameters such as age range, geographic proximity, and shared interests to maximize compatibility and satisfaction.

5. Ethical Considerations:

While machine learning offers significant benefits in optimizing match recommendations, dating apps must address ethical considerations:

- **Transparency:** Providing clear explanations of how machine learning influences match suggestions and the data it uses ensures transparency and builds user trust.

- **Bias Mitigation:** Algorithms should be designed to mitigate biases that could impact match recommendations, such as demographic bias or stereotypes based on user characteristics.

- **Data Privacy:** Safeguarding user data and adhering to privacy regulations are essential to protect user privacy and maintain confidentiality.

Conclusion

Machine learning empowers dating apps to continuously learn from user interactions and feedback, adapting their algorithms to better reflect individual preferences and improve match accuracy. By leveraging data-driven insights and predictive modeling, these algorithms enhance the personalized matchmaking experience, fostering meaningful connections and optimizing user satisfaction. As technology advances and user expectations evolve, the integration of machine learning will continue to shape the future of online dating, offering innovative solutions to meet the diverse needs of users in the digital age.

Factors Influencing Matchmaking in Dating Apps

Matchmaking algorithms in dating apps are designed to analyze multiple factors to suggest potential matches that align with users' preferences and behaviors. Here's a detailed exploration of the key factors influencing matchmaking algorithms:

1. Profile Information:

User profiles serve as foundational elements for matchmaking algorithms, providing essential details that shape match suggestions:

- **Interests and Hobbies:** Algorithms consider users' stated interests, hobbies, and cultural preferences to identify potential matches who share similar passions and lifestyles. Common interests can foster connections and enhance compatibility between users.

- **Relationship Preferences:** Users specify their relationship goals and preferences, such as seeking casual dating, long-term relationships, or specific traits in a partner (e.g., age range, gender identity). Matchmaking algorithms prioritize profiles that align with these preferences to enhance the likelihood of successful matches.

2. Behavioral Data:

Behavioral data captures how users interact with the dating app and informs matchmaking algorithms about user engagement and preferences:

- **Swiping Patterns:** Algorithms analyze users' swiping behaviors (likes and dislikes) to infer preferences and interests. Patterns of swiping indicate which profiles users find appealing, allowing algorithms to adjust match suggestions accordingly.

- **Messaging Frequency and Response Rates:** User activity in messaging, including frequency of interactions and response rates to messages, provides insights into user engagement and communication styles. Algorithms may prioritize profiles with similar messaging behaviors to facilitate meaningful connections.

3. Location:

Geographical proximity is a critical factor in matchmaking algorithms, influencing the likelihood of matches:

- **Proximity to Potential Matches:** Algorithms often prioritize users who are geographically closer to each other. Proximity enhances the feasibility of real-life meetings and dates, promoting convenience and reducing logistical barriers to establishing relationships.

4. Compatibility Scores:

Some dating apps assign compatibility scores or percentages to quantify the likelihood of a successful match based on shared interests and demographics:

- **Shared Interests:** Algorithms calculate compatibility scores based on overlapping interests, hobbies, and values between users. Higher compatibility scores indicate a greater alignment of interests, potentially enhancing relationship compatibility.

- **Demographic Alignment:** Factors such as age, education level, religious beliefs, and lifestyle choices may also influence compatibility scores. Algorithms weigh these demographic factors to prioritize profiles that share similar backgrounds and characteristics.

5. Integration and Optimization:

Matchmaking algorithms integrate these factors through sophisticated algorithms that optimize match suggestions:

- **Algorithmic Optimization:** Algorithms continuously learn and refine their matching criteria based on user feedback and success rates of previous matches. This adaptive approach improves the accuracy and relevance of match suggestions over time, adapting to evolving user preferences and behaviors.

Ethical Considerations:

While matchmaking algorithms enhance user experience, dating apps must address ethical considerations:

- **Transparency:** Providing transparency about how algorithms work and the data they use ensures user trust and understanding.
- **Bias Mitigation:** Algorithms should be designed to mitigate biases, such as demographic bias or stereotypes, to ensure fair and equitable matchmaking.
- **Data Privacy:** Protecting user data and adhering to privacy regulations are essential to maintain user confidentiality and trust in the platform.

Conclusion

Matchmaking algorithms in dating apps leverage profile information, behavioral data, location proximity, and compatibility scores to suggest potential matches that align with users' preferences and increase the likelihood of successful connections. By integrating these factors through advanced algorithms and continuous optimization, dating apps enhance the personalized matchmaking experience, fostering meaningful relationships and user satisfaction in the digital dating landscape. As technology evolves and user expectations shift, the refinement of matchmaking algorithms will continue to shape the future of online dating, catering to diverse preferences and promoting genuine connections in contemporary society.

Ethical Considerations in Dating App Algorithms

As dating apps increasingly rely on sophisticated algorithms to enhance user experience and facilitate matches, ethical considerations play a crucial role in ensuring transparency, user control, and privacy protection. Here's a detailed exploration of these ethical considerations:

1. Transparency:

Transparency involves providing clear explanations of how algorithms operate and the data they utilize to make match suggestions:

- **Algorithm Functionality:** Dating apps should disclose how their algorithms work, including the factors considered (e.g., profile information, behavioral data, location) and how these factors influence match suggestions. Transparent communication helps users understand the matchmaking process and build trust in the platform's operations.

- **Data Usage:** Apps should inform users about the types of data collected (e.g., profile details, interaction history) and how this data is used to personalize their experience. Transparency about data handling practices, such as data storage, processing methods, and data sharing policies, promotes user confidence and informed decision-making.

2. User Control:

Empowering users with control over their experience is essential for respecting individual preferences and ensuring a positive user experience:

- **Preference Adjustment:** Dating apps should allow users to adjust their preferences, such as age range, gender preferences, relationship goals, and other criteria that influence match suggestions. Giving users control over these settings enables them to customize their matchmaking experience according to their personal preferences and comfort levels.

- **Filter Criteria:** Providing robust filtering options allows users to specify desired characteristics in potential matches, such as location proximity, interests, and demographic attributes. Flexible filtering empowers users to refine their search criteria and receive more relevant match suggestions that align with their preferences.

- **Visibility Settings:** Apps should offer options for users to control their visibility on the platform, including settings for profile visibility, online status, and interaction privacy. User-controlled visibility settings enhance privacy and enable individuals to manage their presence on the app in a manner that aligns with their comfort and safety preferences.

3. Privacy Protection:

Protecting user data and ensuring confidentiality are critical to maintaining trust and compliance with privacy laws and regulations:

- **Data Security:** Dating apps should implement robust security measures to safeguard user data against unauthorized access, data breaches, and cyber threats. Encryption protocols, secure data storage practices, and regular security audits are essential to protect sensitive user information.

- **Privacy Policies:** Apps should have clear and comprehensive privacy policies that outline how user data is collected, used, and protected. Privacy policies should be easily accessible to users and written in clear language to facilitate understanding of data handling practices and user rights.

- **Compliance:** Dating apps must adhere to relevant privacy laws and regulations, such as GDPR (General Data Protection Regulation) in Europe or CCPA (California Consumer Privacy Act) in the United States. Compliance ensures that user data is managed ethically and legally, respecting individual rights to privacy and data protection.

Conclusion

Ethical considerations in dating app algorithms encompass transparency, user control, and privacy protection to uphold user trust and promote responsible data management practices. By prioritizing transparency in algorithm functionality, empowering users with control over their preferences and visibility, and implementing robust privacy protections, dating apps can enhance user confidence, foster positive user experiences, and navigate ethical challenges in the digital dating landscape effectively. As technology evolves and regulatory frameworks evolve, ongoing commitment to ethical principles remains essential for sustaining trust and integrity in online matchmaking platforms.

Chapter 3: The Illusion of Choice in Dating Apps

Dating apps offer users a plethora of potential matches, presenting an illusion of abundant choice and control over their dating lives. However, this abundance can lead to psychological phenomena such as the paradox of choice and superficial judgments, influencing user satisfaction and decision-making processes.

1. Paradox of Choice:

The paradox of choice refers to the psychological phenomenon where having too many options can lead to anxiety, dissatisfaction, and decision paralysis rather than enhanced satisfaction:

- **Decision Overload:** When faced with numerous potential matches, users may experience difficulty in making a decision due to the overwhelming number of options available. This can lead to indecision, anxiety about making the wrong choice, and a heightened fear of missing out (FOMO) on better alternatives.

- **Higher Expectations:** With a wide array of choices, users may set higher expectations for potential matches, seeking perfection or idealized traits that may not be realistic. As a result, they may dismiss promising connections prematurely or struggle to commit to a single option, perpetuating a cycle of dissatisfaction.

- **Regret and Comparison:** Users may experience regret after making a choice, wondering if another profile could have been a better match. Continuous comparison between potential matches can diminish satisfaction with chosen partners and perpetuate a sense of dissatisfaction despite having access to many options.

2. Superficial Judgments:

In the context of dating apps, users often make quick, superficial judgments based on limited information, which can impact the quality of interactions and relationship potential:

- **Visual Impressions:** Profiles typically feature photos as the primary visual element, influencing initial impressions and swiping decisions. Users may base their interest or rejection on physical appearance alone, without fully considering other important factors such as personality, values, or compatibility.

- **Profile Details:** While profiles may include additional information such as hobbies, interests, and bio statements, users may skim through these details quickly or prioritize certain characteristics over others. This selective attention can lead to overlooking potentially meaningful connections based on shared interests or values.

- **Instant Gratification:** The convenience of swiping and instant matching fosters a culture of instant gratification, where users seek immediate validation or connections without investing significant time or effort in getting to know potential matches deeply. This can contribute to surface-level interactions and shallow relationships.

3. Impact on User Experience:

The illusion of choice and superficial judgments influence user experience on dating apps in several ways:

- **Reduced Commitment:** Users may hesitate to invest in meaningful conversations or relationships due to the perceived availability of alternative options, leading to a cycle of casual interactions and limited emotional investment.

- **Emotional Toll:** Continuous exposure to rejection or superficial interactions can impact users' self-esteem and emotional well-being, fostering feelings of inadequacy or frustration with the dating process.

- **Navigating Authenticity:** Balancing the desire for choice with the need for genuine connections requires users to navigate authenticity amidst curated profiles and idealized self-presentations common on dating platforms.

Conclusion

The illusion of choice and superficial judgments in dating apps highlight the complex interplay between user expectations, decision-making processes, and relationship outcomes. Understanding the paradox of choice and the tendency for superficial judgments can empower users to approach dating apps mindfully, focusing on meaningful connections rather than quantity or superficial attributes alone. By promoting transparency, encouraging thoughtful engagement, and fostering genuine interactions, dating apps can mitigate the negative effects of choice overload and superficiality, enhancing user satisfaction and supporting meaningful relationships in the digital age.

Paradox of Choice

Decision Overload in Dating Apps: Understanding the Psychological Impact

Decision overload refers to the psychological phenomenon where having too many options can overwhelm individuals, leading to indecision, anxiety, and dissatisfaction. In the context of dating apps, where users are presented with a vast array of potential matches, decision overload can significantly impact user experience and decision-making processes:

1. Psychological Factors:

- **Indecision:** When faced with numerous potential matches, users may struggle to prioritize and make a decision about whom to engage with or pursue further. The abundance of choices can create a sense of uncertainty and hesitation, as users weigh the pros and cons of each option.

- **Anxiety:** The pressure to make the "right" choice among many options can trigger anxiety. Users may worry about selecting a match that may not meet their expectations or missing out on potentially better matches elsewhere on the platform.

- **Fear of Missing Out (FOMO):** With a plethora of options available, users may experience FOMO, fearing that they might overlook a more compatible or attractive match if they commit to one option too quickly. This fear can prolong decision-making and lead to perpetual browsing or swiping without committing to meaningful connections.

2. Cognitive Overload:

- **Processing Complexity:** Evaluating numerous profiles, each presenting varying degrees of information and attractiveness, can overwhelm cognitive resources. Users may find it challenging to compare and contrast different profiles effectively, leading to mental fatigue and reduced decision quality.

- **Information Overload:** The abundance of information presented in profiles (photos, bios, interests) can make it difficult for users to focus on key criteria that are important for relationship compatibility. This information overload can dilute the significance of meaningful factors in favor of superficial attributes.

3. Impact on User Behavior:

- **Reduced Engagement:** Decision overload can lead to passive behavior, where users refrain from actively engaging with potential matches or initiating conversations due to uncertainty or analysis paralysis.

- **Lower Satisfaction:** Difficulty in making decisions and heightened anxiety can diminish user satisfaction with the dating app experience. Users may perceive the process as exhausting or frustrating, leading to disengagement or negative perceptions of the platform.

- **Commitment Issues:** Users may struggle to commit to developing relationships or investing time in getting to know matches more deeply, perpetuating a cycle of superficial interactions and limited emotional investment.

4. Coping Strategies:

- **Setting Priorities:** Encouraging users to prioritize key criteria (e.g., shared values, interests) can help streamline decision-making and focus attention on meaningful connections.

- **Time Management:** Suggesting time limits or structured browsing sessions can prevent users from becoming overwhelmed by continuous exposure to profiles and choices.

- **Mindfulness:** Promoting mindfulness and self-awareness can help users navigate decision overload by encouraging them to reflect on their preferences, values, and relationship goals.

Conclusion

Decision overload in dating apps highlights the challenges users face when presented with a plethora of potential matches. Understanding the psychological impact of decision overload—such as indecision, anxiety, and FOMO—can inform strategies to enhance user experience, promote meaningful connections, and mitigate the negative effects of choice abundance. By fostering a balanced approach to choice and providing tools to support decision-making, dating apps can empower users to navigate the complexities of online dating effectively while promoting satisfaction and genuine relationship outcomes in the digital age.

Higher Expectations in Dating Apps: Impact on User Experience

In the context of dating apps, the abundance of potential matches can lead users to develop heightened expectations for their potential partners. This phenomenon can impact user behavior, satisfaction, and the overall success of forming meaningful connections. Here's a detailed exploration of how higher expectations manifest and their implications:

1. Setting Unrealistic Standards:

● **Idealized Traits:** When users are presented with numerous profiles, they may develop idealized expectations for potential matches. These expectations often revolve around physical appearance, personality traits, lifestyle choices, and other desirable qualities. Users may seek partners who meet a specific set of criteria, aiming for an idealized image of an "ideal" match.

● **Perfectionism:** The abundance of options can foster a perfectionist mindset, where users strive to find a match who ticks all the boxes and fulfills all their expectations perfectly. This pursuit of perfection can lead to overlooking potential connections that may not meet every criterion but could still develop into meaningful relationships.

2. Impact on User Behavior:

● **Dismissal of Promising Connections:** High expectations may cause users to dismiss promising connections prematurely. They may overlook profiles that don't immediately meet their idealized criteria, potentially missing out on compatible matches with genuine potential for compatibility and mutual interest.

● **Commitment Issues:** Users with high expectations may struggle to commit to a single option or invest time in getting to know potential matches beyond superficial attributes. This reluctance to commit can perpetuate a cycle of dissatisfaction, as users continuously seek better alternatives without fully exploring or developing existing connections.

3. Psychological Effects:

● **Frustration and Disappointment:** Unrealistic expectations can lead to frustration and disappointment when users fail to find a match that meets their ideal criteria. This dissatisfaction can diminish user satisfaction with the dating app experience, leading to negative perceptions or reduced engagement over time.

● **Comparison and Regret:** Continuous exposure to a variety of profiles can fuel comparison between potential matches and foster feelings of regret or uncertainty about chosen options. Users may question their decisions or wonder if a more suitable match exists elsewhere on the platform, contributing to emotional turmoil and indecision.

4. Strategies for Mitigation:

● **Encouraging Realistic Expectations:** Dating apps can promote realistic expectations by emphasizing the importance of compatibility beyond superficial traits. Encouraging users to prioritize shared values, communication styles, and relationship goals can facilitate more meaningful connections.

● **Facilitating Communication:** Providing platforms for open communication and meaningful interaction can help users move beyond initial impressions and explore potential matches on a deeper level. Encouraging users to engage in conversations that delve into shared interests and values can foster genuine connections.

● **Education and Guidance:** Offering guidance on navigating the dating app experience, managing expectations, and recognizing the potential for genuine connections can empower users to approach online dating with a balanced perspective.

Conclusion

Higher expectations in dating apps reflect the challenges users face when presented with a wide array of potential matches. By understanding the implications of setting unrealistic standards—such as premature dismissal of promising connections and perpetuation of dissatisfaction—dating apps can implement strategies to promote realistic expectations, facilitate meaningful interactions, and enhance user satisfaction. Empowering users to prioritize compatibility over idealized traits and fostering a supportive environment for genuine connections can contribute to a positive and fulfilling dating app experience in the digital age.

Regret and Comparison in Dating Apps: Understanding the Psychological Impact

Regret and comparison are common psychological experiences among users of dating apps, particularly in environments where there is a wide array of potential matches available. These phenomena can significantly influence user satisfaction, decision-making processes, and emotional well-being. Here's a detailed exploration of how regret and comparison manifest in dating apps and their implications:

1. Experience of Regret:

● **Post-Decision Uncertainty:** After making a choice to engage with or pursue a specific match, users may experience feelings of regret or uncertainty. They may question whether another profile could have been a better fit or if they missed out on a potentially more compatible match elsewhere on the platform.

● **Outcome Comparison:** Users may compare the outcomes of their interactions with chosen matches against hypothetical scenarios with other potential matches. This comparison can amplify feelings of regret if the chosen match does not meet initial expectations or if interactions do not unfold as desired.

2. Continuous Comparison:

● **Endless Options:** The abundance of options on dating apps facilitates continuous comparison between potential matches. Users may feel compelled to continually evaluate new profiles and compare them against existing connections, perpetuating a cycle of uncertainty and dissatisfaction.

● **Comparison Bias:** Continuous exposure to curated profiles and idealized self-presentations can distort perceptions and fuel comparison bias. Users may overestimate the compatibility or attractiveness of other profiles while underestimating the potential of their current connections, leading to unrealistic expectations and dissatisfaction.

3. Implications for User Behavior:

● **Relationship Dissatisfaction:** Persistent comparison between potential matches can diminish satisfaction with chosen partners. Users may struggle to fully invest in developing relationships or may prematurely dismiss promising connections in search of perceived better alternatives.

- **Emotional Toll:** Regret and continuous comparison can take an emotional toll on users, fostering feelings of insecurity, self-doubt, and emotional distress. This emotional turbulence can impact overall well-being and contribute to negative perceptions of the dating app experience.

4. Coping Strategies:

- **Mindfulness and Self-Reflection:** Encouraging users to practice mindfulness and self-reflection can help mitigate feelings of regret and comparison. By focusing on present interactions and recognizing the value of meaningful connections, users can cultivate a more positive and fulfilling dating experience.

- **Managing Expectations:** Educating users about the realities of online dating and the potential for genuine connections can help manage expectations. Emphasizing the importance of compatibility beyond superficial attributes can foster more realistic expectations and reduce the impact of comparison bias.

- **Supportive Environment:** Providing a supportive environment where users feel encouraged to explore connections at their own pace and without pressure to constantly compare or seek alternative options can enhance user satisfaction and well-being.

Conclusion

Regret and comparison in dating apps highlight the challenges users face when navigating a vast array of potential matches. By understanding the psychological impact—such as post-decision uncertainty, continuous comparison, and emotional distress—dating apps can implement strategies to support users in managing these experiences effectively. Promoting mindfulness, managing expectations, and fostering a supportive environment for genuine connections can contribute to a positive and fulfilling dating app experience, enhancing user satisfaction and facilitating meaningful relationships in the digital age.

Superficial Judgments

Visual Impressions in Dating Apps: Impact on Decision-Making

Visual impressions play a significant role in shaping user behavior and decision-making processes on dating apps, where profiles primarily feature photos as the primary visual element. This emphasis on visual presentation can influence initial impressions and swiping decisions, often prioritizing physical appearance over other important factors such as personality, values, and compatibility. Here's a detailed exploration of how visual impressions impact user experience and decision-making:

1. Primacy of Visual Elements:

● **First Impressions:** In dating apps, users typically form initial impressions of potential matches based on profile photos. The visual presentation serves as a primary point of attraction or rejection, influencing users' perceptions and interest in exploring further interactions.

● **Immediate Attraction:** Users may swipe right (like) or left (dislike) based on immediate visual attraction or appeal perceived from profile photos. This rapid evaluation process is driven by visual stimuli and can determine whether users initiate contact or move on to the next profile.

2. Factors Influencing Visual Impressions:

● **Aesthetic Preferences:** Users may be drawn to specific physical features or styles showcased in profile photos, reflecting personal aesthetic preferences or cultural norms of attractiveness.

● **Photographic Quality:** High-quality photos that are well-lit, clear, and visually appealing tend to capture more attention and positive impressions compared to blurry or poorly composed images.

3. Limitations and Biases:

● **Superficial Judgments:** Relying solely on visual impressions can lead to superficial judgments where users prioritize physical appearance over other important aspects of compatibility, such as personality, values, and shared interests.

● **Confirmation Bias:** Users may selectively focus on profile photos that confirm their preconceived notions of attractiveness or desirability, potentially overlooking profiles with promising compatibility but less visually striking photos.

4. Impact on User Experience:

● **Reduced Depth of Interaction:** Emphasizing visual impressions may limit opportunities for meaningful interactions and deeper connections. Users may miss out on exploring potential matches who possess compatible traits and qualities beyond physical appearance.

● **Emotional Responses:** Users' self-esteem and emotional well-being can be influenced by the feedback received based on visual impressions. Repeated rejection or acceptance based solely on appearance may impact users' confidence and perception of self-worth.

5. Strategies for Balanced Engagement:

● **Encouraging Profile Diversity:** Dating apps can encourage users to present a diverse range of photos that showcase different aspects of their personality, interests, and lifestyle beyond physical appearance.

● **Promoting Holistic Evaluation:** Educating users about the importance of considering multiple factors, such as shared values, communication style, and life goals, can foster more balanced decision-making and increase the likelihood of meaningful connections.

● **User Feedback and Interaction:** Providing platforms for meaningful interactions, such as messaging or video calls, encourages users to engage beyond initial visual impressions and explore potential matches on a deeper level.

Conclusion

Visual impressions significantly influence user decision-making on dating apps, where profiles primarily feature photos as the primary visual element. While visual attraction plays a role in initial interest and engagement, emphasizing a balanced approach that considers multiple factors beyond physical appearance—such as personality, values, and compatibility—can enhance user satisfaction and facilitate more meaningful connections in the digital dating landscape. By promoting holistic evaluation and supporting genuine interactions, dating apps can empower users to navigate the complexities of online dating effectively while fostering fulfilling relationships based on mutual understanding and compatibility.

Profile Details in Dating Apps: Importance and Impact on User Engagement

Profile details play a crucial role in providing users with additional information beyond visual impressions on dating apps. While profiles often include details such as hobbies, interests, and bio statements, users may not always thoroughly review or prioritize these elements during their browsing and decision-making processes. This selective attention can potentially lead to overlooking meaningful connections based on shared interests or values. Here's a detailed exploration of how profile details influence user engagement and interaction:

1. Role of Profile Details:

● **Comprehensive Information:** Profile details offer insights into users' personalities, lifestyles, and interests beyond their physical appearance. These details provide a more holistic view of potential matches and facilitate informed decision-making.

● **Contextual Understanding:** Hobbies, interests, and bio statements provide context about users' passions, values, and life experiences, helping to establish common ground and potential areas of compatibility.

2. Challenges in Attention and Prioritization:

● **Attention Bias:** Users may prioritize certain profile details, such as photos or brief descriptions, over comprehensive information such as hobbies or personal anecdotes. This bias can influence initial impressions and swiping decisions, potentially overshadowing compatibility factors like shared values or long-term goals.

● **Skimming Behavior:** In a fast-paced digital environment, users may skim through profile details quickly, focusing on easily digestible information or visually appealing elements. This rapid evaluation process can lead to overlooking nuanced aspects of compatibility that are conveyed through detailed profile content.

3. Impact on User Interaction:

● **Missed Connections:** By overlooking or undervaluing profile details, users may miss opportunities to connect with individuals who share similar interests, values, or life experiences. This oversight can limit the potential for meaningful interactions and compatible relationships.

● **Superficial Engagement:** Emphasizing superficial aspects of profiles, such as photos or brief descriptions, may lead to shallow interactions based on physical attraction rather than deeper connections built on shared values and mutual interests.

4. Strategies for Enhancing Engagement:

● **Encouraging Detailed Profiles:** Dating apps can encourage users to provide comprehensive and authentic profile details that reflect their personalities, interests, and relationship preferences. Prompts or guidelines may help users articulate meaningful aspects of their identity and aspirations.

- **Highlighting Common Ground:** Algorithms or features that highlight shared interests or values between potential matches can facilitate more meaningful connections. Drawing attention to compatibility factors beyond physical attraction promotes genuine interactions and relationship building.
- **Educating Users:** Providing guidance on the importance of considering diverse profile details and engaging in meaningful conversations can empower users to navigate dating apps with intentionality and authenticity. Educating users about the benefits of exploring shared interests and values can enhance the quality of interactions and increase the likelihood of compatible matches.

Conclusion

Profile details in dating apps offer valuable insights into users' personalities, interests, and values, beyond initial visual impressions. While users may prioritize certain aspects of profiles over others, emphasizing the importance of comprehensive profile information and facilitating genuine connections based on shared interests and values can enhance user engagement and satisfaction. By promoting holistic evaluation and encouraging meaningful interactions, dating apps can support users in forming meaningful connections that align with their relationship preferences and aspirations in the digital dating landscape.

Instant Gratification in Dating Apps: Impact on User Behavior

Instant gratification refers to the immediate satisfaction or validation that users seek from the quick and effortless interactions facilitated by dating apps, particularly through features like swiping and instant matching. This convenience-driven culture can influence user behavior, interactions, and the quality of relationships formed. Here's a detailed exploration of how instant gratification manifests in dating apps and its implications:

1. Mechanisms of Instant Gratification:

- **Swiping Interface:** Dating apps often employ a swipe-based interface where users make rapid decisions based on brief visual cues (e.g., profile photos). This interface allows users to quickly swipe right (like) or left (dislike), triggering immediate feedback and potential matches.
- **Instant Matching:** Upon mutual interest (match), users can initiate immediate communication or interactions with minimal effort, fostering a sense of instant validation and connection.

2. Psychological Factors:

- **Validation and Attention:** Swiping and instant matching provide users with instant validation and attention, fulfilling a desire for social acceptance and affirmation. The rapid feedback loop reinforces engagement and can contribute to addictive behaviors.
- **Reduced Investment:** The ease of swiping and instant matching reduces the perceived investment of time and effort required to establish connections. Users may engage in superficial interactions without fully committing to getting to know potential matches beyond initial impressions.

3. Impact on User Interactions:

- **Surface-Level Engagement:** Instant gratification can lead to surface-level interactions characterized by brief exchanges and limited depth. Users may prioritize quantity of matches over quality of interactions, leading to shallow relationships based on superficial attraction rather than meaningful connections.
- **Communication Patterns:** The immediacy of communication channels can encourage casual or flippant messaging behaviors, where users may engage in sporadic or inconsistent communication without sustained effort to develop rapport or intimacy.

4. Consequences for Relationship Development:

- **Lack of Depth:** Relationships formed under the influence of instant gratification may lack depth and emotional intimacy. Users may struggle to move beyond initial attraction or curiosity to cultivate meaningful connections based on shared values and compatibility.

- **Emotional Disconnect:** The pursuit of instant gratification can contribute to emotional detachment or disengagement in relationships. Users may experience difficulty in building trust, vulnerability, and long-term commitment due to a focus on immediate satisfaction and validation.

5. Strategies for Balanced Engagement:

- **Encouraging Intentional Use:** Dating apps can promote intentional use by encouraging users to take time to read profiles thoroughly, consider compatibility factors beyond physical attraction, and engage in meaningful conversations.

- **Emphasizing Quality Interactions:** Platforms can incentivize or highlight interactions that prioritize meaningful communication and shared interests. Features such as prompts for deeper conversation topics or relationship-focused activities can foster genuine connections.

- **Educating About Relationship Building:** Providing educational resources or tips on building healthy relationships can empower users to navigate dating apps with mindfulness and authenticity, promoting long-term satisfaction and fulfillment.

Conclusion

Instant gratification in dating apps reflects the desire for immediate validation and connection through features like swiping and instant matching. While these mechanisms offer convenience and efficiency, they can contribute to surface-level interactions and shallow relationships characterized by limited emotional depth and investment. By promoting intentional use, encouraging quality interactions, and providing resources for relationship building, dating apps can support users in forming meaningful connections based on shared values and genuine compatibility in the digital dating landscape.

Impact on User Experience

Reduced Commitment in Dating Apps: Factors and Implications

Reduced commitment among users of dating apps reflects a tendency to withhold emotional investment and engagement in meaningful relationships. This hesitation often stems from perceptions of abundant alternative options and the convenience of exploring multiple connections simultaneously. Here's a detailed exploration of how reduced commitment manifests in dating apps and its implications:

1. Perceived Availability of Alternatives:

● **Abundance of Options:** Dating apps offer users access to a large pool of potential matches, creating a perception that alternative options are readily available. This abundance can lead users to maintain a mindset of continuous exploration and comparison, delaying commitment to any single relationship.

● **Fear of Missing Out (FOMO):** The availability of alternative matches can exacerbate FOMO, where users fear missing out on potentially better connections by committing too soon or exclusively to one person. This fear drives users to keep their options open and avoid exclusive commitments.

2. Cycle of Casual Interactions:

● **Superficial Engagement:** Users may engage in superficial interactions characterized by casual conversations and minimal emotional investment. The focus on quantity over quality of interactions can perpetuate a cycle of fleeting connections and limited depth in relationships.

● **Avoidance of Vulnerability:** Hesitation to invest emotionally may stem from a reluctance to become vulnerable or emotionally exposed to potential rejection or disappointment. Users may maintain a guarded approach to dating, preferring to keep interactions casual to protect their emotional well-being.

3. Impact on Relationship Development:

● **Stunted Emotional Growth:** Limited emotional investment can hinder the development of intimacy, trust, and mutual understanding in relationships. Without sustained effort and commitment, relationships may struggle to progress beyond surface-level interactions.

● **Difficulty in Building Trust:** Mutual trust and authenticity are essential for fostering meaningful connections. Reduced commitment may lead to skepticism or uncertainty about the intentions and sincerity of potential partners, complicating efforts to build trust and emotional intimacy.

4. Psychological and Social Dynamics:

● **Grass is Greener Mentality:** The perception of limitless options can fuel a "grass is greener" mentality, where users continuously seek better matches or idealized partners. This mentality undermines satisfaction with current relationships and perpetuates a cycle of dissatisfaction.

● **Impact of Digital Interaction:** Interactions mediated through digital platforms may lack the depth and nuance of face-to-face communication, making it easier for users to maintain emotional distance and avoid deeper emotional engagement.

5. Strategies for Promoting Meaningful Connections:

● **Encouraging Intentional Communication:** Dating apps can promote intentional communication by encouraging users to prioritize quality conversations and genuine interactions that align with their relationship goals and values.

● **Educating About Emotional Intelligence:** Providing resources on emotional intelligence and relationship-building skills can empower users to navigate dating apps with empathy, authenticity, and vulnerability.

● **Highlighting Success Stories:** Showcasing success stories of meaningful relationships formed through the app can inspire users to invest in deeper connections and prioritize emotional compatibility over superficial attraction.

Conclusion

Reduced commitment in dating apps reflects users' hesitancy to invest emotionally in meaningful relationships, driven by perceptions of abundant alternative options and the convenience of casual interactions. By promoting intentional communication, educating about emotional intelligence, and highlighting the benefits of genuine connections, dating apps can support users in forming meaningful relationships based on mutual respect, trust, and emotional compatibility in the digital dating landscape.

Emotional Toll in Dating Apps: Impact on Self-Esteem and Well-Being

The emotional toll experienced by users of dating apps encompasses the psychological impact of continuous exposure to rejection, superficial interactions, and the challenges of navigating digital relationships. This toll can significantly affect users' self-esteem, emotional well-being, and overall satisfaction with the dating process. Here's a detailed exploration of how the emotional toll manifests and its implications:

1. Continuous Exposure to Rejection:

● **Impact on Self-Worth:** Repeated rejection or lack of mutual interest from potential matches can erode users' self-esteem and self-confidence. Each instance of rejection may reinforce negative beliefs about one's attractiveness, desirability, or compatibility.

● **Sense of Inadequacy:** Users may internalize rejection as a reflection of personal inadequacies or shortcomings, leading to feelings of unworthiness or self-doubt in the dating context.

2. Superficial Interactions:

● **Lack of Authentic Connection:** Superficial interactions characterized by brief exchanges or emphasis on physical appearance may leave users feeling emotionally disconnected or unfulfilled. The absence of meaningful engagement can contribute to a sense of loneliness or dissatisfaction with the quality of interactions.

● **Validation Seeking:** Seeking validation through superficial interactions or external validation from matches can create dependency on external sources for self-worth, exacerbating feelings of emotional vulnerability.

3. Frustration with the Dating Process:

● **High Expectations vs. Reality:** Discrepancies between idealized expectations and actual experiences in dating apps can lead to frustration or disillusionment with the dating process. Users may struggle to reconcile their desires for meaningful connections with the realities of superficial interactions or frequent disappointments.

● **Negative Spiral:** Persistent frustration or disappointment with the dating process can create a negative spiral where users become increasingly reluctant to engage, leading to withdrawal from the platform or reduced willingness to initiate new connections.

4. Coping Mechanisms and Support:

● **Self-Reflection and Resilience:** Encouraging users to practice self-reflection and cultivate resilience can help mitigate the emotional impact of rejection and superficial interactions. Building self-awareness and affirming personal strengths can bolster self-esteem and promote a healthier approach to dating.

● **Community and Support Networks:** Establishing community forums or support networks within dating apps can provide users with opportunities to share experiences, seek advice, and receive emotional support from peers facing similar challenges.

5. Promoting Positive Experiences:

● **Focus on Meaningful Connections:** Emphasizing the importance of quality over quantity in interactions can shift user focus towards seeking meaningful connections based on shared values, interests, and emotional compatibility.

● **Educational Resources:** Providing resources on emotional well-being, self-care practices, and healthy relationship dynamics can empower users to navigate the emotional challenges of dating apps with greater resilience and self-awareness.

Conclusion

The emotional toll experienced by users of dating apps underscores the challenges of navigating rejection, superficial interactions, and the complexities of digital relationships. By promoting self-reflection, resilience-building strategies, and fostering a supportive community environment, dating apps can mitigate the negative impact on users' self-esteem and emotional well-being. Empowering users to prioritize meaningful connections and providing resources for emotional support can enhance satisfaction and promote healthier dating experiences in the digital age.

Navigating Authenticity in Dating Apps: Balancing Choice and Genuine Connections

Navigating authenticity in the context of dating apps involves the challenge of reconciling users' desire for choice and exploration with the need for meaningful, genuine connections amidst profiles that often present curated or idealized versions of individuals. This dynamic requires users to discern authenticity amidst superficial presentations and curated profiles prevalent on digital dating platforms. Here's a detailed exploration of how users navigate authenticity and its implications:

1. Curated Profiles and Idealized Self-Presentations:

● **Selective Self-Presentation:** Users on dating apps often curate their profiles to highlight positive attributes or aspects of their lives, presenting an idealized version of themselves. This selective self-presentation can create discrepancies between online personas and real-life identities.

● **Visual Representation:** Profile photos and descriptions may emphasize certain traits or lifestyles while omitting others, influencing initial impressions and perceptions of compatibility.

2. Balancing Choice and Authenticity:

● **Desire for Exploration:** The abundance of potential matches and the ease of swiping contribute to users' desire for exploration and variety in their interactions. This desire for choice can lead users to engage with multiple profiles simultaneously, seeking diverse experiences and connections.

● **Seeking Genuine Connections:** Amidst the array of choices, users prioritize authenticity and genuine connections based on shared values, interests, and emotional compatibility. Authenticity involves discerning sincerity and compatibility beyond superficial attributes or curated presentations.

3. Challenges in Discerning Authenticity:

● **Trust and Transparency:** Establishing trust and transparency can be challenging in an environment where profiles may present idealized versions of individuals. Users must navigate initial impressions and interactions to gauge sincerity and alignment with personal values.

● **Communication Dynamics:** Effective communication plays a crucial role in verifying authenticity and building rapport. Users may engage in meaningful conversations that delve beyond superficial topics to assess compatibility and mutual understanding.

4. Implications for Relationship Development:

- **Building Trust and Connection:** Authenticity fosters trust and emotional connection in relationships. Genuine interactions enable users to share authentic experiences, vulnerabilities, and aspirations, fostering deeper understanding and intimacy.
- **Long-Term Compatibility:** Prioritizing authenticity increases the likelihood of forming relationships based on mutual respect, trust, and emotional compatibility. Users can cultivate meaningful connections that align with their relationship goals and aspirations.

5. Strategies for Promoting Authentic Connections:

- **Encouraging Genuine Self-Presentation:** Dating apps can encourage users to present authentic and multidimensional profiles that reflect their true personalities, interests, and values. Providing prompts or guidelines for profile creation can facilitate sincere self-expression.
- **Emphasizing Meaningful Communication:** Platforms can promote meaningful communication by highlighting shared values, encouraging open-ended questions, and facilitating deeper conversations that foster genuine connections.
- **User Education and Empowerment:** Educating users about the importance of authenticity and strategies for discerning sincerity can empower individuals to navigate dating apps with intentionality and authenticity. Resources on effective communication and relationship-building skills can enhance user satisfaction and promote healthier interactions.

Conclusion

Navigating authenticity in dating apps involves balancing the desire for choice and exploration with the pursuit of genuine connections amidst curated profiles and idealized self-presentations. By promoting genuine self-expression, fostering meaningful communication, and empowering users with the tools to discern authenticity, dating apps can support individuals in forming meaningful relationships based on mutual respect, trust, and emotional compatibility in the digital dating landscape. Cultivating an environment that values authenticity enhances user satisfaction and promotes fulfilling interactions that transcend superficial impressions.

Chapter 4: Impact on Communication in Dating Apps

Dating apps have significantly influenced how people communicate, often prioritizing text-based interactions over face-to-face communication. This shift can affect the quality, dynamics, and potential pitfalls of communication, leading to both advantages and challenges in forming relationships. Here's a detailed exploration of these impacts:

1. Text Over Talk:

● **Preference for Text-Based Communication:**

○ **Convenience:** Dating apps offer a convenient platform for users to communicate via text messages at any time and from any location.

○ **Initial Contact:** Text-based interactions provide a low-pressure way for users to initiate contact and gauge interest without the immediate commitment of face-to-face interaction.

○ **Control Over Response:** Users have control over the timing and content of their responses, allowing them to carefully craft messages and manage communication pace.

● **Implications:**

○ **Delayed Emotional Connection:** Text-based communication may delay the development of emotional connection and intimacy compared to face-to-face interactions, where non-verbal cues and tone of voice play significant roles.

○ **Limited Context:** Without visual and auditory cues, users may miss important nuances and emotional expressions, potentially leading to misunderstandings or misinterpretations.

○ **Difficulty in Reading Intentions:** Users may struggle to accurately gauge the intentions and emotions of their matches solely through text, increasing the risk of miscommunication.

2. Miscommunication and Misinterpretation:

● **Potential Challenges:**

○ **Ambiguity:** Text-based messages can be ambiguous, lacking clarity in tone or meaning, which may lead to misinterpretations or unintended implications.

○ **Assumptions:** Users may make assumptions about their matches based on text messages, potentially leading to misunderstandings or jumping to conclusions.

○ **Emotional Expression:** The absence of facial expressions and body language in text-based communication limits the conveyance of emotions, making it challenging to accurately interpret the emotional state of the other person.

● **Impact on Relationships:**

○ **Conflict Resolution:** Miscommunication in text-based conversations can escalate conflicts or disagreements, as nuances and intentions may be misunderstood or overlooked.

○ **Building Trust:** Effective communication is essential for building trust and establishing a deeper connection. Misinterpretations or frequent misunderstandings in text-based interactions may hinder trust-building efforts.

○ **Stress and Anxiety:** Users may experience stress or anxiety related to navigating complex or ambiguous conversations, particularly when trying to convey emotions or sensitive topics through text alone.

3. Strategies for Effective Communication:

• **Use of Emojis and Tone Indicators:** Incorporating emojis, punctuation marks, or tone indicators (e.g., sarcasm tags) can help clarify tone and emotions in text-based messages.

• **Active Listening:** Practicing active listening and seeking clarification when needed can reduce misunderstandings and promote clearer communication.

• **Video or Voice Calls:** Encouraging users to transition from text-based messaging to video or voice calls can facilitate more natural communication, allowing for better emotional connection and understanding.

Conclusion

Dating apps prioritize text-based communication as a primary means of interaction, offering convenience and control over conversations. However, this preference can lead to challenges such as miscommunication, ambiguity, and difficulty in conveying emotions accurately. By promoting strategies for effective communication, including the use of visual cues and active listening, dating apps can support users in building stronger connections and navigating interpersonal dynamics with clarity and empathy in the digital dating landscape. Balancing text-based communication with opportunities for face-to-face interaction can enhance relationship development and foster meaningful connections based on mutual understanding and emotional resonance.

Text Over Talk - Preference for Text-Based Communication

Preference for Text-Based Communication in Dating Apps: Convenience

Dating apps have revolutionized the way people meet and communicate, with text-based communication being a primary mode of interaction. The convenience offered by text messaging on these platforms is a significant factor contributing to its popularity. Here's a detailed exploration of this convenience:

1. Anytime, Anywhere Communication:

● **Accessibility:** Text-based communication on dating apps allows users to send and receive messages at any time, from any location, as long as they have an internet connection. This accessibility is particularly beneficial for individuals with busy schedules, as it enables them to engage in conversations without needing to coordinate real-time interactions.

● **Flexible Timing:** Users can respond to messages at their convenience, without the pressure of immediate replies. This flexibility accommodates different time zones, work schedules, and personal commitments, making it easier for people to stay connected and engaged in conversations.

2. Low Pressure and Control:

● **Reduced Anxiety:** Text-based communication can be less intimidating than face-to-face or phone conversations, especially for initial interactions. It allows users to craft their messages thoughtfully, reducing the pressure of spontaneous responses and potential awkwardness.

● **Control Over Communication:** Users have the opportunity to review and edit their messages before sending them, ensuring clarity and precision in their communication. This control helps in expressing thoughts more accurately and avoiding miscommunication.

3. Managing Multiple Conversations:

● **Simultaneous Interactions:** Text messaging enables users to manage multiple conversations simultaneously, a feature particularly useful on dating apps where users often engage with several potential matches at once. This multitasking capability allows users to explore various connections and gauge compatibility with different individuals.

● **Asynchronous Communication:** Unlike real-time conversations, text-based interactions do not require both parties to be available at the same moment. Users can leave messages for their matches and continue the conversation when the other person is available, making it easier to sustain communication despite busy or conflicting schedules.

4. Privacy and Comfort:

● **Safe Environment:** Text-based communication provides a sense of privacy and comfort, allowing users to interact from familiar and secure environments, such as their homes. This privacy can help users feel more at ease, especially in the early stages of getting to know someone.

● **Reduced Risk:** The initial anonymity and distance afforded by text messaging can reduce the perceived risk of rejection or judgment. Users can gradually build rapport and trust before moving to more personal forms of communication, such as phone calls or in-person meetings.

5. Convenience for Introverted Users:

● **Preferred Communication Style:** For introverted individuals or those who are more comfortable expressing themselves in writing, text-based communication can be a preferred mode of interaction. It allows them to articulate their thoughts and feelings more effectively than in spontaneous verbal exchanges.

● **Time to Reflect:** Introverts often appreciate the opportunity to reflect before responding, which text messaging provides. This reflection time can lead to more meaningful and considered interactions.

6. Integration with Daily Life:

- **Seamless Integration:** Text messaging on dating apps seamlessly integrates into users' daily routines, allowing them to engage in conversations during commutes, breaks, or leisure time without significant disruption to their schedules.
- **Notification Alerts:** Push notifications alert users to new messages, ensuring they stay connected and can promptly respond to their matches, enhancing the fluidity and continuity of conversations.

Conclusion

The convenience of text-based communication on dating apps is a major factor in its widespread use. By offering anytime, anywhere accessibility, low-pressure interactions, control over message crafting, and the ability to manage multiple conversations, text messaging meets the needs of a diverse user base. This convenience fosters ongoing engagement and connection, helping users navigate the complexities of modern dating with greater ease and comfort. While text-based communication provides numerous benefits, balancing it with opportunities for more personal interactions can further enhance the development of meaningful relationships.

Initial Contact in Dating Apps: The Low-Pressure Advantage of Text-Based Interactions

Text-based interactions on dating apps offer a low-pressure way for users to initiate contact and gauge interest, significantly altering the dynamics of initial contact in the dating process. Here's a detailed exploration of how this works and its implications:

1. Lowering the Stakes:

- **Reduced Anxiety:** For many individuals, approaching someone in person or making a phone call can be intimidating and anxiety-inducing. Text-based communication lowers these stakes by allowing users to initiate contact in a less direct and less personal manner. This can be particularly helpful for introverted or shy individuals who might struggle with face-to-face interactions.
- **Safety Net:** The digital barrier provides a sense of safety and comfort. Users can take their time to think about what they want to say and how they want to present themselves without the immediate pressure of real-time reactions.

2. Crafting the Perfect Message:

- **Thoughtful Communication:** Text-based interactions allow users to carefully craft their messages. They can take the time to think about their words, edit for clarity, and avoid the potential awkwardness of spontaneous conversation. This can lead to more thoughtful and intentional communication.
- **First Impressions:** The ability to edit messages before sending helps users put their best foot forward, making a positive first impression. Users can ensure their message is engaging, clear, and free from typos or misstatements.

3. Testing the Waters:

- **Gauge Interest:** Text-based interactions enable users to gauge interest without committing to an immediate face-to-face meeting. They can observe the other person's responsiveness, engagement, and tone through text exchanges before deciding whether to pursue the connection further.
- **Low Commitment:** If a conversation doesn't go well or if the interest isn't mutual, it's easier for users to disengage from a text-based interaction without the social pressure or potential awkwardness of ending an in-person conversation.

4. Building Initial Rapport:

- **Gradual Approach:** Texting allows for a gradual approach to building rapport. Users can start with light, casual conversation topics and gradually move towards more personal or deeper subjects as comfort levels increase.

● **Non-Intrusive:** Text messages are less intrusive than phone calls or in-person meetings. Users can read and respond at their own pace, which respects their time and personal space.

5. Enhancing Communication Skills:

● **Practicing Conversation:** For those who might not feel confident in their conversational skills, text-based interactions provide a way to practice and improve. Users can learn how to ask engaging questions, respond thoughtfully, and develop their communication style in a low-pressure environment.

● **Building Confidence:** Positive text interactions can build confidence, making users more comfortable when they eventually transition to phone or face-to-face communication.

6. Initial Screening:

● **Compatibility Check:** Texting offers a preliminary check on compatibility. Users can discuss interests, values, and basic preferences early on to determine if there's enough common ground to pursue the relationship further.

● **Red Flags:** Early text interactions can reveal red flags, such as poor communication skills, incompatible values, or disinterest, allowing users to make informed decisions about whether to continue engaging with the person.

7. Flexibility and Convenience:

● **Asynchronous Communication:** Texting doesn't require both parties to be available at the same time, making it a convenient way to communicate amidst busy schedules. Users can send messages and respond at their convenience, allowing for flexible and ongoing interactions.

● **Ease of Integration:** Text-based communication easily integrates into daily routines, allowing users to connect with potential matches during breaks, commutes, or downtime without disrupting their day.

Conclusion

Text-based interactions on dating apps provide a low-pressure, convenient way for users to initiate contact and gauge interest. By lowering the stakes of initial contact, allowing for thoughtful message crafting, and providing a gradual approach to building rapport, text messaging helps users navigate the early stages of dating with confidence and ease. This mode of communication respects personal boundaries and schedules, offering a flexible and comfortable environment for users to explore potential connections before committing to more personal forms of interaction. Balancing text-based communication with opportunities for face-to-face interactions can further enhance relationship development and foster meaningful connections.

Control Over Response in Text-Based Communication on Dating Apps

The control over timing and content in text-based communication on dating apps is a significant advantage that enhances user experience and interaction quality. This control allows users to carefully craft their messages and manage the pace of communication, leading to more thoughtful and effective interactions. Here's a detailed exploration of these benefits:

1. Control Over Timing:

● **Asynchronous Communication:** One of the primary advantages of text-based communication is that it's asynchronous, meaning users don't have to be available at the same time to interact. This flexibility allows users to respond when it's convenient for them, accommodating different schedules and time zones.

● **Reduced Pressure:** Unlike real-time conversations, texting doesn't require immediate responses. This reduces the pressure on users to think on their feet, allowing them to take their time to consider their replies.

- **Managing Busy Schedules:** Users with busy lifestyles can fit conversations into their day without having to carve out specific time slots for phone calls or in-person meetings. They can reply during breaks, commutes, or downtime, making it easier to maintain communication.

2. **Control Over Content:**

- **Thoughtful Crafting:** Users have the opportunity to think through their responses and craft messages that accurately convey their thoughts and feelings. This can lead to more meaningful and well-articulated conversations.

- **Editing and Refinement:** Before sending a message, users can edit and refine their text to ensure clarity and avoid misunderstandings. This can help prevent miscommunication and present a polished and thoughtful response.

- **Personalization:** Users can tailor their messages to reflect their personality, interests, and sense of humor, helping to create a stronger connection with their match. This personalization can make interactions more engaging and enjoyable.

3. **Managing Communication Pace:**

- **Setting the Tempo:** Users can control the pace of the conversation by choosing when and how often to respond. This can be especially useful for managing expectations and ensuring the conversation doesn't move too quickly or too slowly.

- **Avoiding Overwhelm:** By controlling the pace, users can prevent themselves from feeling overwhelmed by rapid back-and-forth exchanges. They can take breaks as needed, allowing them to engage more comfortably and sustainably.

- **Building Anticipation:** Deliberately spacing out responses can build anticipation and keep the other person interested and engaged. It creates a rhythm that can make conversations more dynamic and exciting.

4. **Emotional Regulation:**

- **Time to Cool Off:** In situations where a conversation might become tense or emotional, users can take a pause before responding. This cooling-off period allows them to collect their thoughts, avoid impulsive reactions, and respond more calmly and constructively.

- **Managing Emotional Tone:** Users can carefully choose their words to manage the emotional tone of the conversation. They can ensure their messages are supportive, respectful, and considerate, helping to build a positive interaction environment.

5. **Strategic Communication:**

- **Planning Responses:** Users can plan their responses strategically to ask engaging questions, steer the conversation in interesting directions, and highlight shared interests. This can lead to deeper and more meaningful interactions.

- **Addressing Sensitive Topics:** When discussing sensitive or complex topics, users can take the time to formulate their thoughts and approach the conversation delicately. This thoughtful approach can help in navigating difficult subjects more effectively.

6. **Reducing Miscommunication:**

- **Clear and Concise Messaging:** Taking the time to craft messages allows users to be clear and concise, reducing the likelihood of miscommunication. They can ensure their points are made clearly and that their intentions are understood.

- **Using Emojis and Tone Indicators:** Users can incorporate emojis and tone indicators to help convey the emotional context of their messages, adding nuance and clarity that might be lost in plain text.

7. **Enhancing Self-Presentation:**

- **Highlighting Positive Traits:** Users can highlight their positive traits, interests, and values in their messages, helping to create a favorable impression. This controlled self-presentation can make their profile more attractive to potential matches.

- **Avoiding Negative Impressions:** By carefully crafting their messages, users can avoid making negative impressions that might arise from hasty or poorly considered responses.

Conclusion

The control over timing and content in text-based communication on dating apps provides users with significant advantages. By allowing thoughtful crafting of messages, managing the pace of interactions, and reducing the pressure of immediate responses, users can enhance the quality of their conversations. This control fosters more meaningful connections, reduces the risk of miscommunication, and helps users present themselves in the best possible light. Balancing this control with opportunities for more spontaneous and personal interactions can further enrich the dating experience and support the development of deeper, more authentic relationships.

Text Over Talk - Implications

Delayed Emotional Connection in Text-Based Communication on Dating Apps

Text-based communication, while offering convenience and control, may delay the development of emotional connection and intimacy compared to face-to-face interactions. The absence of non-verbal cues and tone of voice, which play significant roles in conveying emotions and building relationships, can impact how users connect emotionally. Here's a detailed exploration of how text-based communication affects emotional connection:

1. Lack of Non-Verbal Cues:

- **Absence of Body Language:** In face-to-face interactions, body language such as facial expressions, gestures, and posture conveys a wealth of information about a person's emotions and intentions. Text-based communication lacks this critical dimension, making it harder to read the emotional undertones of a message.

- **No Eye Contact:** Eye contact is a powerful tool for building trust and intimacy. It helps convey sincerity, interest, and empathy. Without the ability to make eye contact, users may find it more challenging to establish a deep emotional connection.

2. Limited Emotional Expression:

- **Tone of Voice:** The tone of voice adds context and emotional depth to spoken words, helping to convey sarcasm, enthusiasm, affection, and other nuances. Text messages, unless explicitly stated, can be flat and open to interpretation, often missing these subtle emotional cues.

- **Emotional Nuance:** Emotions are complex and multifaceted, often expressed through subtle changes in voice and body language. Text-based communication can struggle to capture these nuances, leading to potential misunderstandings or misinterpretations of the sender's emotional state.

3. Over-Reliance on Words:

- **Word Choice:** In text-based communication, users must rely solely on their choice of words to convey their feelings and intentions. While this can lead to careful and thoughtful message crafting, it can also limit spontaneous and genuine emotional expression.

- **Emojis and Symbols:** While emojis and symbols can help convey emotions, they are not a complete substitute for the richness of human expression available in face-to-face interactions. Overuse or misuse of emojis can also lead to misinterpretation.

4. Delayed Feedback:

- **Asynchronous Responses:** Text messages are often exchanged asynchronously, meaning there can be delays between messages. This delay in feedback can hinder the natural flow of conversation and the immediate emotional responsiveness that characterizes face-to-face interactions.

- **Emotional Misalignment:** Due to the time lag, the emotional state of the participants may change between sending and receiving messages, leading to misalignment and potential misunderstandings in the conversation.

5. Building Trust and Intimacy:

- **Gradual Development:** Building trust and intimacy often requires consistent and emotionally rich interactions. Text-based communication, with its limitations, may slow down this process, requiring more time and effort to achieve the same level of emotional connection as face-to-face interactions.

- **Perceived Distance:** The digital nature of text communication can create a sense of distance, making it harder for users to feel emotionally close to their match. This perceived distance can hinder the development of a deep, emotional bond.

6. Increased Risk of Miscommunication:

- **Ambiguity in Text:** Text messages can be ambiguous, and without the additional context provided by non-verbal cues and tone of voice, users may misinterpret the intent or emotion behind a message. This can lead to confusion and hinder emotional connection.
- **Clarification Needs:** Users may need to spend extra time clarifying their messages to avoid misunderstandings, which can disrupt the natural flow of conversation and delay the development of emotional intimacy.

7. Potential Solutions and Balances:
- **Transitioning to Other Mediums:** To counteract the delay in emotional connection, users can transition from text-based communication to voice or video calls as they become more comfortable with each other. These mediums allow for richer emotional expression and quicker feedback.
- **Using Detailed Messages:** Users can compensate for the lack of non-verbal cues by being more descriptive and expressive in their text messages. Sharing personal stories, experiences, and detailed thoughts can help build a deeper emotional connection.
- **Frequent Communication:** Regular and consistent text communication can help build familiarity and comfort, gradually developing emotional intimacy over time. Frequent exchanges can also create a sense of presence and connection despite the physical distance.

Conclusion

While text-based communication on dating apps offers significant conveniences, it may delay the development of emotional connection and intimacy compared to face-to-face interactions. The absence of non-verbal cues, tone of voice, and immediate feedback can limit emotional expression and lead to potential miscommunication. To foster deeper connections, users can transition to richer communication mediums like voice or video calls, use detailed and expressive messaging, and maintain regular interaction. Balancing text-based communication with these strategies can help bridge the emotional gap and support the development of meaningful, intimate relationships in the digital dating landscape.

Limited Context in Text-Based Communication on Dating Apps

Text-based communication on dating apps, while convenient and controlled, lacks the visual and auditory cues that are essential for conveying nuances and emotional expressions. This limitation can lead to misunderstandings or misinterpretations, affecting the quality of interactions and the development of relationships. Here's a detailed exploration of the impact of limited context in text-based communication:

1. Absence of Visual Cues:
- **Facial Expressions:** Facial expressions convey a wide range of emotions such as happiness, sadness, surprise, and concern. In face-to-face interactions, these expressions provide immediate and clear emotional context to spoken words. Without these visual cues, text messages can seem ambiguous or flat.
- **Body Language:** Body language, including gestures, posture, and movement, plays a crucial role in communication. It can indicate interest, openness, discomfort, or confidence. The lack of body language in text-based communication means that users miss out on these important non-verbal signals, potentially leading to misinterpretations of intent or emotion.

2. Absence of Auditory Cues:
- **Tone of Voice:** Tone of voice adds emotional depth and context to spoken words. It can convey sarcasm, enthusiasm, sincerity, and various other emotions. Text messages, however, do not carry these vocal nuances, making it harder to interpret the sender's true feelings or intentions.

- **Pitch and Volume:** Changes in pitch and volume can emphasize certain points or indicate the emotional intensity behind words. The absence of these auditory cues in text-based communication can result in messages being perceived differently than intended.

3. Ambiguity and Misinterpretation:

- **Literal Interpretation:** Without visual and auditory cues, users are left to interpret messages based solely on the text. This can lead to a more literal interpretation of words, which may not fully capture the sender's intended meaning. For example, a sarcastic comment can be misunderstood as serious if the tone isn't clear.

- **Overlooking Subtleties:** Subtle emotional expressions or underlying tones can be easily overlooked in text-based communication. This can result in important nuances being missed, such as whether a message is meant to be lighthearted or serious.

4. Emotional Misalignment:

- **Different Emotional States:** Text-based communication often occurs asynchronously, meaning users may respond to messages at different times, potentially in different emotional states. This can lead to emotional misalignment, where the emotional context of the message doesn't match the recipient's current state, causing confusion or misinterpretation.

- **Delayed Emotional Response:** The delay in receiving and responding to text messages can disrupt the natural flow of emotional exchange. Users might miss out on immediate emotional reactions that provide context and clarity in face-to-face interactions.

5. Increased Effort for Clarity:

- **Need for Explicit Communication:** To compensate for the lack of non-verbal and auditory cues, users may need to be more explicit in their text messages. This involves using more descriptive language, emoticons, or additional context to ensure their message is understood as intended.

- **Clarifying Questions:** Users might need to ask more clarifying questions to understand the emotional context or intent behind a message. This can add extra steps to the communication process and potentially slow down the interaction.

6. Potential for Misunderstandings:

- **Misinterpretation of Tone:** Without auditory cues, the tone of a message can be easily misinterpreted. A neutral statement might be perceived as harsh, or a joke might be taken seriously, leading to misunderstandings and potential conflicts.

- **Assumptions and Inferences:** In the absence of clear non-verbal and auditory cues, users might make assumptions or inferences about the sender's emotions or intentions. These assumptions can be incorrect and lead to misunderstandings or miscommunications.

7. Strategies to Mitigate Limited Context:

- **Use of Emojis and Emoticons:** Emojis and emoticons can help convey emotions and tone, adding context to text messages. While not a perfect substitute for facial expressions or tone of voice, they can provide additional emotional cues.

- **Detailed and Descriptive Messages:** Being more detailed and descriptive in text messages can help convey the intended emotional context. Users can describe their feelings or thoughts more explicitly to avoid ambiguity.

- **Voice and Video Calls:** Transitioning to voice or video calls can provide the missing auditory and visual cues, helping to convey emotions and nuances more effectively. These mediums offer richer context and can enhance emotional connection.

8. Building Understanding and Patience:

- **Patience and Clarification:** Recognizing the limitations of text-based communication, users should practice patience and seek clarification when needed. Rather than jumping to conclusions, asking follow-up questions can help ensure understanding.
- **Building Trust:** Over time, as users become more familiar with each other's communication styles, the potential for misinterpretation decreases. Building trust and understanding through consistent and clear communication can mitigate the impact of limited context.

Conclusion

The limited context in text-based communication on dating apps can lead to misunderstandings and misinterpretations due to the absence of visual and auditory cues. Without facial expressions, body language, and tone of voice, users must rely solely on text to convey their messages, which can result in ambiguity and emotional misalignment. To mitigate these challenges, users can use emojis, detailed descriptions, and transition to voice or video calls for richer communication. Recognizing the limitations and practicing patience and clarity can help build stronger, more meaningful connections despite the constraints of text-based interactions.

Difficulty in Reading Intentions in Text-Based Communication on Dating Apps

Text-based communication on dating apps presents unique challenges in accurately gauging the intentions and emotions of matches. The absence of non-verbal cues and tone of voice can significantly increase the risk of miscommunication. Here's a detailed exploration of how users may struggle to interpret intentions and emotions solely through text:

1. Lack of Non-Verbal Cues:
- **Facial Expressions and Body Language:** In face-to-face communication, facial expressions and body language provide essential context that helps convey intentions and emotions. Text-based communication lacks these visual cues, making it harder for users to understand the full meaning behind a message.
- **Gestures and Posture:** Gestures and posture also play a significant role in expressing feelings and attitudes. Without these physical cues, text messages can be open to multiple interpretations, leading to potential misunderstandings.

2. Absence of Auditory Cues:
- **Tone of Voice:** The tone of voice adds emotional depth to spoken words, indicating sarcasm, enthusiasm, seriousness, or other emotions. Text lacks this auditory element, making it challenging to discern the sender's emotional state or intention behind their words.
- **Inflection and Emphasis:** Inflection and emphasis in speech can highlight certain parts of a message, providing clues about the speaker's intentions. These nuances are missing in text-based communication, leading to potential ambiguity.

3. Ambiguity and Interpretation:
- **Literal Interpretation:** Without additional context, users might interpret text messages literally, missing out on the subtle emotional cues that would be evident in face-to-face interactions. This can result in misinterpretations of sarcasm, jokes, or light-hearted comments.
- **Variable Contexts:** Each user might have a different interpretation of the same text based on their personal experiences, mood, and current context, which can lead to misunderstandings.

4. Over-Reliance on Words:

- **Limited Expressiveness:** Text messages rely solely on words to convey meaning. This limitation can hinder the expressiveness of communication, especially for complex emotions and intentions that are better conveyed through a combination of verbal and non-verbal cues.

- **Misreading Subtext:** Users may misread or fail to detect subtext and underlying emotions in messages, leading to potential conflicts or confusion about the sender's true intentions.

5. Emotional Misalignment:

- **Delayed Emotional Responses:** As text-based communication often occurs asynchronously, there can be delays in responses. This can result in emotional misalignment, where the sender's emotional context might differ significantly from the recipient's current state.

- **Inconsistent Emotional Cues:** The lack of real-time feedback can cause inconsistencies in emotional cues, making it harder for users to align their emotional states and understand each other's intentions accurately.

6. Increased Risk of Miscommunication:

- **Ambiguity in Tone:** The tone of a text message can be easily misinterpreted. A message intended to be friendly or humorous might be perceived as rude or dismissive without the correct tonal context.

- **Misunderstanding Intentions:** Without clear indicators of intention, users might misconstrue the purpose or seriousness of a message, leading to confusion about the sender's motives or feelings.

7. Strategies to Mitigate Difficulties:

- **Use of Emojis and Emoticons:** Emojis and emoticons can help convey emotions and tone, providing additional context that can clarify the sender's intentions. However, they should be used thoughtfully to avoid over-reliance and potential misinterpretation.

- **Explicit Communication:** Being explicit and detailed in messages can help reduce ambiguity. Users can describe their feelings, intentions, and context more clearly to ensure their message is understood as intended.

- **Clarifying Questions:** Asking follow-up questions and seeking clarification can help ensure understanding. Rather than making assumptions, users can verify their interpretations of a message.

8. Transition to Richer Communication Mediums:

- **Voice and Video Calls:** To overcome the limitations of text-based communication, transitioning to voice or video calls can provide the missing auditory and visual cues. These mediums allow for more nuanced and expressive interactions, helping to convey intentions and emotions more accurately.

- **Face-to-Face Meetings:** Whenever possible, moving from online interactions to face-to-face meetings can significantly enhance understanding and emotional connection. In-person communication provides the full range of non-verbal and auditory cues, reducing the risk of miscommunication.

Conclusion

The difficulty in reading intentions and emotions in text-based communication on dating apps stems from the absence of non-verbal and auditory cues. This limitation can lead to misinterpretations and increased risk of miscommunication. To mitigate these challenges, users can utilize emojis, provide explicit context, and ask clarifying questions. Transitioning to richer communication mediums like voice or video calls can also enhance understanding and emotional connection. By adopting these strategies, users can navigate the limitations of text-based communication and build more meaningful and accurate interactions on dating apps.

Miscommunication and Misinterpretation - Potential Challenges

Ambiguity in Text-Based Communication on Dating Apps

Text-based communication on dating apps, while convenient, often suffers from ambiguity due to the absence of non-verbal cues and tone of voice. This ambiguity can lead to misinterpretations and unintended implications, affecting the quality of interactions and relationships. Here's a detailed exploration of how text-based messages can be ambiguous and the potential consequences:

1. Lack of Non-Verbal Cues:

● **Facial Expressions and Body Language:** In face-to-face communication, facial expressions, gestures, and body language provide essential context that helps clarify the speaker's intent and emotions. Text messages lack these visual cues, making it harder for the recipient to fully understand the sender's meaning.

● **Tone of Voice:** Tone of voice adds emotional depth to spoken words, indicating sarcasm, enthusiasm, seriousness, or other emotions. Text lacks this auditory element, making it challenging to discern the sender's emotional state or the intended tone behind their words.

2. Multiple Interpretations:

● **Literal vs. Figurative Meaning:** Without additional context, text messages can be interpreted literally, figuratively, or in various other ways. A simple statement like "I'm fine" can be interpreted as genuinely fine, sarcastic, or dismissive, depending on the context which is often missing in text-based communication.

● **Lack of Emotional Nuance:** Text-based messages may not convey the full range of emotions that the sender intends. For example, a joke or playful comment might be misunderstood as rude or offensive if the recipient doesn't recognize the intended humor.

3. Context Dependency:

● **Recipient's State of Mind:** The recipient's mood, previous experiences, and current context can significantly influence how they interpret a text message. A neutral message might be perceived negatively if the recipient is in a bad mood or has had a negative experience earlier.

● **Cultural and Personal Differences:** Cultural background and personal communication styles can also affect interpretation. What might be a harmless joke in one culture could be seen as offensive in another, leading to misunderstandings.

4. Ambiguity in Content:

● **Vague Language:** The use of vague or ambiguous language can contribute to misunderstandings. Phrases like "we should hang out sometime" or "let's see how it goes" can be interpreted in various ways, leading to confusion about the sender's true intentions.

● **Short and Abrupt Messages:** Short messages or responses, such as "ok" or "sure," can come across as disinterested or dismissive, even if that's not the sender's intention. The brevity of these messages often lacks the context needed to convey the sender's true feelings.

5. Potential Consequences:

● **Misinterpretations:** Ambiguous text messages can lead to misinterpretations, where the recipient misunderstands the sender's intentions, emotions, or meaning. This can cause unnecessary confusion, frustration, or conflict.

● **Unintended Implications:** Messages that are not clear can be perceived in ways the sender did not intend. For example, a message meant to be light-hearted might be taken seriously, leading to unintended consequences in the relationship.

6. Strategies to Mitigate Ambiguity:

- **Use of Emojis and Emoticons:** Emojis and emoticons can help convey emotions and tone, providing additional context that can clarify the sender's intentions. For example, a smiley face can indicate that a message is meant to be friendly or humorous.
- **Explicit Communication:** Being explicit and detailed in messages can help reduce ambiguity. Users can describe their feelings, intentions, and context more clearly to ensure their message is understood as intended.
- **Asking Clarifying Questions:** If a message is unclear, recipients can ask follow-up questions to seek clarification. This helps ensure understanding and avoids making incorrect assumptions.
- **Using Voice and Video Calls:** Whenever possible, transitioning to voice or video calls can provide the missing auditory and visual cues. These mediums allow for more nuanced and expressive interactions, helping to convey intentions and emotions more accurately.

7. **Building Understanding and Patience:**
- **Practicing Patience:** Recognizing that text-based communication has limitations, users should practice patience and avoid jumping to conclusions. Giving the benefit of the doubt can help prevent unnecessary conflicts.
- **Building Familiarity:** Over time, as users become more familiar with each other's communication styles, the potential for misinterpretation decreases. Building trust and understanding through consistent and clear communication can mitigate the impact of ambiguity.

Conclusion

Text-based communication on dating apps often suffers from ambiguity due to the absence of non-verbal and auditory cues. This can lead to misinterpretations and unintended implications, affecting the quality of interactions. To mitigate these challenges, users can utilize emojis, provide explicit context, and ask clarifying questions. Transitioning to richer communication mediums like voice or video calls can also enhance understanding and emotional connection. By adopting these strategies, users can navigate the limitations of text-based communication and build more meaningful and accurate interactions on dating apps.

Assumptions in Text-Based Communication on Dating Apps

Text-based communication on dating apps often leads users to make assumptions about their matches based on limited information. These assumptions can result in misunderstandings or premature conclusions, affecting the dynamics of potential relationships. Here's a detailed exploration of how assumptions arise and their potential consequences:

1. **Limited Information:**
- **Profiles and Bios:** Dating profiles typically include photos, brief bios, and a few details about interests and preferences. This limited information can lead users to fill in the gaps with assumptions, which may not accurately reflect the person's true character or intentions.
- **Short Messages:** Initial conversations are usually brief and focused on getting to know basic facts about each other. The lack of depth in these interactions can result in assumptions about a match's personality, values, and compatibility.

2. **Interpretation of Text:**
- **Ambiguous Language:** Text messages often lack the clarity and nuance of face-to-face communication. Words and phrases can be interpreted in various ways, leading users to make assumptions based on their own perspectives and experiences.

- **Tone and Intent:** Without auditory and visual cues, it's challenging to discern the tone and intent behind a message. Users might assume a certain tone (e.g., sarcasm, seriousness) that wasn't intended by the sender, leading to potential misunderstandings.

3. Personal Biases and Experiences:

- **Past Experiences:** Users' past experiences can heavily influence how they interpret messages. For example, someone who has been hurt in previous relationships might assume negative intentions in a message that was meant to be neutral or positive.

- **Cognitive Biases:** Cognitive biases, such as confirmation bias (favoring information that confirms pre-existing beliefs), can lead users to interpret messages in ways that align with their expectations or fears.

4. Assumptions About Compatibility:

- **Interests and Hobbies:** Users might assume that sharing similar interests or hobbies automatically means compatibility. However, shared interests don't always translate to deeper compatibility in values, goals, or lifestyle.

- **First Impressions:** First impressions based on profile pictures and initial messages can be misleading. Users might assume someone is a perfect match or completely unsuitable based on these limited interactions.

5. Potential Consequences:

- **Misunderstandings:** Assumptions can lead to misunderstandings about a match's intentions, feelings, or personality. This can cause unnecessary conflicts or discomfort in the interaction.

- **Premature Judgments:** Making quick judgments based on assumptions can result in dismissing potentially good matches too soon or pursuing matches that might not be genuinely compatible in the long run.

- **Emotional Reactions:** Assumptions can evoke strong emotional reactions, such as excitement, disappointment, or frustration, which might not be warranted if the full context were known.

6. Strategies to Mitigate Assumptions:

- **Clarification and Communication:** Encouraging open and honest communication can help clarify intentions and reduce assumptions. Asking questions and seeking clarification about ambiguous messages can prevent misunderstandings.

- **Taking Time:** Allowing more time to get to know a match before making conclusions can help build a more accurate understanding of their personality and compatibility.

- **Checking Biases:** Being aware of personal biases and past experiences that might color interpretations can help users approach conversations with a more open mind.

- **Transitioning to Richer Communication:** Moving from text-based interactions to voice or video calls can provide additional context and help users better understand tone, intent, and emotional nuances.

7. Building Empathy and Understanding:

- **Giving Benefit of the Doubt:** Assuming positive intentions and giving matches the benefit of the doubt can help prevent premature negative judgments. Approaching conversations with empathy and understanding can create a more positive interaction environment.

- **Focusing on Consistency:** Looking for consistency in a match's communication and behavior over time can provide a more accurate picture of their intentions and character. Consistent actions and words are more reliable indicators than isolated messages.

8. Educating Users:

- **Awareness of Limitations:** Educating users about the limitations of text-based communication and the common pitfalls of making assumptions can help them navigate interactions more effectively.

- **Promoting Patience:** Encouraging users to be patient and take the time to build a deeper understanding of their matches can lead to more meaningful connections.

Conclusion

Assumptions in text-based communication on dating apps often arise from limited information, ambiguous language, personal biases, and the lack of non-verbal cues. These assumptions can lead to misunderstandings, premature judgments, and emotional reactions that may not be warranted. To mitigate these challenges, users can focus on open communication, seek clarification, allow more time to understand their matches, and transition to richer communication mediums like voice or video calls. By building empathy, checking biases, and promoting patience, users can navigate the complexities of text-based interactions more effectively and build more meaningful connections.

Emotional Expression in Text-Based Communication on Dating Apps

Text-based communication on dating apps poses unique challenges, particularly when it comes to conveying and interpreting emotions. The absence of facial expressions, body language, and other non-verbal cues can significantly limit emotional expression, leading to potential misunderstandings and difficulties in forming deeper connections. Here's a detailed exploration of how the lack of non-verbal cues impacts emotional expression and communication:

1. Limitations of Text-Based Communication:

● **Facial Expressions:** Facial expressions are crucial for conveying emotions such as happiness, sadness, anger, or surprise. Without seeing a person's face, it's challenging to understand their true emotional state, making it harder to empathize and respond appropriately.

● **Body Language:** Gestures, posture, and movements add context to verbal communication. For example, crossed arms might indicate defensiveness, while a relaxed posture can suggest openness. Text messages lack these physical indicators, leaving room for misinterpretation.

2. Challenges in Conveying Emotions:

● **Tone and Intonation:** In spoken communication, tone and intonation help express emotions and nuances. For instance, the same sentence can sound supportive or sarcastic depending on how it's said. Text messages can't convey these subtleties, leading to potential misinterpretation of the sender's intent.

● **Subtle Emotional Cues:** Small emotional cues, such as a slight smile or a furrowed brow, often go unnoticed in text-based communication. These subtle cues play a significant role in understanding how someone feels in a given moment.

3. Impact on Interpretation:

● **Ambiguity in Messages:** Text messages can be ambiguous, and without non-verbal cues, it's easy to misinterpret the emotional undertone. A message like "I'm fine" can be interpreted in multiple ways—genuinely fine, sarcastically fine, or reluctantly fine—without additional context.

● **Over-Reliance on Assumptions:** In the absence of clear emotional indicators, users may rely on assumptions based on their own feelings, experiences, and biases. This can lead to incorrect conclusions about the other person's emotional state.

4. Strategies to Enhance Emotional Expression:

● **Use of Emojis and Emoticons:** Emojis and emoticons can help convey emotions more effectively in text-based communication. A smiley face, for example, can indicate friendliness or happiness, while a sad face can convey disappointment or empathy.

● **Detailed and Descriptive Language:** Using detailed and descriptive language can help convey emotions more clearly. Instead of saying "I'm fine," a more descriptive response like "I'm feeling a bit overwhelmed but managing" provides better emotional context.

● **Clarifying Questions:** Asking clarifying questions can help ensure accurate interpretation of emotional states. For example, if a message seems ambiguous, asking "How are you really feeling?" can prompt a more detailed response.

5. Emotional Connection and Authenticity:

● **Building Trust:** Consistently expressing emotions honestly and openly can help build trust and authenticity in text-based interactions. Sharing personal experiences and feelings can foster a deeper emotional connection.

● **Active Listening:** Demonstrating active listening skills, such as summarizing what the other person has said and responding thoughtfully, can enhance emotional connection. Phrases like "It sounds like you're feeling..." can show empathy and understanding.

6. Transitioning to Richer Communication Mediums:

● **Voice and Video Calls:** Transitioning from text messages to voice or video calls can significantly enhance emotional expression. Voice calls add tone and intonation, while video calls provide visual cues like facial expressions and body language, offering a more holistic view of the other person's emotions.

● **Balanced Communication:** Combining text messages with occasional voice or video calls can balance convenience with the need for richer emotional expression. This approach helps maintain continuous communication while allowing for more nuanced emotional interactions when needed.

7. Mitigating Misunderstandings:

● **Clarifying Intentions:** Being clear about intentions and emotions in text messages can help reduce misunderstandings. Phrases like "I'm joking" or "I'm serious" can clarify the tone of a message.

● **Providing Context:** Sharing context around a message can help the recipient understand the emotional state behind it. For example, explaining a stressful day at work can provide context for a seemingly curt message.

Conclusion

Text-based communication on dating apps, while convenient, often limits emotional expression due to the absence of facial expressions, body language, and tone of voice. This can lead to ambiguity, misinterpretation, and reliance on assumptions, affecting the quality of interactions and emotional connections. To mitigate these challenges, users can employ strategies such as using emojis, detailed language, and clarifying questions. Transitioning to richer communication mediums like voice and video calls can also enhance emotional expression and understanding. By being mindful of these limitations and adopting effective communication practices, users can navigate text-based interactions more successfully and build deeper, more meaningful connections.

Miscommunication and Misinterpretation - Impact on Relationships

Conflict Resolution in Text-Based Conversations on Dating Apps

Text-based communication on dating apps, while convenient, can lead to miscommunication that escalates conflicts or disagreements. The absence of non-verbal cues and tone of voice makes it challenging to convey and interpret nuances and intentions accurately. Here's a detailed exploration of how miscommunication in text-based conversations can escalate conflicts and strategies for effective conflict resolution:

1. Challenges in Text-Based Communication:

● **Lack of Non-Verbal Cues:** Text messages lack facial expressions, body language, and tone of voice, which are essential for understanding emotions and intentions accurately.

● **Ambiguity:** Messages can be ambiguous or open to interpretation, leading to misunderstandings about the sender's intentions or emotional state.

● **Assumptions:** Users may make assumptions based on their own biases or past experiences, which can lead to misinterpretations of messages.

2. Causes of Escalated Conflicts:

● **Misinterpreted Tone:** Without auditory cues, text messages can be misinterpreted as hostile, sarcastic, or indifferent, even if the sender didn't intend such tones.

● **Delayed Responses:** Delayed responses in text-based conversations can create tension or anxiety, with recipients interpreting the delay as disinterest or rudeness.

● **Emotional Responses:** Strong emotions, such as frustration or disappointment, can escalate conflicts when they're expressed through text without the moderating influence of face-to-face interaction.

3. Strategies for Effective Conflict Resolution:

● **Clarity and Directness:** Communicate clearly and directly to avoid ambiguity. Clearly express thoughts, feelings, and intentions to minimize misunderstandings.

● **Use of Emojis and Emoticons:** Emojis and emoticons can add emotional context to messages, helping to convey tone and reduce misinterpretations.

● **Active Listening:** Practice active listening by paraphrasing and summarizing the other person's messages to ensure understanding before responding.

● **Avoid Assumptions:** Avoid making assumptions about the other person's intentions or feelings. Instead, ask clarifying questions to gain a better understanding.

● **Take Breaks:** If emotions are escalating, take a break from the conversation. Stepping away temporarily can provide space for reflection and prevent further escalation.

● **Seek Common Ground:** Focus on finding common ground and areas of agreement rather than dwelling on differences. This approach can help de-escalate conflicts and foster constructive dialogue.

● **Apologize When Necessary:** If misunderstandings or miscommunications occur, apologize sincerely. Acknowledging mistakes or misunderstandings can help rebuild trust and rapport.

● **Transition to Voice or Video Calls:** If a conflict persists or becomes complex, consider transitioning to voice or video calls. These mediums allow for richer communication with tone of voice and visual cues, facilitating clearer understanding and resolution.

● **Learn from Conflicts:** Use conflicts as opportunities for growth and learning. Reflect on what contributed to the misunderstanding and discuss ways to improve communication in future interactions.

4. Building Trust and Understanding:

● **Consistency:** Consistently demonstrating honesty, respect, and empathy in communication can build trust and understanding over time.

● **Patience:** Be patient with each other's perspectives and communication styles. Recognize that misunderstandings are common in text-based conversations and approach conflicts with patience and understanding.

5. Cultural and Personal Considerations:

● **Cultural Sensitivity:** Be mindful of cultural differences that may influence communication styles and interpretations of messages.

● **Personal Boundaries:** Respect each other's boundaries and preferences for communication. Discuss and establish boundaries early in the relationship to avoid misunderstandings.

6. Conflict as a Growth Opportunity:

● **Resolution Through Understanding:** Use conflicts as opportunities to deepen understanding and strengthen communication skills. Discussing and resolving conflicts can lead to stronger connections and mutual respect.

Conclusion

Miscommunication in text-based conversations on dating apps can escalate conflicts due to the lack of non-verbal cues, ambiguity, and assumptions. Effective conflict resolution strategies include clear communication, active listening, using emojis for emotional context, and seeking common ground. Taking breaks, transitioning to voice or video calls when needed, and learning from conflicts can foster trust, understanding, and stronger relationships. By approaching conflicts with patience, empathy, and a willingness to resolve misunderstandings, users can navigate text-based interactions more effectively and build healthier connections on dating apps.

Building Trust Through Effective Communication on Dating Apps

Building trust on dating apps relies heavily on effective communication, which can be challenging due to the limitations of text-based interactions. Misinterpretations and misunderstandings can hinder trust-building efforts. Here's a detailed exploration of how effective communication fosters trust and strategies to overcome communication challenges:

1. Importance of Effective Communication:

● **Clarity and Transparency:** Clear and transparent communication helps build trust by conveying honesty and openness. Clearly expressing thoughts, feelings, and intentions reduces the likelihood of misunderstandings.

● **Consistency:** Consistently demonstrating respect, empathy, and reliability in communication builds trust over time. Consistent behavior and messaging reinforce reliability and sincerity.

2. Challenges in Text-Based Interactions:

● **Lack of Non-Verbal Cues:** Text messages lack facial expressions, body language, and tone of voice, which are crucial for interpreting emotions and intentions accurately.

● **Ambiguity:** Messages can be ambiguous or open to interpretation, leading to misunderstandings about the sender's intentions or emotional state.

● **Assumptions:** Users may make assumptions based on their own biases or past experiences, which can lead to misinterpretations of messages.

3. Strategies for Building Trust:

● **Clear Communication:** Be clear and direct in your communication to avoid ambiguity. Clearly express your thoughts, feelings, and expectations to minimize misunderstandings.

- **Active Listening:** Practice active listening by summarizing and paraphrasing the other person's messages to ensure understanding before responding. This demonstrates attentiveness and respect for their perspective.
- **Use of Emojis and Emoticons:** Emojis and emoticons can add emotional context to messages, helping to convey tone and reduce the risk of misinterpretation.
- **Ask Clarifying Questions:** If a message is unclear or raises doubts, ask clarifying questions to gain a better understanding of the other person's perspective and intentions.
- **Avoid Assumptions:** Avoid making assumptions about the other person's feelings or intentions. Instead, seek clarification to ensure mutual understanding.
- **Share Personal Insights:** Sharing personal insights, experiences, and perspectives fosters openness and authenticity, which are key to building trust.
- **Be Reliable:** Demonstrate reliability by following through on commitments, responding promptly to messages, and being consistent in your interactions.
- **Apologize and Repair:** If misunderstandings or conflicts arise, apologize sincerely and work together to resolve issues. Addressing and repairing trust breaches demonstrates accountability and commitment to the relationship.

4. Overcoming Communication Challenges:

- **Transition to Richer Communication:** Consider transitioning from text messages to voice or video calls when appropriate. These mediums allow for richer communication with tone of voice and non-verbal cues, enhancing understanding and emotional connection.
- **Educate Yourself:** Learn about communication styles and preferences. Understanding cultural differences or personal communication preferences can improve mutual understanding and trust.
- **Build Emotional Intelligence:** Develop emotional intelligence to recognize and manage emotions effectively. Being emotionally aware helps navigate sensitive topics and foster empathy in interactions.

5. Consistency and Patience:

- **Consistency in Behavior:** Consistently demonstrating honesty, respect, and empathy builds trust over time. Reliable behavior and communication reinforce sincerity and reliability.
- **Patience and Understanding:** Approach misunderstandings or communication challenges with patience and understanding. Building trust takes time and effort, especially in text-based interactions where nuances can be easily missed.

6. Building a Foundation of Trust:

- **Mutual Respect:** Show respect for each other's perspectives, boundaries, and communication preferences. Respecting personal boundaries and preferences builds a foundation of trust and mutual respect.
- **Authenticity and Vulnerability:** Share authentic thoughts, feelings, and experiences to foster vulnerability and deepen emotional connection. Being genuine and vulnerable encourages reciprocity and trust.

Conclusion

Effective communication is essential for building trust and establishing a deeper connection on dating apps. Misinterpretations and frequent misunderstandings in text-based interactions can hinder trust-building efforts. By practicing clear communication, active listening, using emotional cues like emojis, and avoiding assumptions, users can foster trust, authenticity, and mutual understanding. Overcoming communication challenges through patience, consistency, and empathy builds a strong foundation of trust that enhances relationships on dating apps.

Stress and Anxiety in Text-Based Conversations on Dating Apps

Navigating conversations on dating apps can be stressful and anxiety-inducing, especially when trying to convey emotions or discuss sensitive topics through text alone. The inherent limitations of text-based communication, such as the absence of non-verbal cues and potential for misinterpretation, contribute to these feelings. Here's a detailed exploration of how stress and anxiety manifest in text-based conversations and strategies to manage them effectively:

1. Challenges in Text-Based Communication:

● **Ambiguity:** Text messages can be ambiguous, making it difficult to accurately convey or interpret emotions, intentions, and nuances.

● **Misinterpretation:** Without non-verbal cues like facial expressions and tone of voice, messages can be misinterpreted, leading to misunderstandings and heightened anxiety.

● **Pressure to Respond:** There may be pressure to respond quickly to messages, especially if there's anticipation or uncertainty about the other person's expectations.

2. Sources of Stress and Anxiety:

● **Complex Conversations:** Discussions involving emotions, sensitive topics, or relationship expectations can be challenging to navigate through text alone.

● **Fear of Miscommunication:** Anxiety may arise from the fear of being misunderstood or unintentionally causing offense due to the limitations of text-based communication.

● **Overthinking:** Users may overanalyze messages, trying to discern hidden meanings or intentions, which can heighten stress and anxiety.

3. Strategies to Manage Stress and Anxiety:

● **Clear Communication:** Be clear and direct in your messages to minimize ambiguity and reduce the risk of misunderstandings. Use straightforward language to convey your thoughts and feelings effectively.

● **Use of Emojis and Emoticons:** Emojis and emoticons can add emotional context to messages, helping to convey tone and reduce the likelihood of misinterpretation. They can also lighten the mood and ease tension in conversations.

● **Take Breaks:** If you feel overwhelmed or anxious during a conversation, take breaks to regroup and gather your thoughts. Stepping away momentarily can provide perspective and reduce stress.

● **Manage Expectations:** Clarify expectations around response times and communication frequency to alleviate pressure. Set boundaries that prioritize your mental well-being while maintaining respectful communication.

● **Practice Active Listening:** Focus on understanding the other person's perspective before responding. Summarize and paraphrase their messages to ensure clarity and demonstrate empathy.

● **Seek Clarification:** If a message is unclear or causes anxiety, ask for clarification. It's okay to seek additional information to better understand the other person's intentions or feelings.

● **Engage in Self-Care:** Engage in activities that promote relaxation and reduce stress outside of dating app interactions. Practicing self-care, such as exercise, meditation, or hobbies, can help manage anxiety levels.

● **Share Vulnerabilities:** Be open about your feelings and vulnerabilities in a respectful manner. Sharing your concerns or anxieties can foster understanding and empathy in the conversation.

4. Building Resilience:

● **Learn from Experiences:** Reflect on past interactions to identify patterns or triggers that contribute to stress and anxiety. Use these insights to develop strategies for future conversations.

● **Set Realistic Expectations:** Recognize that misunderstandings and challenges are common in text-based communication. Setting realistic expectations for yourself and others can reduce pressure and anxiety.

5. Seeking Support:

● **Talk to Friends or Counselors:** If feelings of stress or anxiety persist, consider talking to friends, family, or a counselor. Discussing your concerns with a supportive person can provide perspective and alleviate anxiety.

6. Transition to Richer Communication:

● **Voice or Video Calls:** Consider transitioning from text messages to voice or video calls for more complex or emotional conversations. Hearing tone of voice and seeing facial expressions can enhance understanding and reduce anxiety.

Conclusion

Stress and anxiety in text-based conversations on dating apps stem from the challenges of conveying emotions, navigating ambiguity, and managing expectations without non-verbal cues. By practicing clear communication, using emotional cues like emojis, taking breaks when needed, and engaging in self-care, users can manage stress and anxiety effectively. Building resilience through reflection, setting realistic expectations, and seeking support when necessary can enhance confidence and well-being in navigating conversations on dating apps.

Strategies for Effective Communication

Use of Emojis and Tone Indicators in Text-Based Messages

In text-based communication, such as on dating apps, incorporating emojis, punctuation marks, or tone indicators like sarcasm tags can significantly enhance clarity and convey emotions effectively. Here's a detailed exploration of how these tools can be used to clarify tone and emotions in messages:

1. Enhancing Clarity and Emotion:

- **Emojis as Emotional Cues:** Emojis serve as visual representations of emotions, allowing users to convey feelings such as happiness 😊, sadness 😞, excitement ✨, or affection ❤. They add emotional context to messages, helping recipients interpret the intended tone and mood accurately.

- **Punctuation Marks:** Punctuation, such as exclamation points (!) or ellipses (...), can emphasize emotions or indicate pauses in speech. For example, "I'm so excited!" versus "I'm so excited..." can convey different levels of enthusiasm or anticipation.

- **Tone Indicators:** Tone indicators like "/s" (for sarcasm) or "/j" (for joking) clarify the intended tone of a message, reducing the risk of misinterpretation. These tags explicitly denote sarcasm, humor, or seriousness, ensuring that the message is received as intended.

2. Practical Applications:

- **Conveying Humor:** Emojis and tone indicators are particularly useful for conveying humor or sarcasm, which can be challenging to interpret in text alone. For instance, adding a laughing emoji 😄 or "/j" after a humorous comment ensures that the recipient understands it as a joke.

- **Expressing Emotions:** Emojis allow users to express a wide range of emotions beyond words alone. Whether it's excitement, gratitude, love, or disappointment, emojis provide a quick and visual way to convey feelings accurately.

- **Softening Statements:** Emojis can soften statements that may otherwise appear blunt or harsh. For example, adding a smiley face ✨ at the end of constructive feedback can make it sound more supportive and encouraging.

- **Clarifying Intentions:** Tone indicators such as "/s" clarify when a statement is meant sarcastically, preventing misunderstandings that could arise from literal interpretation.

3. Strategies for Effective Use:

- **Match Emoji to Context:** Choose emojis that match the context and tone of your message. For example, use celebratory emojis like ✨ for good news or sympathy emojis like 😞 for condolences.

- **Avoid Overuse:** While emojis are effective for conveying emotions, avoid overusing them, which can detract from the clarity of your message. Use them selectively to enhance rather than overwhelm communication.

- **Consider Cultural Context:** Be mindful of cultural differences in emoji interpretations. Emojis may have different meanings or connotations across cultures, so choose emojis that are widely understood in your intended audience.

- **Use Tone Indicators Appropriately:** Use tone indicators sparingly and only when necessary to clarify the tone of a message. Overuse of tone indicators can detract from the natural flow of conversation.

- **Combine with Words:** Emojis and tone indicators should complement, not replace, clear and articulate communication. Use them alongside well-worded messages to ensure complete understanding.

4. Benefits in Dating Contexts:

- **Building Rapport:** Emojis and tone indicators help build rapport and emotional connection by effectively conveying emotions and intentions. They add warmth and personality to messages, enhancing the overall dating experience.

● **Reducing Miscommunication:** By clarifying tone and emotions, emojis and tone indicators reduce the likelihood of misinterpretation or misunderstandings in potentially sensitive or nuanced conversations.

● **Expressing Affection:** Emojis like ❤, 😊, or ☺ are commonly used to express affection and interest in dating contexts, fostering positive interactions and enhancing romantic communication.

5. Cultural Sensitivity and Adaptation:

● **Understand Cultural Nuances:** Be aware of cultural nuances in emoji usage. Some emojis may have different meanings or cultural connotations, so consider the cultural background of the recipient when choosing emojis.

● **Respect Preferences:** Respect individual preferences regarding emoji usage. Some people may prefer minimal emoji use, while others may enjoy expressive and colorful messages. Adapt your communication style based on the recipient's preferences.

Conclusion

Incorporating emojis, punctuation marks, and tone indicators enhances clarity and emotional expression in text-based messages on dating apps. These tools help convey emotions, clarify intentions, and reduce the risk of miscommunication. By using emojis and tone indicators strategically, users can foster effective communication, build rapport, and enhance the overall quality of interactions in dating contexts.

Active Listening in Communication

Active listening is a crucial skill that enhances understanding, reduces misunderstandings, and promotes clearer communication in various contexts, including conversations on dating apps. Here's a detailed exploration of active listening and its benefits in fostering effective communication:

1. Understanding Active Listening:

● **Definition:** Active listening involves fully concentrating on what the other person is saying, understanding their message, responding thoughtfully, and confirming understanding through paraphrasing or clarifying questions.

● **Key Elements:**

○ **Pay Attention:** Focus on the speaker's words, tone of voice, and non-verbal cues to grasp their message fully.

○ **Show Interest:** Demonstrate interest and engagement through verbal cues (e.g., nodding, verbal affirmations) and non-verbal cues (e.g., eye contact, body posture).

○ **Reflect Understanding:** Reflect back on what the speaker has said by paraphrasing or summarizing their message to confirm mutual understanding.

○ **Seek Clarification:** Ask questions to clarify any points that are unclear or ambiguous, ensuring that both parties are on the same page.

2. Benefits of Active Listening:

● **Reduced Misunderstandings:** By actively listening, you're better able to understand the speaker's intentions, emotions, and perspectives, reducing the likelihood of misinterpretation or misunderstanding.

● **Enhanced Empathy:** Active listening fosters empathy by allowing you to see situations from the speaker's point of view and understand their feelings and concerns more deeply.

- **Improved Communication:** Clearer understanding leads to more effective responses and exchanges, creating a more productive and respectful communication environment.
- **Building Trust:** Active listening demonstrates respect and genuine interest in the speaker's thoughts and feelings, building trust and rapport over time.

3. Practices for Practicing Active Listening on Dating Apps:

- **Focus on the Conversation:** Minimize distractions and give your full attention to the messages you receive on dating apps. This shows respect and enhances understanding.
- **Validate Emotions:** Acknowledge the emotions expressed by the other person. For example, respond with empathy to statements of excitement, concern, or joy.
- **Paraphrase or Summarize:** Repeat or summarize key points to ensure you've understood the message correctly. This technique confirms understanding and encourages the other person to clarify if needed.
- **Ask Open-Ended Questions:** Encourage deeper conversation by asking open-ended questions that prompt the other person to share more about their thoughts, experiences, or preferences.
- **Clarify Ambiguities:** If a message is unclear or ambiguous, politely ask for clarification. For example, "Could you clarify what you meant by...?"
- **Avoid Interrupting:** Allow the other person to finish speaking before responding. Interrupting can disrupt the flow of conversation and indicate a lack of respect for their viewpoint.

4. Applying Active Listening in Dating Contexts:

- **Understanding Intentions:** Actively listening helps you discern the other person's intentions behind their messages, whether they're seeking casual conversation, friendship, or a serious relationship.
- **Building Emotional Connection:** By listening actively, you can connect emotionally with the other person, showing genuine interest in their personality, interests, and values.
- **Resolving Conflicts:** Active listening facilitates conflict resolution by enabling both parties to express their concerns, understand each other's viewpoints, and work towards mutually acceptable solutions.
- **Developing Trust:** Consistently practicing active listening on dating apps demonstrates your sincerity, reliability, and respect for the other person's feelings, contributing to the development of trust and rapport.

5. Cultivating Active Listening Skills:

- **Practice Regularly:** Actively listen in all your interactions, not just on dating apps. Practice with friends, family, or colleagues to refine your skills over time.
- **Seek Feedback:** Ask for feedback from others on your listening skills. They can provide insights into areas for improvement and reinforce your strengths.
- **Reflect and Adjust:** Reflect on your conversations to identify areas where active listening was effective and where you can improve. Adjust your approach based on what you learn.

Conclusion

Active listening is a powerful tool for enhancing communication on dating apps by fostering understanding, empathy, and clarity. By focusing on the speaker's messages, validating emotions, seeking clarification, and demonstrating genuine interest, active listening reduces misunderstandings and builds trust in dating contexts. Practicing active listening regularly improves communication skills, strengthens relationships, and contributes to meaningful connections on dating apps and beyond.

Transitioning to Video or Voice Calls on Dating Apps

Encouraging users to transition from text-based messaging to video or voice calls on dating apps can significantly enhance communication by fostering more natural interactions, emotional connection, and deeper understanding. Here's a detailed exploration of the benefits and considerations involved in making this transition:

1. Benefits of Video or Voice Calls:

- **Enhanced Communication:** Video or voice calls allow for real-time, synchronous communication where participants can hear each other's voices, see facial expressions, and observe non-verbal cues such as body language and gestures.

- **Facilitating Emotional Connection:** Seeing and hearing the other person adds depth to conversations, allowing for a more genuine emotional connection compared to text-based messaging alone.

- **Building Trust:** Face-to-face interactions, even through video calls, help build trust by providing a more personal and authentic way to communicate and interact with potential partners.

- **Clarifying Intentions and Personality:** Video or voice calls offer insights into the other person's personality, communication style, and mannerisms that may not be fully conveyed through text messages.

2. Considerations for Transitioning:

- **Mutual Comfort:** Ensure both parties are comfortable with the transition to video or voice calls. Respect each other's preferences and readiness to engage in more personal forms of communication.

- **Timing:** Introduce the idea of transitioning to calls at an appropriate time in your conversations. This could be after establishing some rapport and mutual interest through text-based messaging.

- **Privacy and Safety:** Prioritize privacy and safety considerations when exchanging contact information or connecting on external platforms for calls. Use reputable apps or platforms that offer security features and protect user privacy.

- **Respect Boundaries:** Be mindful of each other's boundaries and preferences regarding the frequency and duration of calls. Respect any discomfort or hesitation expressed by the other person.

3. Strategies for Encouraging Calls:

- **Express Interest:** Express genuine interest in getting to know the other person better and suggest transitioning to a call to facilitate more meaningful conversations.

- **Highlight Benefits:** Emphasize the benefits of video or voice calls, such as clearer communication, deeper connection, and the opportunity to build rapport more effectively.

- **Schedule Calls:** Propose specific times or schedules for calls that are convenient for both parties. This demonstrates consideration for each other's time and availability.

- **Initiate Openly:** Be proactive in initiating the transition to calls if you feel it would enhance your connection. Communicate openly about your preferences and willingness to engage in calls.

4. Tips for Effective Video or Voice Calls:

- **Prepare Environment:** Choose a quiet and well-lit environment for calls to minimize distractions and ensure clear audio and video quality.

- **Active Listening:** Practice active listening during calls by focusing on the speaker, responding thoughtfully, and asking clarifying questions to deepen understanding.

- **Be Yourself:** Be authentic and genuine during calls, allowing your personality to shine through naturally. Avoid putting on a facade or trying to impress excessively.

- **Enjoy the Interaction:** Approach calls with a positive mindset and enjoy the opportunity to connect with the other person on a more personal level.

5. Overcoming Challenges:

- **Technical Issues:** Anticipate and troubleshoot potential technical issues such as poor internet connection or audio/video problems to ensure smooth communication.
- **Nervousness:** If either party feels nervous about calls, acknowledge the discomfort and take it slow. Gradually ease into conversations to build comfort and confidence.
- **Language or Cultural Differences:** Respect and navigate any language or cultural differences that may affect communication during calls. Be patient and willing to clarify or explain when needed.

Conclusion

Transitioning from text-based messaging to video or voice calls on dating apps enhances communication by allowing for more natural interactions, deeper emotional connections, and improved understanding of each other's personalities. By respecting each other's comfort levels, prioritizing privacy and safety, and embracing the benefits of face-to-face communication, users can foster meaningful connections and build rapport effectively in dating contexts.

Chapter 5: The Gamification of Dating

Dating apps have revolutionized the way people meet and interact, often through gamification elements like swiping and instant gratification. This approach not only transforms the dating experience but also impacts user behavior and mental health. Here's a detailed exploration of the gamification of dating, focusing on swipe culture and the addictive nature of these platforms:

Swipe Culture: Gamifying the Dating Experience

1. Mechanics of Swiping:

○ **Simple and Engaging:** The swipe feature, popularized by apps like Tinder, allows users to quickly indicate interest or disinterest by swiping right or left. This simple, game-like mechanic is highly engaging and easy to use, making it accessible to a broad audience.

○ **Instant Feedback:** Swiping provides immediate feedback. A right swipe that results in a match gives an instant sense of validation, while a left swipe allows users to quickly move on, keeping the interaction dynamic and fast-paced.

2. Game Elements in Dating:

○ **Points and Rewards:** Matches can be seen as rewards, similar to earning points in a game. The more matches one gets, the more "points" they accumulate, driving users to keep playing.

○ **Levels and Progress:** Users may feel a sense of progression as they accumulate matches or conversations, similar to advancing levels in a game. This progression keeps users engaged and motivated to continue using the app.

3. Instant Gratification:

○ **Quick Decisions:** Swiping encourages users to make rapid decisions based on limited information, primarily photos and brief bios. This can lead to superficial judgments, as the focus is on immediate attraction rather than deeper compatibility.

○ **Immediate Rewards:** The potential for instant matches and conversations provides immediate gratification, reinforcing the behavior and encouraging continuous use of the app.

Addiction and Dependency: The Impact on Mental Health and Behavior

1. Addictive Nature of Dating Apps:

○ **Dopamine Hits:** The brain releases dopamine, a neurotransmitter associated with pleasure and reward, each time a user gets a match or receives a message. This creates a cycle of seeking these pleasurable hits, similar to the mechanism behind gambling addiction.

○ **Variable Rewards:** The unpredictability of matches (not knowing when the next match will occur) makes the process more addictive. This concept, known as variable ratio reinforcement, is also used in slot machines and other gambling devices.

2. **Psychological Impact:**

○ **Rejection and Validation:** The constant cycle of swipes, matches, and messages can lead to a rollercoaster of emotions. Rejection (lack of matches or negative interactions) can harm self-esteem, while validation (matches and positive interactions) can create dependency on external approval.

○ **Fear of Missing Out (FOMO):** The vast number of potential matches and the constant influx of new profiles can create a fear of missing out on a better match, driving users to continuously check and engage with the app.

3. **Behavioral Changes:**

○ **Increased Screen Time:** The addictive nature of dating apps can lead to excessive screen time, reducing time spent on other meaningful activities and potentially affecting physical health (e.g., poor posture, eye strain).

○ **Casual Interactions:** The gamified nature of swiping may encourage more casual, short-term interactions rather than meaningful, long-term relationships. This can perpetuate a cycle of superficial connections.

4. **Mental Health Concerns:**

○ **Anxiety and Depression:** The highs and lows of the dating app experience can contribute to anxiety and depression. The pressure to present oneself in the best light, coupled with the potential for rejection, can take a toll on mental health.

○ **Self-Worth Issues:** Users may begin to equate their self-worth with the number of matches or positive interactions they receive, leading to issues with self-esteem and self-image.

Conclusion

The gamification of dating through features like swiping and instant gratification has transformed the dating landscape. While these elements make dating apps engaging and widely popular, they also introduce significant risks related to addiction and mental health. The addictive nature of the gamified experience, characterized by dopamine hits and variable rewards, can lead to dependency, increased screen time, and superficial interactions. Additionally, the psychological impacts, including anxiety, depression, and self-worth issues, highlight the need for users to be mindful of their app usage and seek balance in their digital and real-life interactions. By understanding these dynamics, users can better navigate the world of online dating while safeguarding their mental and emotional well-being.

Mechanics of Swiping

Swipe Feature in Dating Apps

The swipe feature, popularized by apps like Tinder, revolutionized the way users interact with potential matches on dating platforms. Here's an in-depth exploration of how this simple and engaging mechanic works and why it has become a staple in modern dating apps:

1. Functionality of the Swipe Feature:

● **User Interaction:** The swipe feature allows users to view profiles one at a time and make quick decisions based on visual cues. A swipe to the right indicates interest ('like'), while a swipe to the left indicates disinterest ('pass').

● **Simplicity:** The mechanics are straightforward: users swipe right if they are interested in someone or left if they are not. This simplicity eliminates the need for complex navigation or interaction patterns, making the app intuitive and user-friendly.

● **Instant Feedback:** Each swipe provides instant feedback as the user sees an immediate response — a match notification if both parties swipe right, or a move to the next profile if not.

2. Engagement and User Experience:

● **Game-Like Element:** The swipe feature incorporates a game-like element, akin to playing cards or making quick decisions in a game. This gamification adds an element of fun and excitement to the dating experience, appealing to a broad audience, including younger demographics.

● **Accessibility:** Its ease of use makes the swipe feature accessible to users of all ages and technological backgrounds. It requires minimal effort and time commitment to navigate profiles and make decisions, fitting into the fast-paced lifestyles of many users.

● **Reduced Time Investment:** Users can efficiently browse through potential matches without investing significant time in each profile, which is particularly appealing to those with busy schedules or limited patience for lengthy browsing.

3. Psychological Appeal and Behavior:

● **Instant Gratification:** Swiping offers immediate gratification as users receive immediate feedback on their actions. This quick feedback loop reinforces engagement and encourages continued use of the app.

● **Decision-Making Efficiency:** The swipe feature supports rapid decision-making based on initial impressions, leveraging visual cues such as profile photos and brief descriptions. Users can quickly assess potential matches and prioritize those who align with their preferences.

● **Psychological Investment:** Despite its simplicity, swiping creates a sense of psychological investment as users actively participate in selecting potential matches. This involvement enhances user satisfaction and perceived control over their dating experience.

4. Evolution and Integration:

● **Industry Standard:** The success of the swipe feature has made it an industry standard in dating apps, influencing the design and functionality of numerous platforms that followed Tinder.

● **Continuous Innovation:** While the basic swipe remains popular, dating apps continue to innovate by adding variations such as super likes, rewind options, or enhanced algorithms to refine match suggestions.

● **User Feedback Loop:** Feedback from users continues to shape the evolution of the swipe feature, leading to improvements in usability, inclusivity, and overall user experience over time.

5. Impact on Dating Culture:

- **Shift in Interaction Norms:** The swipe feature has influenced dating culture by promoting a more visual and immediate approach to matchmaking, shifting emphasis from detailed profiles to initial attraction and compatibility cues.
- **Normalization of Online Dating:** Its widespread adoption has contributed to the normalization of online dating as a mainstream method for meeting potential partners, especially among younger generations.
- **Social Interaction Patterns:** Users adapt their social interaction patterns to align with the swipe mechanic, influencing offline behavior and expectations regarding dating dynamics and initial meetings.

Conclusion

The swipe feature in dating apps like Tinder has redefined how users engage with potential matches by offering a simple, engaging, and efficient method for indicating interest or disinterest. Its game-like mechanics, ease of use, and psychological appeal have made it a cornerstone of modern dating platforms, shaping user behavior, industry standards, and broader societal norms surrounding online dating. As dating apps continue to evolve, the swipe feature remains a fundamental component in facilitating connections and shaping the digital dating landscape.

Instant Feedback in Dating App Swiping

The instant feedback mechanism in dating app swiping, such as on Tinder, plays a crucial role in shaping user engagement, satisfaction, and interaction dynamics. Here's a detailed exploration of how instant feedback influences user behavior and the overall experience:

1. Immediate Response Mechanism:

- **Right Swipe (Like):** When a user swipes right on a profile, indicating interest, and the other person reciprocates with a right swipe as well, a match is created. This mutual interest triggers an immediate notification, providing users with instant validation of their attractiveness or compatibility.
- **Left Swipe (Pass):** Conversely, swiping left indicates disinterest or lack of compatibility. This action allows users to swiftly move on to the next profile without dwelling on potential matches that do not align with their preferences.

2. Psychological Impact:

- **Validation and Satisfaction:** A right swipe that results in a match delivers a sense of validation and satisfaction to the user, affirming their attractiveness or appeal to potential partners. This positive reinforcement encourages continued use of the app and reinforces positive self-perception.
- **Efficiency and Decision-Making:** The swift nature of left swipes enables users to efficiently filter through profiles based on initial impressions. This rapid decision-making process aligns with the fast-paced nature of modern dating, where users prioritize efficiency and instant results.

3. Engagement and User Experience:

- **Gamification Element:** Instant feedback incorporates a gamification element into the dating experience, resembling a rewarding feedback loop seen in games. This gamified approach enhances user engagement by making the interaction dynamic and interactive.
- **Feedback Loop:** The immediate notification of matches or rejections keeps users engaged and interested in the app. It encourages them to continue swiping and exploring potential matches, driven by the anticipation of positive outcomes.

4. Impact on Interaction Dynamics:

- **Dynamic Interaction:** The rapid exchange of swipes and instant feedback shapes the overall interaction dynamics on dating apps. It fosters a dynamic environment where users actively participate in selecting and engaging with potential matches based on immediate responses.
- **User Behavior:** Users adapt their swiping behavior based on instant feedback. Positive outcomes (matches) reinforce certain swiping patterns or preferences, while negative outcomes (no matches) prompt users to adjust their criteria or approach.

5. Evolution and User Expectations:

- **Industry Standard:** Dating apps have adopted instant feedback mechanisms as an industry standard, influencing user expectations and shaping the design of new features and functionalities.
- **Continuous Innovation:** App developers continuously innovate to enhance the instant feedback experience, integrating features like super likes or real-time notifications to further engage users and improve user satisfaction.

6. User Satisfaction and Retention:

- **Enhanced User Satisfaction:** The immediacy of feedback contributes to higher user satisfaction by meeting the need for validation and recognition. Satisfied users are more likely to continue using the app and recommend it to others.
- **Retention Strategy:** Providing instant feedback is a retention strategy for dating apps, as it enhances user experience and encourages regular app usage. It contributes to the app's success by maintaining user engagement and loyalty over time.

Conclusion

Instant feedback through swiping in dating apps not only accelerates the decision-making process but also enhances user engagement and satisfaction. By delivering immediate validation or rejection, dating apps create a dynamic environment where users actively participate in selecting potential matches. This feedback mechanism influences user behavior, interaction dynamics, and app design, shaping the modern digital dating experience and setting expectations for user engagement across the industry.

Game Elements in Dating

Matches as Points and Rewards in Dating Apps

In dating apps, matches often function as rewards, akin to earning points in a game. This gamification strategy not only enhances user engagement but also influences behavior and interaction dynamics. Here's an in-depth exploration of how matches serve as points and rewards in the context of dating apps:

1. Concept of Matches as Rewards:

● **Positive Reinforcement:** When a user swipes right and matches with another user who reciprocates interest, it serves as immediate positive reinforcement. This validation reinforces the user's actions and encourages continued use of the app to accumulate more matches.

● **Accumulation of "Points":** Each match can be metaphorically seen as earning a point or achieving a milestone within the app. Users may perceive accumulating matches as a measure of their attractiveness or success in the dating realm, similar to achieving higher scores in a game.

2. Psychological Impact:

● **Sense of Achievement:** Successfully obtaining matches can create a sense of achievement and accomplishment for users. It validates their profile, interests, and attractiveness, boosting self-esteem and satisfaction with the app experience.

● **Motivation to Engage:** The prospect of earning more matches motivates users to actively participate in swiping and interacting within the app. This motivation stems from the desire to increase their "points" and maximize their success in connecting with potential partners.

3. Gamification Elements:

● **Game-Like Dynamics:** Dating apps integrate gamification elements, such as matches as rewards, to enhance user engagement. Similar to gaming strategies, these elements create a competitive or goal-oriented environment where users strive to achieve positive outcomes (matches).

● **Feedback Loop:** Matches as rewards create a feedback loop where the anticipation of achieving more matches drives continued app usage. This cycle of action (swiping) and reward (matches) reinforces user behavior and promotes sustained engagement.

4. Impact on User Behavior:

● **Swiping Behavior:** Users may adjust their swiping behavior based on the perceived value of matches as rewards. They may swipe more selectively or actively enhance their profiles to attract more matches, aiming to optimize their "score" within the app.

● **App Engagement:** The concept of matches as rewards encourages prolonged app engagement as users seek to maximize their success rate and accumulate more matches. This engagement contributes to the app's popularity and user retention.

5. Industry Standards and Innovation:

● **Standard Practice:** Matches as rewards have become a standard practice in dating app design, influencing user expectations and app features. Developers continually innovate by introducing features that enhance the match-making process and reward system.

● **Enhancing User Experience:** By leveraging matches as rewards, dating apps enhance user experience and satisfaction. This gamification strategy makes the app more enjoyable and compelling for users, contributing to its long-term success.

Conclusion

In dating apps, matches serve not only as indicators of mutual interest but also as rewards that drive user engagement and satisfaction. By gamifying the matchmaking process, apps create a dynamic where users actively seek matches to accumulate points and achieve personal milestones. This gamification strategy influences user behavior, interaction patterns, and app design, shaping the modern digital dating landscape and setting expectations for engagement and success within the dating app industry.

Levels and Progress in Dating Apps

In dating apps, users often experience a sense of progression similar to advancing levels in a game as they accumulate matches or engage in conversations. This concept of levels and progress enhances user motivation, engagement, and satisfaction within the app. Here's an in-depth exploration of how levels and progress influence user behavior and interaction dynamics:

1. Concept of Levels and Progress:

● **Accumulation of Matches:** Each match or successful interaction with another user can be perceived as achieving a level or milestone within the app. Users may interpret accumulating matches as progressing towards their dating goals or enhancing their status within the app's community.

● **Conversation Milestones:** Progress can also be measured by the advancement of conversations from initial messages to deeper interactions or potential dates. Each stage of conversation completion may signify a new level of engagement or connection achieved.

2. Psychological Impact:

● **Sense of Achievement:** Similar to leveling up in games, achieving matches or progressing in conversations provides users with a sense of achievement and accomplishment. This positive reinforcement boosts self-esteem and motivates continued use of the app.

● **Motivation to Engage:** The prospect of reaching higher levels or achieving more matches motivates users to actively participate in swiping, messaging, and profile optimization. This motivation stems from the desire to advance their status or success within the dating app environment.

3. Gamification Elements:

● **Game-Like Dynamics:** Dating apps integrate gamification elements, such as levels and progress indicators, to enhance user engagement. These elements create a competitive or goal-oriented framework where users strive to achieve and surpass their previous milestones.

● **Feedback Loop:** Levels and progress create a feedback loop where users are encouraged to continue using the app in pursuit of reaching higher levels or achieving more matches. This cycle of action (swiping, messaging) and reward (matches, conversations) reinforces user behavior and promotes sustained engagement.

4. Impact on User Behavior:

● **Optimized Interactions:** Users may adjust their interaction strategies to optimize their progress within the app. They may prioritize engaging with profiles that are likely to result in matches or invest more effort in conversations that contribute to their perceived progression.

● **Increased Engagement:** The concept of levels and progress fosters increased app engagement as users actively pursue their dating objectives. This engagement contributes to the app's popularity and user retention by providing a structured and rewarding experience.

5. Industry Standards and Innovation:

● **Standard Practice:** Levels and progress indicators have become standard features in many dating apps, influencing user expectations and app design. Developers continually innovate by introducing features that enhance the progression system and user experience.

● **Enhancing User Satisfaction:** By incorporating levels and progress, dating apps enhance user satisfaction by providing a clear path to achievement and success within the app. This gamification strategy makes the app more engaging and enjoyable for users, contributing to its long-term success.

Conclusion

Levels and progress in dating apps function as motivational tools that enhance user engagement and satisfaction. By mimicking the progression systems seen in gaming, apps create a dynamic environment where users actively pursue matches and conversations to achieve higher levels or milestones. This gamification strategy influences user behavior, interaction patterns, and app design, shaping the modern digital dating experience and setting expectations for engagement and success within the dating app industry.

Instant Gratification

Quick Decisions in Dating App Swiping

Swiping in dating apps encourages users to make rapid decisions based on limited information, primarily focusing on photos and brief bios. This quick decision-making process can lead to superficial judgments where immediate attraction takes precedence over deeper compatibility considerations. Here's a comprehensive exploration of how quick decisions influence user behavior and interaction dynamics:

1. Mechanism of Swiping:

- **Visual-Based Interaction:** Dating apps employ a swipe-based mechanism where users view profiles, typically consisting of photos and short bios, and swipe right to indicate interest (like) or left to pass (dislike).

- **Simplified Decision-Making:** The swipe feature simplifies the decision-making process by presenting profiles one at a time and requiring users to quickly assess each based on initial visual impressions.

2. Psychological Impact:

- **First Impressions:** Users form first impressions based on photos and brief bios, which can shape their initial attraction or interest in potential matches. This initial attraction often dictates whether a user swipes right or left, influencing subsequent interaction possibilities.

- **Superficial Judgments:** The emphasis on immediate visual appeal can lead to superficial judgments where users prioritize physical attractiveness over other factors such as personality, values, or long-term compatibility.

3. Behavioral Patterns:

- **Impulse Decision-Making:** The rapid nature of swiping encourages impulse decision-making, where users may quickly swipe based on gut reactions or snap judgments rather than a thorough consideration of profile details.

- **Selective Attention:** Users may focus primarily on certain visual cues, such as appearance or style, while overlooking or giving less weight to other profile information that could be crucial for establishing meaningful connections.

4. Impact on Interaction Dynamics:

- **Interaction Pacing:** Swiping fosters a fast-paced interaction environment where users rapidly cycle through profiles, leading to a high volume of swipes within short periods. This dynamic can influence how users engage with the app and manage their time spent swiping.

- **Surface-Level Interactions:** The focus on quick decisions and initial attraction can promote surface-level interactions where conversations may initially revolve around physical appearance rather than deeper, more substantive topics.

5. User Experience and Satisfaction:

- **Efficiency vs. Depth:** While swiping offers efficiency in browsing potential matches, it may compromise depth and thoroughness in assessing compatibility factors beyond initial attraction. This trade-off can impact user satisfaction depending on individual dating preferences.

- **Behavioral Adaptation:** Users may adapt their swiping behavior based on perceived success rates or feedback, adjusting their criteria for swiping right or left to optimize match potential or satisfaction with the app experience.

6. Industry Trends and Evolution:

- **User Feedback and Innovation:** Dating apps continually evolve based on user feedback and behavioral insights, introducing features or adjustments to balance quick decisions with the need for meaningful connections and user satisfaction.

Conclusion

Swiping in dating apps facilitates quick decision-making based on limited information, primarily photos and brief bios. This approach encourages users to make rapid judgments and prioritize initial attraction over deeper compatibility considerations. While swiping enhances efficiency in browsing potential matches, it can also lead to superficial interactions and potentially impact user satisfaction depending on individual preferences for depth and connection in dating experiences. As dating apps evolve, balancing quick decisions with fostering meaningful connections remains a key challenge and focus area for enhancing user engagement and satisfaction.

Immediate Rewards in Dating Apps

Immediate rewards in dating apps refer to the potential for instant matches and conversations, which provide users with immediate gratification. This concept of instant rewards reinforces user behavior and encourages continuous engagement with the app. Here's a thorough exploration of how immediate rewards influence user behavior and interaction dynamics:

1. Concept of Immediate Rewards:

● **Instant Gratification:** Dating apps offer the possibility of immediate matches and conversations when users swipe right and mutually express interest. This instant gratification satisfies the user's desire for validation and connection in real-time.

● **Positive Reinforcement:** When a user receives an instant match or starts a conversation, it serves as positive reinforcement for their actions (e.g., swiping right), encouraging them to continue using the app to seek similar rewards.

2. Psychological Impact:

● **Reward Pathway Activation:** Immediate rewards trigger the brain's reward pathway, releasing dopamine—a neurotransmitter associated with pleasure and reward. This neurological response reinforces the behavior (using the app) that led to the reward (match or conversation).

● **Motivation to Engage:** The prospect of achieving instant rewards motivates users to actively participate in swiping, messaging, and profile interactions within the app. This motivation stems from the anticipation of positive outcomes and the enjoyment derived from immediate gratification.

3. Behavioral Patterns:

● **Continued Engagement:** Users are more likely to engage with the app consistently when they experience frequent instant rewards. The desire to replicate or exceed previous positive experiences drives ongoing app usage and interaction.

● **Optimized Swiping Behavior:** Users may adjust their swiping behavior to maximize the likelihood of receiving instant rewards. For instance, they may swipe right more selectively or enhance their profiles to attract matches quickly.

4. Impact on Interaction Dynamics:

● **Dynamic Interaction:** Immediate rewards create a dynamic interaction environment where users actively seek and respond to matches and conversations. This dynamic keeps the app experience engaging and reinforces user satisfaction.

● **Communication Flow:** Instant matches and conversations facilitate the flow of communication, allowing users to quickly transition from interest to interaction without delays. This immediacy enhances user experience by reducing wait times and fostering real-time connections.

5. User Experience and Satisfaction:

- **Enhanced Satisfaction:** Immediate rewards contribute to user satisfaction by meeting their desire for instant validation and connection. Satisfied users are more likely to continue using the app and recommend it to others, contributing to app popularity and growth.
- **Retention Strategy:** Providing immediate rewards is a retention strategy for dating apps, as it enhances user engagement and encourages habitual use. The consistent delivery of positive experiences maintains user interest and loyalty over time.

6. Industry Trends and Evolution:

- **Innovation and User Feedback:** Dating apps evolve by integrating features that enhance the delivery of immediate rewards, such as real-time notifications or personalized match suggestions. These innovations align with user expectations and preferences for instant gratification.

Conclusion

Immediate rewards in dating apps, such as instant matches and conversations, play a crucial role in shaping user behavior and interaction dynamics. By providing immediate gratification, these rewards activate the brain's reward system and reinforce user engagement with the app. This positive reinforcement motivates users to continue using the app, contributing to enhanced satisfaction, retention, and overall user experience. As dating apps evolve, leveraging immediate rewards remains a key strategy for optimizing user engagement and fostering meaningful connections in the digital dating landscape.

Addictive Nature of Dating Apps

Dopamine Hits in Dating Apps

Dopamine hits in dating apps refer to the release of dopamine—a neurotransmitter associated with pleasure and reward—in response to receiving matches or messages. This neurological response creates a cycle where users seek these pleasurable hits, akin to the mechanisms observed in addictive behaviors such as gambling. Here's an in-depth exploration of how dopamine hits influence user behavior and interaction dynamics in dating apps:

1. Neurological Basis:

● **Dopamine Release:** When users receive a match notification or message on a dating app, their brain releases dopamine. This release occurs in anticipation of and upon receiving a reward (e.g., a match), reinforcing the behavior (using the app) that led to the reward.

● **Pleasure and Reward:** Dopamine is known as the "feel-good" neurotransmitter because it plays a crucial role in experiencing pleasure and reinforcing behaviors that lead to rewards. In the context of dating apps, dopamine release contributes to the enjoyment and satisfaction users derive from matching with others.

2. Psychological Impact:

● **Positive Reinforcement:** Dopamine serves as a form of positive reinforcement, reinforcing the behavior of swiping right or engaging with the app. This reinforcement strengthens the neural pathways associated with using the app, making it more likely for users to repeat these behaviors to experience dopamine release again.

● **Cycle of Seeking:** The pleasurable experience of receiving matches or messages creates a cycle where users actively seek these dopamine hits by using the app consistently. This cycle mirrors addictive behaviors where individuals seek rewarding stimuli to maintain pleasurable feelings.

3. Behavioral Patterns:

● **Increased Engagement:** Dopamine hits contribute to increased user engagement with dating apps. Users are motivated to spend more time swiping, messaging, and interacting within the app to replicate the positive experiences associated with dopamine release.

● **Behavioral Adaptation:** Users may adapt their app usage patterns based on previous experiences of dopamine release. For example, they may adjust their swiping strategy or profile presentation to increase their chances of receiving matches and triggering dopamine release.

4. Comparison to Gambling Addiction:

● **Similar Mechanisms:** The cycle of seeking dopamine hits in dating apps shares similarities with the mechanisms observed in gambling addiction. Both involve the anticipation of rewards (matches or wins) and the release of dopamine upon achieving these rewards, reinforcing the behavior that led to them.

● **Risk of Overuse:** Like gambling, the pursuit of dopamine hits in dating apps can lead to overuse or compulsive behaviors, where users spend excessive time and effort seeking matches to maintain pleasurable feelings associated with dopamine release.

5. Impact on User Experience and Satisfaction:

● **Enhanced Satisfaction:** Dopamine hits contribute to user satisfaction by providing pleasurable experiences associated with matching and interacting within the app. Satisfied users are more likely to continue using the app and engage in positive interactions with others.

● **Retention Strategy:** Dating apps leverage dopamine hits as a retention strategy to maintain user interest and loyalty. By consistently delivering rewarding experiences, apps encourage habitual use and foster long-term engagement.

6. Ethical Considerations and User Well-being:

● **Balance and Moderation:** While dopamine hits enhance user experience, dating apps must balance providing rewards with promoting healthy app usage habits. Educating users about the potential effects of dopamine release and promoting moderation can mitigate risks associated with overuse.

Conclusion

Dopamine hits in dating apps play a significant role in shaping user behavior and interaction dynamics by providing pleasurable experiences associated with matching and receiving messages. The release of dopamine reinforces app usage behaviors and motivates users to seek rewarding interactions. While these dopamine-driven experiences enhance user satisfaction and engagement, dating apps must also consider ethical implications and promote responsible usage to ensure user well-being in the digital dating environment.

Variable Rewards in Dating Apps

Variable rewards in dating apps refer to the unpredictability of receiving matches or messages, where users do not know when the next match will occur. This uncertainty makes the matching process more addictive by leveraging the concept of variable ratio reinforcement, similar to techniques used in gambling devices such as slot machines. Here's an in-depth exploration of how variable rewards influence user behavior and interaction dynamics in dating apps:

1. Concept of Variable Rewards:

● **Unpredictable Matching:** In dating apps, users experience variable rewards because they cannot predict when they will receive a match or message. This unpredictability adds an element of excitement and anticipation to the matching process.

● **Variable Ratio Reinforcement:** Variable rewards operate on a variable ratio reinforcement schedule, where rewards (matches) are delivered at unpredictable intervals after a certain number of swipes or interactions. This reinforcement schedule is highly effective in reinforcing behavior and maintaining engagement.

2. Psychological Impact:

● **Anticipation and Excitement:** The unpredictability of variable rewards creates a sense of anticipation and excitement among users. They remain engaged and motivated to continue swiping and interacting within the app in anticipation of the next rewarding match.

● **Behavioral Conditioning:** Variable ratio reinforcement conditions users to associate app usage with the potential for rewarding outcomes (matches). This conditioning strengthens the habit of using the app regularly to seek these unpredictable rewards.

3. Comparison to Gambling Devices:

● **Similar Mechanisms:** Dating apps leverage variable rewards in a manner similar to gambling devices like slot machines. Both use unpredictable rewards to maintain user interest and encourage repetitive behaviors (swiping or pulling the lever) to achieve rewarding outcomes (matches or wins).

● **Psychological Hooks:** Variable ratio reinforcement exploits psychological hooks by providing occasional, unpredictable rewards that stimulate the release of dopamine—a neurotransmitter associated with pleasure and reward. This stimulation reinforces the behavior of using the app.

4. Behavioral Patterns:

● **Increased Engagement:** Variable rewards increase user engagement by keeping users actively involved in swiping and interacting within the app. Users are motivated to spend more time and effort to maximize their chances of receiving rewarding matches.

- **App Habit Formation:** The unpredictable nature of variable rewards contributes to habit formation, where users develop regular app usage patterns to satisfy their desire for rewarding experiences. This habituation fosters long-term engagement with the app.

5. Impact on User Experience and Satisfaction:

- **Enhanced Satisfaction:** Variable rewards contribute to user satisfaction by providing exciting and rewarding experiences associated with matching and interacting within the app. The element of unpredictability adds value to each match and reinforces positive user experiences.

- **Retention Strategy:** Dating apps strategically use variable rewards as a retention strategy to maintain user interest and loyalty over time. By delivering unpredictable yet rewarding experiences, apps encourage continued app usage and interaction.

6. Ethical Considerations and User Well-being:

- **Awareness and Transparency:** While variable rewards enhance user engagement, dating apps must ensure transparency about their use of reinforcement schedules. Educating users about the psychological mechanisms of variable rewards and promoting mindful app usage can mitigate potential risks associated with overuse.

Conclusion

Variable rewards in dating apps leverage the unpredictability of matching outcomes to enhance user engagement and satisfaction. By employing a variable ratio reinforcement schedule, apps stimulate anticipation and excitement among users, reinforcing app usage behaviors to seek rewarding matches. While variable rewards contribute to a positive user experience, it is essential for dating apps to prioritize user well-being by promoting responsible usage practices and maintaining transparency about their use of psychological reinforcement techniques.

Psychological Impact

Rejection and Validation in Dating Apps

Rejection and validation in dating apps describe the emotional impact of the continuous cycle of swiping, matching, and messaging. This process can evoke strong emotional responses, where rejection diminishes self-esteem, while validation fosters dependency on external approval. Here's a comprehensive exploration of how rejection and validation influence user emotions and behavior in dating apps:

1. Emotional Dynamics:

- **Cycle of Emotions:** Using dating apps involves a constant cycle of swiping right (expressing interest), waiting for matches, and engaging in conversations. This cycle can evoke a range of emotions, from anticipation and excitement to disappointment and frustration.

- **Impact of Rejection:** Rejection on dating apps occurs when users do not receive matches or experience negative interactions (unmatched or ignored messages). Rejection can harm self-esteem and lead to feelings of inadequacy or undesirability.

- **Dependency on Validation:** Validation in dating apps refers to receiving matches, positive interactions, or compliments from matches. This validation can create a dependency on external approval, where users seek reassurance and affirmation from matches to boost their self-esteem.

2. Psychological Impact:

- **Self-Esteem Issues:** Repeated rejection or lack of matches can negatively impact self-esteem and self-worth. Users may question their attractiveness or desirability based on their perceived success or failure in obtaining matches.

- **Validation Seeking Behavior:** The desire for validation can drive users to prioritize matches and positive interactions as sources of self-worth. This dependency on external approval may lead to seeking constant reassurance and validation from matches to feel valued.

3. Behavioral Responses:

- **Behavioral Adjustment:** Users may adjust their swiping strategies or profile presentation in response to rejection or validation experiences. For example, they may become more selective in swiping or modify their profile content to increase their chances of receiving validation through matches.

- **Emotional Responses:** Emotional responses to rejection or validation can vary widely among users. Some may become discouraged and decrease app usage, while others may become more determined to improve their profile or interaction skills to enhance validation experiences.

4. Relationship with App Engagement:

- **Impact on App Engagement:** Rejection and validation significantly influence user engagement with dating apps. Positive validation (matches and positive interactions) reinforces app usage behaviors, while repeated rejection may deter users from continuing to engage with the app.

- **Retention Strategy:** Dating apps may leverage validation as a retention strategy by enhancing user satisfaction through positive experiences and interactions. Apps aim to mitigate the negative effects of rejection by promoting a supportive community and positive user interactions.

5. Coping Mechanisms and Support:

- **Coping with Rejection:** Users may develop coping mechanisms to manage rejection, such as focusing on self-improvement, seeking support from friends, or taking breaks from app usage to maintain emotional well-being.

- **Balancing Validation:** To mitigate dependency on external validation, users can focus on developing self-confidence and deriving self-worth from personal achievements and relationships beyond dating apps.

6. Ethical Considerations:

● **Promoting Positive Interaction:** Dating apps have a responsibility to promote positive interaction environments and support users' emotional well-being. This includes addressing issues of rejection sensitively and encouraging respectful communication among users.

Conclusion

Rejection and validation are integral aspects of the dating app experience, influencing user emotions and behavior. While validation can enhance self-esteem and engagement, repeated rejection can have detrimental effects on self-worth. Dating apps must balance promoting positive validation experiences with mitigating the negative impact of rejection to foster a supportive and emotionally healthy environment for users. Encouraging self-confidence and providing resources for coping with rejection are essential for promoting positive user experiences and maintaining ethical standards in digital dating platforms.

Fear of Missing Out (FOMO) in Dating Apps

Fear of Missing Out (FOMO) in dating apps refers to the anxiety or apprehension users feel about potentially missing out on better matches or opportunities due to the vast number of potential profiles and the constant influx of new users. This fear drives users to continuously check and engage with the app to avoid the perceived loss of a potentially ideal match. Here's an in-depth exploration of how FOMO influences user behavior and emotions in dating apps:

1. Psychological Dynamics:

● **Anxiety and Apprehension:** FOMO in dating apps manifests as anxiety or apprehension about missing out on potential matches that could be more compatible or attractive. Users worry that by not actively engaging with the app, they may miss opportunities for meaningful connections.

● **Comparison and Uncertainty:** The abundance of profiles and the variety of potential matches contribute to feelings of uncertainty and comparison. Users may compare their own matches or interactions with those of others, fueling a sense of urgency to find the "best" match.

2. Behavioral Responses:

● **Continuous Engagement:** FOMO motivates users to engage with the app frequently and consistently. They may check the app multiple times a day, swipe extensively, or respond quickly to messages to ensure they do not miss potential opportunities.

● **Overwhelming Choices:** The abundance of choices can overwhelm users, making it challenging to make decisions or commit to a single match. This indecision stems from the fear of missing out on better options that may appear among the many profiles available.

3. Impact on User Experience:

● **Stress and Pressure:** FOMO creates stress and pressure as users feel compelled to keep up with the app's activities to avoid missing potential matches. This constant pressure can lead to burnout or fatigue from app usage.

● **Emotional Rollercoaster:** The emotional impact of FOMO includes fluctuations between hopefulness (anticipating a great match) and disappointment (missing out on perceived opportunities). Users may experience heightened emotions based on their app interactions and outcomes.

4. Relationship with App Engagement:

● **Increased App Usage:** FOMO contributes to increased app engagement and usage frequency. Users spend more time swiping, messaging, and exploring profiles to maximize their chances of finding desirable matches and minimizing the fear of missing out.

- **Retention Strategy:** Dating apps may capitalize on FOMO as a retention strategy by creating features or notifications that encourage frequent app usage. This strategy aims to keep users engaged and active on the platform to reduce the likelihood of missing potential matches.

5. Coping Strategies:

- **Setting Boundaries:** Users can mitigate FOMO by setting boundaries on app usage, such as limiting daily swiping sessions or disabling notifications to reduce constant engagement pressure.

- **Focus on Quality over Quantity:** Emphasizing quality connections over the quantity of matches can help users manage FOMO. By focusing on meaningful interactions rather than constantly seeking new matches, users may reduce anxiety and stress associated with FOMO.

6. Ethical Considerations:

- **Promoting Healthy Usage:** Dating apps should promote healthy app usage habits and awareness of FOMO's impact on user well-being. Educating users about managing expectations and setting realistic goals can foster a more positive and balanced app experience.

Conclusion

Fear of Missing Out (FOMO) in dating apps reflects users' anxiety about missing potential matches or opportunities due to the vast array of profiles and constant influx of new users. This fear drives users to engage frequently with the app, seeking to maximize their chances of finding ideal matches and avoiding feelings of regret or missed opportunities. While FOMO can increase app engagement, it is essential for dating apps to prioritize user well-being by promoting balanced app usage and providing resources for managing anxiety associated with FOMO. Helping users navigate the abundance of choices and emphasizing quality interactions can contribute to a more positive and fulfilling experience on dating platforms.

Behavioral Changes

Increased Screen Time Due to Dating Apps

Increased screen time due to dating apps refers to the prolonged use of mobile devices or computers for swiping, messaging, and interacting within dating platforms. This behavior is driven by the addictive nature of dating apps, which can negatively impact users' time management, physical health, and overall well-being. Here's a comprehensive exploration of how increased screen time on dating apps affects users:

1. Addiction and Engagement:

● **Continuous Engagement:** Dating apps are designed to be engaging, with features like swiping, matching, and messaging that encourage frequent interaction. Users may spend extended periods on the app to maximize matches and interactions.

● **Addictive Features:** Features such as variable rewards (unpredictable matches), instant gratification (immediate matches), and gamification (swiping as a game) contribute to addictive behaviors, prolonging app usage sessions.

2. Impact on Time Management:

● **Time Sink:** Excessive screen time on dating apps can consume significant portions of users' daily routines, reducing time allocated to productive or meaningful activities such as work, hobbies, or social interactions offline.

● **Distraction:** Users may become distracted by dating apps, checking their devices frequently throughout the day to monitor matches or respond to messages, potentially disrupting focus on other tasks or responsibilities.

3. Physical Health Concerns:

● **Poor Posture:** Prolonged use of mobile devices or computers while engaging with dating apps can lead to poor posture, especially when users hunch over their screens for extended periods.

● **Eye Strain:** Staring at screens for prolonged periods may cause eye strain or discomfort, exacerbated by the small text and visual elements typical of dating app interfaces.

4. Psychological Effects:

● **Emotional Impact:** Increased screen time on dating apps can contribute to emotional fluctuations, including feelings of frustration, disappointment from unsuccessful matches, or anxiety related to maintaining app engagement.

● **Dependency:** Users may develop a dependency on dating apps for social validation or emotional fulfillment, relying on matches and interactions as sources of self-esteem or validation.

5. Social and Relationship Impact:

● **Reduced Face-to-Face Interaction:** Excessive screen time on dating apps may reduce opportunities for face-to-face interactions and meaningful connections offline, impacting social skills and relationship-building in real-life settings.

● **Isolation:** Users may experience social isolation or withdrawal from offline social activities as they prioritize app usage, potentially leading to feelings of loneliness or disconnection from others.

6. Mitigation Strategies:

● **Setting Limits:** Establishing boundaries on app usage, such as designated times for swiping or messaging, can help manage screen time and balance app engagement with other activities.

● **Digital Detox:** Taking periodic breaks from dating apps or reducing overall screen time can promote mental well-being and reduce dependency on digital interactions.

7. Ethical Considerations:

- **User Well-being:** Dating apps should prioritize user well-being by promoting healthy app usage habits, providing tools for managing screen time, and educating users about the potential impact of excessive screen time on physical and mental health.
- **Transparency:** App developers should be transparent about the addictive features of their platforms and empower users with settings or notifications that encourage responsible usage and breaks from prolonged screen time.

Conclusion

Increased screen time due to dating apps reflects the addictive nature of these platforms, driven by engaging features and the pursuit of social validation or connection. While screen time on dating apps can enhance accessibility and interaction opportunities, it is crucial to recognize its potential impact on time management, physical health, and overall well-being. By promoting responsible app usage and providing support for managing screen time, dating apps can foster a balanced and positive user experience that prioritizes both digital interaction and offline well-being.

Casual Interactions in Dating Apps

Casual interactions in dating apps refer to the tendency for users to engage in superficial or short-term connections rather than pursuing meaningful, long-term relationships. This phenomenon is often influenced by the gamified nature of swiping and matching, which emphasizes quick decisions and instant gratification over deeper compatibility or emotional connection. Here's a comprehensive exploration of how casual interactions are perpetuated in dating apps:

1. Gamification and Swiping Dynamics:

- **Quick Decisions:** Dating apps employ a swipe-based interface where users make rapid decisions (swipe right for interest, swipe left for disinterest) based primarily on visual cues such as photos and brief bios. This gamified approach encourages users to prioritize initial attraction and immediate gratification over deeper compatibility or relationship potential.
- **Superficial Judgments:** The emphasis on swiping and matching can lead to superficial judgments, where users base their interest or disinterest on physical appearance or limited profile information rather than personality traits, values, or long-term compatibility.

2. Cycle of Superficial Connections:

- **Short-Term Focus:** The gamified nature of swiping fosters a culture of casual interactions where users may engage in brief conversations or casual dates without the intention of forming meaningful, long-term relationships. This cycle perpetuates a pattern of superficial connections that prioritize novelty and immediate satisfaction over emotional depth or commitment.
- **Lack of Investment:** Casual interactions in dating apps may involve minimal emotional investment or commitment, as users may quickly move on to new matches or interactions in search of novelty or excitement.

3. Psychological and Behavioral Aspects:

- **Instant Gratification:** The instant feedback and validation provided by matches and messages can reinforce casual interactions by rewarding quick swiping and superficial engagement. Users may seek immediate gratification without investing time or effort in building meaningful connections.
- **Fear of Missing Out (FOMO):** The fear of missing out on potentially better matches or experiences can encourage users to prioritize quantity (number of matches) over quality (depth of connection), perpetuating a cycle of casual interactions driven by FOMO.

4. Impact on Relationship Goals:

- **Shift in Priorities:** The prevalence of casual interactions in dating apps may influence users' relationship goals, with some prioritizing casual dating or short-term encounters over the pursuit of long-term relationships or emotional intimacy.
- **Communication Patterns:** Casual interactions may be characterized by less meaningful communication or depth in conversations, focusing more on light-hearted topics or surface-level interests rather than personal values or life goals.

5. Social and Cultural Influences:

- **Normalization of Casual Dating:** The widespread use and acceptance of dating apps have contributed to the normalization of casual dating and non-committal interactions within contemporary dating culture. This cultural shift may influence users' expectations and behaviors on dating platforms.
- **Peer Influence:** Social norms and peer behaviors within dating app communities can reinforce casual interactions by promoting a casual dating mindset or emphasizing the enjoyment of casual encounters without expectations of long-term commitment.

6. Ethical Considerations:

- **User Expectations:** Dating apps should be transparent about the potential for casual interactions and provide users with tools or features that support their relationship goals, whether casual or serious. This includes promoting respectful communication and managing user expectations regarding the nature of interactions on the platform.
- **Safety and Well-being:** Ensuring user safety and emotional well-being involves addressing issues such as consent, boundaries, and respectful behavior in casual interactions. Dating apps have a responsibility to create a positive and inclusive environment that respects diverse relationship preferences and intentions.

Conclusion

Casual interactions in dating apps are influenced by the gamified nature of swiping, which encourages quick decisions and superficial judgments based on visual cues. This dynamic fosters a cycle of short-term connections characterized by minimal emotional investment or commitment, prioritizing novelty and immediate gratification over deeper compatibility or long-term relationship goals. While dating apps offer accessibility and convenience in meeting new people, understanding the implications of casual interactions is essential for promoting a balanced and positive user experience that respects diverse relationship preferences and encourages meaningful connections based on mutual respect and compatibility.

Mental Health Concerns

Anxiety and Depression in the Context of Dating Apps

Anxiety and depression can significantly impact users of dating apps due to the emotional highs and lows associated with seeking connections, managing self-presentation, and navigating potential rejections. Here's a thorough exploration of how these mental health challenges manifest within the dating app experience:

1. Pressure to Present:

● **Self-Presentation:** Users often feel pressured to present the best versions of themselves through curated profiles, appealing photos, and engaging bios. This pressure stems from the desire to attract matches and establish a positive impression, potentially leading to anxiety about how they are perceived by others.

● **Social Comparison:** The process of swiping and matching invites comparisons with others, which can exacerbate feelings of inadequacy or self-doubt if users perceive themselves as less attractive or successful compared to their matches.

2. Fear of Rejection:

● **Vulnerability:** Engaging with dating apps requires users to put themselves out there emotionally, making them vulnerable to potential rejection or dismissal. The fear of rejection can lead to heightened anxiety about initiating conversations, expressing interest, or pursuing meaningful connections.

● **Impact of Rejection:** Experiencing rejection or lack of matches can trigger feelings of disappointment, sadness, or low self-esteem, particularly if users internalize rejection as a reflection of their worth or attractiveness.

3. Emotional Rollercoaster:

● **Highs and Lows:** The unpredictable nature of dating apps, where users experience highs (e.g., getting matches or positive interactions) and lows (e.g., unanswered messages or unmatched expectations), can contribute to emotional instability and mood swings.

● **Dependency on Validation:** Seeking validation through matches or positive interactions can create a cycle of emotional dependence on external approval, where users' self-worth becomes intertwined with their dating app experiences.

4. Perceived Expectations:

● **Idealized Relationships:** Users may internalize societal or app-driven expectations of idealized relationships or perfect matches, leading to unrealistic standards or heightened pressure to find a "perfect" partner through dating apps.

● **Comparison with Others:** Comparing one's dating app experiences with those of others can amplify feelings of inadequacy or dissatisfaction, especially if peers appear to have more successful or fulfilling interactions.

5. Coping Mechanisms:

● **Cognitive Distortions:** Negative thinking patterns, such as catastrophizing rejection or overgeneralizing lack of matches, can exacerbate anxiety and depression. Recognizing and challenging these cognitive distortions is essential for managing emotional well-being.

● **Seeking Support:** Engaging with friends, support networks, or mental health professionals can provide emotional support and perspective, offering strategies for coping with dating app-related stressors and fostering resilience.

6. Ethical Considerations:

● **User Well-being:** Dating apps have a responsibility to prioritize user well-being by promoting healthy app usage habits, providing resources for managing anxiety and depression, and fostering a supportive community environment that values inclusivity and respect.

● **Privacy and Safety:** Protecting user privacy and safety includes safeguarding against harmful behaviors such as harassment or abuse, which can exacerbate anxiety and depression among vulnerable users.

Conclusion

Anxiety and depression in the context of dating apps are influenced by the pressures of self-presentation, fear of rejection, and the emotional rollercoaster of seeking connections. These challenges can impact users' mental health, contributing to feelings of anxiety, low self-esteem, and emotional instability. Understanding the psychological implications of dating app usage is crucial for promoting a positive user experience that prioritizes mental well-being, resilience, and healthy relationship-building practices. By addressing these concerns ethically and supporting users with resources for managing stress and emotional challenges, dating apps can contribute to a more balanced and supportive digital dating environment.

Self-Worth Issues in the Context of Dating Apps

Self-worth issues can arise in users of dating apps when they equate their value or attractiveness with the number of matches, positive interactions, or validation they receive within the app. This phenomenon is influenced by the dynamics of seeking external validation and comparison with others, which can impact users' self-esteem and self-image. Here's an in-depth exploration of how self-worth issues manifest within the context of dating apps:

1. External Validation:

● **Dependency on Matches:** Users may develop a dependency on receiving matches or positive interactions as a source of validation. The perception that more matches equate to higher attractiveness or desirability can lead to a cycle of seeking external approval to validate one's self-worth.

● **Impact of Rejection:** Experiencing rejection or lack of matches may be internalized as a reflection of personal inadequacy or unattractiveness. This negative feedback can contribute to feelings of diminished self-worth and self-doubt.

2. Comparison with Others:

● **Social Comparison:** Comparing one's success or attractiveness on dating apps with that of others can exacerbate self-worth issues. Users may perceive themselves as less desirable or attractive if they believe their matches or interactions pale in comparison to those of their peers.

● **Idealized Standards:** Internalizing societal or app-driven standards of attractiveness or relationship success can create unrealistic expectations, leading users to question their own worth if they do not meet these perceived ideals.

3. Psychological Impact:

● **Self-Esteem:** Equating self-worth with dating app outcomes can undermine users' self-esteem, as their sense of value becomes contingent upon external feedback rather than intrinsic qualities or personal achievements.

● **Emotional Vulnerability:** Relying on external validation for self-worth makes users emotionally vulnerable to fluctuations in app interactions. Positive feedback may temporarily boost self-esteem, while negative feedback or lack of validation can trigger feelings of insecurity or unworthiness.

4. Behavioral Patterns:

● **Validation-Seeking Behaviors:** Users may engage in behaviors aimed at maximizing matches or positive interactions, such as editing profiles, choosing flattering photos, or altering messaging strategies to appeal to perceived preferences.

- **Risk of Over-Engagement:** Over-engaging with dating apps to seek validation may detract from other aspects of life, leading to reduced focus on personal goals, relationships offline, or overall well-being.

5. Coping Strategies:

- **Self-Awareness:** Recognizing and challenging thoughts linked to external validation can promote self-awareness and reduce reliance on dating app outcomes for self-worth.

- **Healthy Perspective:** Developing a balanced perspective on dating app interactions, recognizing that matches or interactions do not define one's worth, can help mitigate self-worth issues and promote resilience.

6. Ethical Considerations:

- **Promoting Positive User Experience:** Dating apps have a responsibility to promote positive user experiences by fostering a supportive environment that values authenticity, respect, and inclusivity. This includes discouraging behaviors that may exacerbate self-worth issues, such as comparison or unrealistic expectations.

- **User Education:** Providing resources or guidance on maintaining healthy self-esteem and managing validation-seeking behaviors can empower users to navigate dating apps in ways that prioritize their mental well-being.

Conclusion

Self-worth issues in the context of dating apps are influenced by the tendency to equate personal value with external validation, such as matches or positive interactions. These issues can impact users' self-esteem, emotional well-being, and behavior within the app. By promoting self-awareness, healthy coping strategies, and a supportive digital environment, dating apps can contribute to a positive user experience that values intrinsic qualities and promotes resilience in managing self-worth issues.

Chapter 6: Dehumanization and Objectification in the Context of Dating Apps

Dating apps, while facilitating connections between individuals, can also inadvertently contribute to the dehumanization and objectification of potential partners. This phenomenon arises from the app's interface, user behavior, and the dynamics of online interactions. Here's a detailed exploration of how dehumanization and objectification manifest on dating apps, and their impact on users' self-esteem and self-worth:

1. Treating People as Products:

● **Profile Representation:** Users often present themselves through curated profiles, focusing on attractive photos, brief bios, and selected interests. This presentation can reduce individuals to mere representations of their best qualities, akin to marketing products rather than presenting their full, nuanced selves.

● **Swipe Mechanism:** The swipe feature, where users make rapid judgments based on visual appeal and limited profile information, can reinforce a transactional mindset where potential partners are evaluated and discarded with ease. This process can lead to viewing others as disposable commodities rather than individuals with complex personalities and emotions.

2. Impact on Self-Esteem:

● **Rejection Sensitivity:** Users may experience heightened sensitivity to rejection due to the volume of interactions and the ease with which matches can be dismissed. Repeated rejection or lack of matches may contribute to feelings of inadequacy, loneliness, or diminished self-worth.

● **Superficial Validation:** Conversely, superficial acceptance based solely on physical appearance or initial attraction may provide fleeting validation. However, this validation can be shallow and may not contribute to a genuine sense of self-worth or fulfillment.

3. Psychological Dynamics:

● **Reduced Empathy:** The digital interface of dating apps, which prioritizes brief interactions and visual cues, can diminish opportunities for empathetic connection. Users may focus more on surface-level characteristics rather than engaging deeply with others' emotions or perspectives.

● **Objectification:** Objectification occurs when individuals are treated as objects of desire rather than respected as individuals with inherent dignity and autonomy. This can lead to interactions where personal boundaries are disregarded or where individuals are valued primarily for their physical attributes.

4. Gender Dynamics:

● **Gender Stereotyping:** Dating apps can reinforce traditional gender stereotypes or biases, where men and women may be evaluated based on stereotypical notions of attractiveness or desirability. This can perpetuate societal norms that prioritize physical appearance over other qualities.

● **Safety Concerns:** Objectification and dehumanization can contribute to unsafe or disrespectful behaviors, such as harassment or unsolicited advances, which further impact users' sense of safety and well-being.

5. Ethical Considerations:

● **Promoting Respectful Interactions:** Dating apps have a responsibility to promote respectful interactions that prioritize individuals' dignity and autonomy. This includes implementing features to discourage objectification, educating users on respectful behavior, and addressing harassment or inappropriate conduct promptly.

● **User Education:** Providing resources on healthy relationship dynamics, consent, and the impact of objectification can empower users to navigate dating apps in ways that promote mutual respect and genuine connection.

Conclusion

Dehumanization and objectification on dating apps can stem from the platform's design, user behaviors, and societal dynamics. These phenomena can impact users' self-esteem and self-worth by influencing how they perceive themselves and others within the digital dating landscape. By fostering a culture of empathy, respect, and inclusivity, dating apps can mitigate the negative effects of dehumanization and objectification, promoting healthier interactions and enhancing users' overall well-being.

Treating People as Products

Profile Representation on Dating Apps

Profile representation on dating apps involves how users present themselves through curated profiles, which often emphasize attractive photos, brief bios, and selected interests. This process can inadvertently reduce individuals to mere representations of their best qualities, akin to marketing products rather than presenting their full, nuanced selves. Here's a detailed exploration of this phenomenon:

1. Visual Emphasis:

● **Attractive Photos:** Users typically select photos that highlight their best physical attributes or convey a specific image. These photos are often chosen to attract attention and convey a favorable first impression, emphasizing physical appearance over other personal qualities.

● **Visual Presentation:** The layout and design of dating app profiles prioritize visual appeal, encouraging users to present themselves in a visually compelling manner. This can lead to a focus on aesthetics rather than deeper aspects of personality or character.

2. Brief Bios and Selected Interests:

● **Curated Information:** Users craft brief bios that highlight key aspects of their personality or interests. These bios are often designed to be concise yet engaging, offering a snapshot of the user's identity that may not capture the full complexity of their personality or life experiences.

● **Selected Interests:** Users may selectively highlight interests or hobbies that they believe will resonate positively with potential matches. This selective presentation may omit aspects of their identity that are less socially desirable or do not align with perceived dating app norms.

3. Representation vs. Authenticity:

● **Marketing Analogy:** The process of profile curation can be likened to marketing, where individuals strategically present themselves to attract attention and generate interest. This approach may prioritize marketability over authenticity, leading to a portrayal that may not fully reflect the user's true self.

● **Nuanced Identity:** Dating apps may inadvertently encourage users to present simplified or idealized versions of themselves, omitting nuances, vulnerabilities, or aspects that they perceive as less appealing. This can contribute to a disconnect between the curated profile and the user's authentic self.

4. Psychological Impact:

● **Self-Presentation Pressure:** The pressure to present an attractive or appealing profile can create stress or anxiety, as users seek to meet perceived standards of attractiveness or desirability set by the app or social norms.

● **Expectations and Disappointment:** Curated profiles may set expectations that do not align with reality, leading to disappointment or frustration when users' offline interactions do not match the idealized image presented online.

5. Ethical Considerations:

● **Authenticity and Honesty:** Dating apps have a responsibility to promote authenticity and honesty in profile representation. This includes discouraging deceptive practices or misrepresentation that may mislead potential matches and undermine trust within the app community.

● **Encouraging Diversity:** Supporting diverse expressions of identity and personality on dating apps can foster a more inclusive environment that values individuals for their unique qualities rather than conforming to narrow standards of attractiveness or presentation.

Conclusion

Profile representation on dating apps involves the strategic curation of photos, bios, and interests to attract potential matches. While this process aims to present users in a positive light, it can inadvertently reduce individuals to simplified representations of their best qualities, akin to marketing products. Recognizing the tension between curated profiles and authentic self-expression is essential for promoting genuine connections and fostering a positive user experience on dating apps. By encouraging authenticity, transparency, and respect for diverse identities, dating apps can contribute to a more inclusive and fulfilling digital dating landscape.

Swipe Mechanism on Dating Apps

The swipe mechanism on dating apps, popularized by platforms like Tinder, involves users making rapid judgments based on visual appeal and limited profile information. This feature allows users to swipe right to indicate interest or left to pass on a potential match. Here's a detailed exploration of how the swipe mechanism can reinforce a transactional mindset and lead to viewing others as disposable commodities:

1. Rapid Judgments Based on Visual Appeal:

● **Visual Focus:** The swipe feature prioritizes visual impressions over deeper aspects of personality or compatibility. Users typically make split-second decisions based on photos that convey physical attractiveness or a specific aesthetic.

● **Superficial Evaluation:** Limited profile information, such as brief bios or selected interests, may not provide enough context for meaningful evaluation. As a result, users often rely on initial visual appeal to determine interest, potentially overlooking important qualities that contribute to relationship compatibility.

2. Transactional Mindset:

● **Ease of Evaluation:** The ease and speed of swiping encourage a transactional approach to evaluating potential partners. Users may view the process as akin to browsing through products, where matches are sought based on immediate visual appeal rather than deeper connection or compatibility.

● **Disposable Nature:** Swiping left to reject a potential match can reinforce a perception of disposability, where individuals are quickly discarded if they do not meet specific visual or superficial criteria. This mindset can lead to minimizing the value of each individual interaction and reducing empathy towards potential matches.

3. Impact on Perception of Others:

● **Commoditization:** The swipe mechanism can contribute to viewing potential partners as commodities to be evaluated and selected based on perceived attractiveness or superficial traits. This can undermine recognition of each person's unique identity, personality, and emotional complexity.

● **Dehumanization:** Rapid swiping and superficial judgments may dehumanize potential matches by reducing them to visual stimuli or simplistic characteristics. This can hinder genuine empathy and understanding of each person's individuality beyond their profile presentation.

4. Psychological Dynamics:

● **Desensitization:** Continuous use of the swipe feature can desensitize users to the potential impact of their actions on others. The repetitive nature of swiping may lead to a detachment from the emotional consequences of rejecting or matching with individuals.

● **Impulse Control:** The ease of swiping and the immediate feedback (match or rejection) can influence users' impulse control, leading to hasty decisions without fully considering the implications or potential for meaningful connection.

5. Ethical Considerations:

● **Promoting Mindful Interaction:** Dating apps have a responsibility to encourage mindful interaction that goes beyond superficial judgments. This includes promoting features or guidelines that prompt users to consider compatibility factors beyond visual appeal and to engage in respectful, thoughtful communication.

● **User Education:** Providing education on the potential impact of swiping behaviors can help users navigate the app in a way that values each person's dignity and fosters genuine connections. This may include promoting empathy, authenticity, and respectful engagement within the digital dating environment.

Conclusion

The swipe mechanism on dating apps facilitates rapid judgments based on visual appeal and limited profile information, potentially reinforcing a transactional mindset where potential partners are evaluated and discarded with ease. This process can lead to viewing others as disposable commodities rather than individuals with complex personalities and emotions. Recognizing these dynamics is crucial for promoting more meaningful interactions and fostering empathy within the digital dating landscape. By encouraging thoughtful engagement and valuing authenticity over superficial criteria, dating apps can contribute to a more respectful and fulfilling user experience.

Impact on Self-Esteem

Rejection Sensitivity on Dating Apps

Rejection sensitivity on dating apps refers to users' heightened emotional response to perceived rejection, which can be amplified by the high volume of interactions and the ease with which matches can be dismissed. This phenomenon can lead to feelings of inadequacy, loneliness, or diminished self-worth. Here's a detailed exploration of how rejection sensitivity manifests and its impact on users' emotional well-being:

1. Volume of Interactions:

● **High Frequency:** Dating apps facilitate numerous interactions where users swipe through potential matches or receive notifications of interest. The sheer volume of these interactions increases the likelihood of experiencing rejection or perceived rejection.

● **Continuous Exposure:** Users are exposed to a continuous stream of potential matches, each representing an opportunity for connection but also a potential source of rejection if interest is not mutual. This constant exposure can heighten sensitivity to rejection.

2. Ease of Dismissal:

● **Swipe Culture:** The swipe feature allows users to quickly dismiss potential matches with a simple gesture, often based on superficial criteria such as physical appearance or initial impressions from a brief bio. This ease of dismissal can contribute to a sense of disposability and reduced empathy for others' feelings.

● **Impersonal Nature:** The digital interface of dating apps can make rejections feel impersonal, as they often occur without direct communication or explanation. This lack of personal interaction can exacerbate feelings of rejection and inadequacy.

3. Emotional Impact:

● **Feelings of Inadequacy:** Repeated rejections or lack of matches may lead users to question their attractiveness, likability, or compatibility with potential partners. This self-doubt can erode self-esteem and contribute to feelings of inadequacy.

● **Loneliness and Isolation:** Persistent rejection or perceived lack of interest from potential matches can intensify feelings of loneliness and social isolation. Users may feel disconnected from others or struggle to establish meaningful connections within the digital dating environment.

4. Cognitive and Behavioral Responses:

● **Negative Self-Talk:** Users may engage in negative self-talk, interpreting rejections as personal failures or evidence of their unworthiness. This cognitive response can perpetuate a cycle of self-criticism and undermine confidence in initiating new interactions.

● **Withdrawal:** In response to rejection sensitivity, some users may withdraw from active engagement on dating apps or avoid initiating new connections altogether. This withdrawal can further exacerbate feelings of loneliness or social exclusion.

5. Coping Strategies and Support:

● **Self-Care:** Encouraging users to practice self-care and self-compassion can help mitigate the emotional impact of rejection sensitivity. This includes engaging in activities that promote emotional well-being and nurturing positive self-esteem.

● **Community Support:** Building a supportive community within dating apps or providing access to resources for coping with rejection can empower users to navigate challenges and maintain resilience in the face of setbacks.

Conclusion

Rejection sensitivity on dating apps reflects users' heightened emotional response to perceived rejection, influenced by the volume of interactions and the ease with which matches can be dismissed. This phenomenon can significantly impact users' emotional well-being, contributing to feelings of inadequacy, loneliness, or diminished self-worth. Recognizing and addressing rejection sensitivity involves promoting empathy, resilience, and self-care strategies within the digital dating environment to foster a more supportive and fulfilling user experience.

Superficial Validation on Dating Apps

Superficial validation on dating apps refers to the validation or approval that users may receive based solely on physical appearance or initial attraction. While this validation can provide a sense of acceptance, it is often shallow and may not contribute to a genuine sense of self-worth or fulfillment. Here's a detailed exploration of how superficial validation manifests and its implications for users:

1. Basis of Validation:

● **Physical Appearance:** Dating apps often prioritize photos as the primary means of attracting interest and making initial impressions. Users may receive validation or approval based solely on their physical appearance, which is highlighted in profile pictures.

● **Superficial Criteria:** Validation may be contingent upon meeting superficial criteria such as attractiveness, fashion sense, or presentation in photos. This form of validation focuses on external attributes rather than deeper qualities or personal characteristics.

2. Fleeting Nature:

● **Short-Lived:** Superficial validation based on physical appearance or initial attraction tends to be fleeting. It may provide a temporary boost in confidence or self-esteem but lacks longevity or meaningful impact on one's sense of self-worth.

● **Surface-Level Interaction:** Interactions that are primarily based on superficial validation may lack depth or emotional connection. Users may feel that these interactions do not contribute to building meaningful relationships or fulfilling social connections.

3. Impact on Self-Worth:

● **Dependency on External Approval:** Relying on superficial validation for self-worth can create a dependency on external approval. Users may seek validation through continued engagement on dating apps or by modifying their profile presentation to enhance attractiveness.

● **Diminished Fulfillment:** Despite receiving superficial validation, users may not experience genuine fulfillment or satisfaction. This form of validation may leave individuals feeling empty or dissatisfied, as it does not address deeper emotional needs or desires for meaningful connection.

4. Psychological Dynamics:

● **Comparison and Competition:** Superficial validation can contribute to a sense of competition or comparison among users. Individuals may compare themselves to others based on perceived attractiveness or success in receiving validation, which can exacerbate feelings of insecurity or inadequacy.

● **Emotional Disconnection:** Focusing on superficial validation may detract from authentic emotional connections or meaningful interactions. Users may prioritize surface-level impressions over compatibility or shared values, limiting the potential for genuine relationship development.

5. Promoting Authenticity and Self-Worth:

- **Encouraging Authenticity:** Dating apps can promote authenticity by emphasizing the value of genuine self-expression and connection beyond physical appearance. This includes encouraging users to highlight their interests, values, and personality traits in addition to photos.
- **Supporting Self-Worth:** Building self-worth involves fostering internal validation based on personal strengths, values, and achievements. Dating apps can support users in developing a healthy self-concept that is not solely reliant on external validation or superficial criteria.

Conclusion

Superficial validation on dating apps refers to approval or acceptance based primarily on physical appearance or initial attraction. While this validation may provide a temporary boost in confidence, it tends to be shallow and lacks lasting fulfillment or genuine connection. Recognizing the limitations of superficial validation involves promoting authenticity, supporting self-worth based on internal factors, and encouraging users to seek meaningful connections that transcend surface-level impressions within the digital dating environment.

Psychological Dynamics

Reduced Empathy on Dating Apps

Reduced empathy on dating apps refers to the diminished ability or opportunity for users to connect empathetically with others due to the digital interface, which often emphasizes brief interactions and visual cues over deeper emotional engagement. Here's a detailed exploration of how reduced empathy manifests and its implications within the context of dating apps:

1. Digital Interface:

● **Brief Interactions:** Dating apps typically facilitate brief interactions, such as swiping through profiles or exchanging short messages. These interactions may prioritize efficiency and quick judgments over meaningful engagement or emotional connection.

● **Visual Focus:** The emphasis on visual cues, such as profile photos or brief bios, can lead users to prioritize physical appearance or initial impressions rather than deeper emotional understanding or empathy.

2. Surface-Level Engagement:

● **Superficial Criteria:** Users may focus on superficial criteria, such as attractiveness or presentation in photos, when evaluating potential matches. This surface-level engagement can detract from deeper exploration of personality, values, or shared interests.

● **Limited Context:** Without face-to-face interaction or non-verbal cues, users may struggle to interpret others' emotions or perspectives accurately. This limited context can hinder empathetic understanding and connection.

3. Psychological Dynamics:

● **Dehumanization:** The digital format of dating apps can contribute to dehumanization, where users perceive others as profiles or images rather than individuals with complex emotions, experiences, and perspectives.

● **Transactional Mindset:** Users may adopt a transactional mindset, where interactions are viewed as exchanges of information or opportunities for validation rather than opportunities for genuine emotional connection or empathy.

4. Impact on Relationships:

● **Emotional Disconnect:** Reduced empathy may result in emotional disconnect or difficulty establishing meaningful relationships. Users may struggle to empathize with others' feelings or perspectives, limiting the potential for deeper emotional bonds.

● **Miscommunication:** Misinterpretation or misunderstanding of others' emotions or intentions can arise due to the lack of non-verbal cues or context in digital interactions. This can further hinder empathetic communication and connection.

5. Promoting Empathetic Connection:

● **Encouraging Meaningful Engagement:** Dating apps can promote empathetic connection by encouraging users to engage meaningfully with others' profiles and bios, beyond superficial impressions. This includes fostering curiosity about shared interests, values, and life experiences.

● **Facilitating Communication:** Incorporating features that support richer communication, such as video calls or voice messages, can enhance opportunities for empathetic understanding and emotional connection.

Conclusion

Reduced empathy on dating apps reflects the diminished ability or opportunity for users to connect empathetically with others, influenced by the digital interface that prioritizes brief interactions and visual cues. Recognizing the implications of reduced empathy involves promoting deeper engagement beyond superficial criteria, fostering understanding of others' emotions and perspectives, and enhancing communication channels that support meaningful emotional connection within the digital dating environment.

Objectification in the Context of Dating Apps

Objectification on dating apps refers to the treatment of individuals as objects of desire, focusing primarily on their physical attributes rather than respecting them as individuals with inherent dignity and autonomy. This phenomenon can lead to interactions where personal boundaries are disregarded or where individuals are valued primarily for their superficial qualities. Here's a detailed exploration of how objectification manifests and its implications within the context of dating apps:

1. Focus on Physical Appearance:

● **Primary Criterion:** Dating apps often prioritize photos as the primary means of making initial impressions and attracting interest. Users may evaluate potential matches based primarily on physical attractiveness, reducing individuals to their appearance rather than considering their personality, values, or interests.

● **Superficial Judgments:** Objectification can lead to superficial judgments where individuals are valued or dismissed based solely on their perceived attractiveness or physical presentation in profile photos.

2. Disregard for Personal Boundaries:

● **Boundary Crossing:** Objectification can contribute to interactions where personal boundaries are disregarded or violated. Users may prioritize their own desires or preferences without considering or respecting the boundaries, comfort levels, or consent of others.

● **Transactional Interactions:** Interactions driven by objectification may be transactional, focusing on immediate gratification or validation rather than mutual respect, consent, or emotional connection.

3. Dehumanization:

● **Reduction to Objects:** Treating individuals as objects of desire can lead to their dehumanization, where their worth is determined primarily by their perceived attractiveness or suitability as a romantic or sexual partner.

● **Diminished Autonomy:** Objectification can diminish individuals' autonomy by reducing them to stereotypes or idealized images, rather than recognizing their multifaceted identities and personal agency.

4. Psychological and Emotional Impact:

● **Self-Objectification:** Individuals who experience objectification may internalize these perceptions, viewing themselves through the lens of external validation or physical appearance. This self-objectification can impact self-esteem, self-worth, and overall well-being.

● **Emotional Harm:** Objectification can contribute to emotional harm, including feelings of objectified individuals being used or valued solely for their physical attributes rather than respected for their holistic qualities.

5. Promoting Respect and Dignity:

● **Encouraging Respectful Interactions:** Dating apps can promote respectful interactions by emphasizing mutual respect, consent, and recognition of individuals' inherent dignity. This includes fostering conversations that prioritize personality, values, and shared interests alongside physical attraction.

● **Educational Initiatives:** Implementing educational initiatives within dating apps can raise awareness about objectification, boundaries, and healthy relationship dynamics. These initiatives can empower users to navigate interactions with greater empathy, respect, and consideration for others' autonomy.

Conclusion

Objectification on dating apps reflects the treatment of individuals as objects of desire, focusing primarily on their physical attributes rather than respecting their inherent dignity and autonomy. Recognizing the implications of objectification involves promoting interactions that prioritize mutual respect, consent, and recognition of individuals' multifaceted identities within the digital dating environment. By fostering a culture of respect and dignity, dating apps can contribute to creating more positive and fulfilling user experiences that prioritize meaningful connections beyond superficial criteria.

Gender Dynamics

Gender Stereotyping on Dating Apps

Gender stereotyping on dating apps refers to the reinforcement of traditional societal norms and biases where individuals, particularly men and women, are evaluated based on stereotypical notions of attractiveness or desirability. This phenomenon can perpetuate existing gender norms that prioritize physical appearance and reinforce traditional roles. Here's a detailed exploration of how gender stereotyping manifests and its implications within the context of dating apps:

1. Reinforcement of Traditional Norms:

- **Appearance Standards:** Dating apps often emphasize visual impressions through profile photos, where users may be judged based on conventional standards of attractiveness. Men and women may feel pressure to conform to stereotypical ideals of physical appearance to attract matches.

- **Role Expectations:** Stereotypes regarding gender roles may influence how individuals present themselves on dating apps. For instance, men may feel pressured to display confidence or assertiveness, while women may feel compelled to emphasize femininity or attractiveness in their profiles.

2. Evaluation Based on Stereotypical Traits:

- **Physical Attractiveness:** Users may prioritize physical appearance when swiping through profiles or making initial judgments. This emphasis can reinforce stereotypes about men as providers of status or women as objects of desire, based on appearance.

- **Personality Traits:** Stereotypical expectations about personality traits, such as men being assertive or women being nurturing, may influence how users perceive potential matches. This can lead to overlooking individuals who do not fit traditional stereotypes.

3. Impact on User Experience:

- **Pressure to Conform:** Gender stereotyping can create pressure for users to conform to societal expectations regarding appearance, behavior, or personality traits. This pressure may limit individual expression and authenticity in profile presentations.

- **Stereotype Threat:** Individuals who do not align with traditional gender stereotypes may experience stereotype threat, where their self-perception or confidence is negatively affected by perceived expectations or biases within the dating app environment.

4. Reinforcement of Bias:

- **Biased Algorithms:** Dating app algorithms that prioritize certain profiles or suggest matches based on stereotypical criteria can reinforce existing biases or preferences. This can perpetuate inequalities and limit opportunities for diverse connections.

- **Social Validation:** Users may seek social validation or acceptance by conforming to gender stereotypes that are reinforced within the dating app community. This can reinforce societal norms rather than challenging or expanding perspectives on gender and identity.

5. Promoting Diversity and Inclusivity:

- **Diverse Representation:** Dating apps can promote diversity and inclusivity by showcasing a wide range of profiles that challenge traditional gender stereotypes. This includes highlighting individuals with diverse interests, backgrounds, and identities beyond physical appearance.

- **Education and Awareness:** Implementing educational initiatives within dating apps can raise awareness about gender stereotyping, biases, and their impact on user experiences. These initiatives can empower users to engage in more respectful, inclusive interactions that value individuality and authenticity.

Conclusion

Gender stereotyping on dating apps reflects the reinforcement of traditional societal norms and biases regarding attractiveness, desirability, and gender roles. Recognizing the implications of gender stereotyping involves promoting interactions that value diversity, inclusivity, and authenticity within the digital dating environment. By challenging stereotypes and promoting awareness, dating apps can contribute to creating more positive and equitable user experiences that prioritize genuine connections based on shared interests, values, and mutual respect.

Safety Concerns in the Context of Dating Apps

Safety concerns on dating apps encompass a range of issues related to objectification, dehumanization, and their implications for user experiences. These concerns can contribute to unsafe or disrespectful behaviors, impacting users' sense of safety and well-being. Here's a detailed exploration of how safety concerns manifest and their implications within the context of dating apps:

1. **Objectification and Dehumanization:**

• **Disregard for Boundaries:** Objectification can lead to interactions where individuals are treated as objects of desire rather than respected as autonomous persons with boundaries. This disregard for personal boundaries can contribute to unsafe or coercive behaviors, such as pressuring or manipulating others into unwanted interactions.

• **Diminished Respect:** Dehumanization reduces individuals to superficial qualities, such as physical appearance or perceived desirability, rather than acknowledging their full humanity. This lack of respect can foster environments where users may feel vulnerable to disrespectful or exploitative behavior.

2. **Harassment and Unsolicited Advances:**

• **Impact of Objectification:** Objectifying attitudes may contribute to behaviors such as harassment or unsolicited advances, where individuals feel entitled to pursue or comment on others without regard for their comfort or consent.

• **Boundary Violations:** Unsafe behaviors, such as sending explicit messages or persistent unwanted contact, can violate personal boundaries and contribute to feelings of discomfort, anxiety, or fear among users.

3. **Psychological and Emotional Impact:**

• **Impact on Well-Being:** Users may experience emotional distress, anxiety, or diminished self-esteem as a result of objectification or disrespectful interactions on dating apps. These negative experiences can erode trust in online interactions and impact users' willingness to engage in dating app communities.

• **Safety Concerns:** Persistent or threatening behaviors, such as stalking or intimidation, can escalate safety concerns for users. Safety features and reporting mechanisms on dating apps are crucial for addressing these issues and protecting user well-being.

4. **Addressing Safety Challenges:**

• **Platform Responsibility:** Dating apps have a responsibility to implement robust safety measures, including moderation, reporting mechanisms, and user education on respectful behavior. Clear guidelines and community standards can help mitigate risks and promote a safer online environment.

• **User Empowerment:** Empowering users with tools to control their visibility, block or report abusive behavior, and access support resources can enhance their sense of safety and agency within dating app communities.

5. **Promoting Respectful Interactions:**

• **Educational Initiatives:** Implementing educational initiatives within dating apps can raise awareness about respectful communication, consent, and healthy boundaries. These initiatives encourage users to engage in interactions that prioritize mutual respect and safety.

- **Community Norms:** Fostering community norms that reject objectification, harassment, and coercive behaviors promotes a culture of respect and safety within dating app platforms. Encouraging positive interactions based on genuine connection and mutual consent supports a more inclusive and supportive online dating environment.

Conclusion

Safety concerns on dating apps related to objectification and dehumanization highlight the importance of promoting respectful interactions and prioritizing user well-being. By addressing these issues through robust safety measures, user empowerment, and community education, dating apps can cultivate environments that foster genuine connections while mitigating risks associated with unsafe or disrespectful behaviors. Enhancing safety features and promoting a culture of respect contribute to creating positive and inclusive user experiences within the digital dating landscape.

Ethical Considerations

Promoting Respectful Interactions on Dating Apps

Dating apps play a crucial role in fostering a culture of respect and safety by implementing features and policies that prioritize individuals' dignity and autonomy. Promoting respectful interactions involves several strategies aimed at discouraging objectification, educating users on respectful behavior, and addressing harassment promptly. Here's a detailed exploration of how dating apps can promote respectful interactions:

1. Feature Implementation:

- **Profile Guidelines:** Dating apps can establish clear guidelines for profile content to discourage objectification. This includes policies against explicit or inappropriate photos, hate speech, or discriminatory language that devalues individuals based on gender, ethnicity, or other characteristics.

- **Reporting Mechanisms:** Robust reporting mechanisms empower users to flag inappropriate behavior, including harassment, spam, or other forms of misconduct. Prompt responses to reports are essential for addressing concerns swiftly and maintaining a safe environment.

- **Blocking and Filtering:** Providing users with tools to block or filter unwanted contacts helps them control their interactions and maintain boundaries. This feature is critical for users to feel empowered in managing their online experience.

2. User Education:

- **Guidelines and Tips:** Offering guidelines and educational resources within the app educates users on respectful communication, consent, and healthy boundaries. Tips on initiating conversations, recognizing red flags, and respecting personal space can promote positive interactions.

- **Community Standards:** Establishing community standards that promote inclusivity, tolerance, and respect reinforces expectations for user behavior. Clear communication of these standards encourages users to contribute to a welcoming and safe community.

3. Addressing Harassment and Misconduct:

- **Prompt Action:** Taking immediate action on reported incidents of harassment or misconduct demonstrates the app's commitment to user safety. This may include suspending or permanently banning accounts that violate community guidelines.

- **Transparent Communication:** Communicating openly with users about policies, enforcement actions, and updates on safety measures builds trust and accountability. Transparency in how the app handles safety issues fosters a sense of security among its user base.

4. Cultivating a Respectful Culture:

- **Promoting Empathy:** Encouraging empathy and consideration for others in online interactions can reduce instances of objectification or insensitive behavior. Features that prompt users to consider the impact of their messages or actions on others can foster empathy.

- **Inclusivity Initiatives:** Actively promoting inclusivity through diverse representation in marketing, features, and community events reinforces the app's commitment to respecting all users. Celebrating diversity contributes to a welcoming environment where individuals feel valued and respected.

5. Continuous Improvement:

- **Feedback Mechanisms:** Regularly seeking feedback from users about their experiences and suggestions for improvement allows dating apps to evolve in addressing emerging challenges. Incorporating user input into policy updates and feature enhancements demonstrates responsiveness to community needs.

- **Collaboration with Experts:** Partnering with experts in psychology, sociology, and digital ethics can inform best practices for promoting respectful interactions and mitigating risks of harm. Collaboration helps dating apps stay informed about evolving trends and societal norms.

Conclusion

Promoting respectful interactions on dating apps involves a multifaceted approach that includes feature implementation, user education, proactive management of harassment, and fostering a culture of inclusivity and empathy. By prioritizing user safety and dignity, dating apps can create environments where individuals feel empowered to engage authentically and respectfully. Continuous efforts to improve policies and practices ensure that dating apps evolve in addressing challenges while upholding principles of respect and integrity within the digital dating landscape.

User Education on Dating Apps

User education plays a pivotal role in empowering individuals to navigate dating apps responsibly and ethically. By providing resources on healthy relationship dynamics, consent, and the impact of objectification, dating apps can foster an environment that promotes mutual respect, genuine connection, and user safety. Here's a detailed exploration of how user education can be implemented effectively:

1. Healthy Relationship Dynamics:

- **Understanding Boundaries:** Education on healthy relationship dynamics includes guidance on setting and respecting personal boundaries. This helps users recognize the importance of consent and autonomy in interactions with others on dating platforms.

- **Effective Communication:** Resources can educate users on effective communication skills, such as active listening, empathy, and clear expression of intentions. These skills are crucial for fostering meaningful connections and avoiding misunderstandings.

- **Conflict Resolution:** Providing tips on resolving conflicts constructively encourages users to address disagreements or misunderstandings in a respectful manner. This promotes healthier interactions and reduces the likelihood of escalation or harm.

2. Consent Education:

- **Definition of Consent:** Clear explanations of what constitutes consent and the importance of enthusiastic, ongoing consent in all interactions are essential. Users should understand that consent is freely given, reversible, informed, and enthusiastic.

- **Recognizing Coercion:** Education should highlight the signs of coercion or pressure in online interactions and emphasize the need for all parties to feel comfortable and respected throughout their communication.

- **Empowerment in Consent:** Empowering users to assert their boundaries and preferences, as well as to recognize and respect the boundaries of others, fosters a culture of mutual respect and safety.

3. Impact of Objectification:

- **Awareness of Objectifying Behaviors:** Users benefit from learning about the negative impact of objectification on individuals' self-esteem, mental health, and overall well-being. Understanding how objectification reduces individuals to superficial qualities can encourage more empathetic and respectful interactions.

- **Promoting Authenticity:** Encouraging users to present themselves authentically and appreciate the full personality and humanity of others helps combat objectification. Emphasizing the value of genuine connections over superficial judgments reinforces positive online dating behaviors.

4. Promoting User Safety:

● **Recognizing Red Flags:** Education should include information on recognizing red flags or warning signs of potentially harmful behaviors, such as manipulation, gaslighting, or abusive language. Empowering users to trust their instincts and take action if they feel unsafe is crucial.

● **Reporting and Support:** Clear guidance on how to report abusive behavior and access support resources within the app promotes user safety. Prompt responses to reports of misconduct demonstrate the platform's commitment to maintaining a safe environment.

5. Continuous Learning and Feedback:

● **Updating Resources:** Regularly updating educational resources based on user feedback, emerging trends, and expert advice ensures that information remains relevant and effective in addressing evolving challenges.

● **Collaboration with Experts:** Partnering with experts in psychology, relationship counseling, and digital ethics enhances the quality and credibility of educational content. Expert input informs best practices for promoting healthy online interactions and addressing complex issues.

Conclusion

User education on dating apps is essential for promoting responsible, respectful, and safe interactions among users. By providing resources on healthy relationship dynamics, consent, and the impact of objectification, dating apps empower individuals to navigate online dating with awareness, empathy, and integrity. Educated users are better equipped to foster genuine connections, respect boundaries, and contribute to a positive and inclusive digital dating community. Continuous improvement and collaboration with experts ensure that user education initiatives effectively address the evolving needs and challenges of online dating platforms.

Chapter 7: Hookup Culture vs. Long-Term Relationships on Dating Apps

Dating apps have significantly influenced contemporary dating dynamics, often leading to the prominence of hookup culture alongside challenges in pursuing serious, long-term relationships. Here's a detailed exploration of these contrasting aspects:

1. Casual Encounters:

- **Rise of Hookup Culture:** Dating apps have facilitated a rise in hookup culture by providing a platform where users can easily connect for casual, non-committal encounters. Features like swiping and instant messaging encourage quick, spontaneous interactions based primarily on physical attraction.

- **Transactional Nature:** Hookup culture often emphasizes the transactional nature of relationships, where the primary focus is on immediate gratification and physical intimacy rather than emotional connection or long-term commitment.

- **Social Acceptance:** The normalization of casual encounters through dating apps has contributed to a broader social acceptance of non-committal relationships, challenging traditional dating norms that prioritize emotional connection and long-term commitment.

2. Finding Serious Relationships:

- **Challenges and Misalignment:** In an environment dominated by hookup culture, individuals seeking serious, long-term relationships may face challenges. The emphasis on casual encounters can lead to misunderstandings or misaligned expectations between users looking for different relationship outcomes.

- **Superficial Judgments:** Dating apps' reliance on profile photos and brief bios for matchmaking can promote superficial judgments, making it challenging for users to assess compatibility beyond physical appearance. This can hinder the development of meaningful connections necessary for long-term relationships.

- **Navigating Intentions:** Clarifying intentions early in interactions becomes crucial for users seeking serious relationships. Clear communication about relationship goals, values, and expectations helps mitigate the ambiguity prevalent in a hookup-centric dating environment.

3. Impact on Traditional Dating:

- **Shift in Dating Norms:** Dating apps have contributed to a shift in traditional dating norms, where the pace and expectations of relationships are influenced by digital interactions rather than face-to-face encounters or shared social circles.

- **Diverse Preferences:** While hookup culture is prominent, dating apps also cater to diverse preferences, including those seeking meaningful connections. Some platforms offer features like detailed profiles, compatibility assessments, and relationship-oriented filters to facilitate serious dating.

- **Balancing Choices:** Users navigating dating apps must navigate between casual encounters and the pursuit of long-term relationships, often requiring careful consideration of profiles, communication styles, and shared values.

4. Psychological Impact:

- **Emotional Well-being:** The prevalence of hookup culture and the challenges of finding serious relationships can impact users' emotional well-being. Repeated experiences of casual encounters or difficulties in forming lasting connections may contribute to feelings of loneliness, frustration, or disillusionment.

- **Self-Esteem:** Users may experience fluctuations in self-esteem based on their success in achieving desired relationship outcomes on dating apps. Rejection or the perception of being valued solely for physical attributes can influence self-worth and confidence.

5. Cultural and Societal Influences:

● **Generational Differences:** Generational attitudes towards dating, influenced by technology and social norms, shape the prevalence of hookup culture versus the pursuit of long-term relationships. Younger generations, accustomed to digital interactions, may approach dating apps with different expectations than older generations.

● **Social Validation:** The instant feedback and validation provided by dating apps, whether through matches or messages, can influence users' perceptions of their desirability and attractiveness within the dating pool. This social validation may reinforce behaviors aligned with hookup culture or long-term relationship goals.

Conclusion

Dating apps have transformed the dating landscape by popularizing hookup culture while presenting challenges for those seeking serious, long-term relationships. Understanding the dynamics of hookup culture versus the pursuit of meaningful connections requires navigating differences in user intentions, communication styles, and societal influences. By acknowledging these contrasts, dating apps can cater to diverse relationship preferences while fostering environments that promote respect, clear communication, and emotional well-being among users. Balancing the impact of hookup culture with opportunities for meaningful relationships remains a key challenge and opportunity in the evolving digital dating realm.

Casual Encounters

Rise of Hookup Culture on Dating Apps

Dating apps have significantly contributed to the rise of hookup culture by providing a digital platform that facilitates quick and casual encounters. Here's a detailed exploration of how dating apps have fostered hookup culture:

1. Accessibility and Convenience:

● **Digital Connectivity:** Dating apps leverage technology to connect users instantly, transcending geographical barriers and facilitating interactions that may not occur otherwise. This accessibility lowers traditional barriers to meeting new people, making casual encounters more feasible and immediate.

● **Swiping Mechanism:** The swipe feature popularized by apps like Tinder simplifies the process of indicating interest or disinterest based on superficial criteria such as profile photos and brief bios. This gamified approach encourages rapid decision-making and facilitates a high volume of interactions.

2. Focus on Physical Attraction:

● **Visual Primacy:** Dating apps prioritize visual elements, such as profile photos, as the initial basis for attraction and interaction. Users often make split-second decisions based on these visuals, which can emphasize physical appearance over other qualities like personality or shared interests.

● **Instant Messaging:** Features like instant messaging enable users to initiate conversations immediately upon mutual interest (a match). This immediacy encourages spontaneous interactions centered on immediate attraction rather than long-term compatibility or emotional connection.

3. Norms and Acceptance:

● **Normalization:** Over time, hookup culture facilitated by dating apps has become more normalized and socially accepted, particularly among younger demographics. The ease and convenience of digital interactions contribute to a cultural shift where casual encounters are viewed as a viable and legitimate way of meeting new people.

● **Social Validation:** Positive reinforcement through matches and interactions reinforces the behavior associated with hookup culture, creating a cycle where users seek validation and gratification through casual interactions.

4. Transactional Nature:

● **Non-Committal Approach:** Hookup culture on dating apps often reflects a non-committal approach to relationships, where users engage in brief, often one-time encounters without the expectation of emotional intimacy or long-term commitment.

● **Transactional Relationships:** Interactions facilitated by dating apps can adopt a transactional nature, where users exchange attention, validation, or physical intimacy in a manner that mirrors consumerist behaviors rather than emotional connections.

5. Impact on Dating Dynamics:

● **Shift in Norms:** The prevalence of hookup culture has contributed to a shift in dating norms, where traditional expectations of courtship and relationship progression may be replaced by more casual and immediate interactions.

● **Challenges for Serious Relationships:** While hookup culture caters to immediate gratification and casual encounters, it can present challenges for individuals seeking serious, long-term relationships. The emphasis on physical attraction and spontaneous interactions may overshadow the development of deeper emotional connections or shared values.

Conclusion

Dating apps have revolutionized dating dynamics by facilitating hookup culture through features that prioritize accessibility, physical attraction, and instant gratification. The rise of hookup culture reflects broader shifts in societal norms towards casual relationships and digital interactions. Understanding these dynamics is essential for navigating dating apps and recognizing the influences of hookup culture on personal preferences, relationship expectations, and societal attitudes towards dating and intimacy.

Transactional Nature in Hookup Culture

Hookup culture, fostered significantly by dating apps, often emphasizes a transactional approach to relationships. Here's a detailed exploration of its characteristics and impact:

1. Emphasis on Immediate Gratification:

● **Instantaneous Interactions:** Dating apps facilitate quick, often impulsive interactions based on immediate attraction or physical appeal. Users can engage in spontaneous conversations or arrange meetings swiftly, prioritizing immediate gratification over long-term emotional connection.

● **Physical Intimacy:** The transactional nature of hookup culture places a strong emphasis on physical intimacy as a primary goal of interactions. Users may seek short-term encounters or casual relationships that fulfill immediate physical desires without the expectation of emotional bonding or commitment.

2. Limited Emotional Investment:

● **Surface-Level Connections:** Relationships in hookup culture tend to remain superficial, focusing on the present moment rather than long-term emotional investment. Users may prioritize fun, excitement, or sexual satisfaction over developing deeper emotional connections or understanding each other's personal histories and aspirations.

● **Avoidance of Emotional Vulnerability:** The transactional approach often involves avoiding emotional vulnerability or attachment, as these elements can complicate casual relationships or detract from the simplicity and immediacy of physical interactions.

3. Exchange-Based Dynamics:

● **Transactional Exchanges:** Interactions within hookup culture can resemble transactional exchanges, where individuals exchange attention, validation, or physical intimacy in a manner that mirrors economic transactions. This exchange-based dynamic may involve clear expectations and boundaries regarding the duration and nature of the relationship.

● **Quid Pro Quo Mentality:** Participants in hookup culture may adopt a quid pro quo mentality, expecting reciprocation of attention or favors in exchange for physical intimacy or validation. This approach reinforces the transactional nature of relationships, where each party evaluates the benefits and costs of engaging in casual encounters.

4. Challenges for Emotional Connection:

● **Limited Communication:** Communication within hookup culture may focus primarily on arranging meetings or discussing immediate desires, rather than engaging in meaningful conversations that foster emotional intimacy or understanding.

● **Difficulty in Vulnerability:** Establishing emotional connection or vulnerability can be challenging within hookup culture, as the emphasis on casual interactions may discourage individuals from expressing deeper emotions or personal vulnerabilities.

5. Impact on Relationship Expectations:

- **Shift in Priorities:** The prevalence of hookup culture can influence individuals' relationship expectations, shifting priorities away from emotional connection or long-term commitment towards immediate physical satisfaction and recreational companionship.
- **Navigating Expectations:** For individuals seeking serious relationships, navigating hookup culture can present challenges in identifying compatible partners who share similar relationship goals and values. The transactional nature of casual encounters may complicate efforts to establish trust, mutual respect, and shared understanding.

Conclusion

Hookup culture, characterized by its transactional nature, emphasizes immediate gratification and physical intimacy over emotional connection or long-term commitment. Facilitated by dating apps, this cultural shift reflects broader societal attitudes towards relationships and intimacy, influencing how individuals approach dating, communication, and personal fulfillment. Understanding the transactional dynamics of hookup culture is essential for navigating contemporary dating landscapes and recognizing its impact on personal values, relationship expectations, and emotional well-being.

Social Acceptance of Casual Encounters Through Dating Apps

The normalization of casual encounters facilitated by dating apps has reshaped societal attitudes towards relationships, emphasizing non-committal interactions over traditional values of emotional connection and long-term commitment. Here's a detailed exploration of this phenomenon:

1. Evolution of Social Norms:

- **Shifting Perceptions:** Dating apps have played a pivotal role in shifting societal perceptions of relationships, particularly among younger generations. Casual encounters, once stigmatized or viewed as unconventional, are now increasingly normalized and accepted as legitimate ways of meeting potential partners.
- **Generational Influence:** Young adults, in particular, have embraced dating apps as a mainstream method for socializing and forming connections. The prevalence of digital interactions has normalized casual dating practices, challenging older, more conservative views that prioritize courtship and commitment.

2. Accessibility and Convenience:

- **Digital Accessibility:** Dating apps provide accessible platforms for individuals to explore their dating preferences and engage in casual interactions without geographical limitations. This accessibility broadens social circles and introduces users to diverse perspectives and relationship dynamics.
- **Convenience:** The convenience of dating apps enables users to initiate and maintain connections effortlessly, facilitating spontaneous meetups and casual encounters that align with contemporary lifestyles characterized by mobility and flexibility.

3. Cultural and Media Influence:

- **Media Portrayal:** Popular media, including television shows, films, and online content, often depict casual relationships and hookups as normative behaviors among young adults. This media representation reinforces the perception that non-committal interactions are common and acceptable in modern dating culture.
- **Social Media Integration:** Social media platforms amplify the visibility and acceptance of casual encounters, with users sharing experiences, preferences, and opinions that contribute to shaping societal attitudes towards relationship dynamics and personal fulfillment.

4. Redefining Relationship Expectations:

- **Alternative Relationship Models:** The normalization of casual encounters challenges traditional relationship models that prioritize exclusivity, emotional intimacy, and long-term commitment. Individuals may explore alternative relationship structures, such as open relationships or polyamory, that accommodate diverse emotional and sexual needs.

- **Personal Agency:** Dating apps empower individuals to define their relationship goals and preferences, encouraging autonomy in navigating romantic connections based on personal values, desires, and aspirations.

5. Impact on Dating Practices:

- **Diversification of Dating Practices:** The acceptance of casual encounters diversifies dating practices, allowing individuals to experiment with different relationship dynamics and intimacy levels. This diversity promotes inclusivity and respect for diverse expressions of romantic and sexual identities.

- **Challenges and Considerations:** While casual encounters are increasingly accepted, navigating dating apps requires consideration of consent, communication, and mutual respect to ensure positive and fulfilling interactions for all participants.

Conclusion

The normalization of casual encounters through dating apps reflects evolving societal norms and values regarding relationships and intimacy. By challenging traditional dating expectations, dating apps have broadened opportunities for individuals to explore diverse relationship dynamics and define their own paths to personal fulfillment. Understanding the social acceptance of casual encounters is essential for navigating contemporary dating landscapes and embracing the diversity of relationship experiences and expressions in today's digital age.

Finding Serious Relationships

Challenges and Misalignment in Hookup Culture

In an environment where hookup culture predominates, individuals seeking serious, long-term relationships may encounter significant challenges. Here's a detailed exploration of these challenges and the potential misalignment of expectations:

1. Different Relationship Goals:

- **Casual vs. Long-Term:** Hookup culture often prioritizes casual, non-committal encounters focused on immediate gratification and physical intimacy. Individuals seeking serious relationships may have contrasting priorities, prioritizing emotional connection, commitment, and long-term compatibility.

- **Communication Challenges:** Misaligned expectations can arise when users fail to communicate their relationship goals clearly or interpret interactions differently. Casual encounters may be perceived as ambiguous, leading to misunderstandings about the nature and expectations of the relationship.

2. Emotional Dissonance:

- **Emotional Investment:** Individuals seeking serious relationships may invest emotionally in interactions, expecting reciprocity and mutual investment from their partners. In contrast, hookup culture may discourage emotional vulnerability or attachment, potentially leaving individuals feeling emotionally unfulfilled or disconnected.

- **Impact on Well-being:** Emotional dissonance can contribute to feelings of disillusionment, loneliness, or frustration among individuals seeking meaningful connections within a hookup-oriented environment. The discrepancy between desired and experienced emotional intimacy may impact self-esteem and overall well-being.

3. Trust and Commitment Issues:

- **Building Trust:** Trust is foundational in establishing meaningful relationships. In hookup culture, where interactions may be brief and transient, individuals seeking long-term commitments may struggle to build trust and establish emotional security with potential partners.

- **Commitment Phobia:** The transient nature of casual encounters in hookup culture can perpetuate commitment phobia or reluctance to invest in relationships that require long-term emotional and logistical commitments. This reluctance may stem from past experiences, fear of vulnerability, or uncertainty about future relationship outcomes.

4. Compatibility Assessment:

- **Surface-Level Interactions:** Hookup culture often emphasizes physical attraction and immediate chemistry over deeper compatibility factors such as shared values, life goals, and interpersonal dynamics. Individuals seeking long-term relationships may find it challenging to assess compatibility beyond initial attraction or superficial interactions.

- **Navigating Expectations:** Clarifying expectations and discussing relationship goals early in the dating process can mitigate misunderstandings and align expectations between individuals seeking casual encounters and those prioritizing serious relationships. Open communication promotes transparency and mutual understanding in navigating diverse relationship intentions.

5. Personal Growth and Reflection:

- **Self-Discovery:** Individuals navigating hookup culture while seeking serious relationships may undergo personal growth and reflection. Clarifying personal values, relationship priorities, and desired relationship outcomes can guide intentional dating practices and foster resilience in navigating dating challenges.

● **Adapting Dating Strategies:** Adapting dating strategies to prioritize authentic connections and compatibility can enhance resilience and empower individuals to pursue relationships aligned with their long-term goals and aspirations.

Conclusion

Navigating hookup culture while seeking serious, long-term relationships involves recognizing challenges related to misaligned expectations, emotional dissonance, trust-building, and compatibility assessment. By fostering clear communication, self-reflection, and intentional dating practices, individuals can navigate dating landscapes effectively, align relationship intentions, and cultivate meaningful connections that support their emotional and relational well-being. Understanding these challenges is essential for individuals seeking to establish fulfilling, long-term relationships within a cultural context that may prioritize casual encounters and non-committal interactions.

Superficial Judgments on Dating Apps

Dating apps often rely heavily on profile photos and brief bios as primary criteria for matchmaking, which can lead to superficial judgments among users. Here's a detailed exploration of how this phenomenon occurs and its impact on forming meaningful connections:

1. Visual Bias:

● **Immediate Impressions:** Profile photos are typically the first impression users have of potential matches. This initial visual encounter can heavily influence users' perceptions and decisions, often prioritizing physical attractiveness as a key determinant of interest.

● **Limited Information:** Brief bios accompanying photos may provide minimal context or insight into a person's personality, values, interests, or life experiences. Users may rely on visual cues alone to gauge compatibility, overlooking nuanced aspects that contribute to meaningful connections.

2. Impact on Compatibility Assessment:

● **Surface-Level Criteria:** Relying on superficial judgments based on photos can hinder users' ability to assess deeper compatibility factors essential for long-term relationships. Shared values, communication styles, life goals, and emotional intelligence are crucial aspects that contribute to relationship satisfaction but may not be apparent from a profile photo.

● **Mismatched Expectations:** Superficial judgments may lead to mismatches between users' perceived and actual compatibility. Users may find themselves interacting with individuals whose values, interests, or relationship goals do not align with their own, despite initial physical attraction.

3. Psychological Effects:

● **Self-Esteem Impact:** Users may experience fluctuations in self-esteem based on the validation or lack thereof received from matches. Rejection or lack of matches based on physical appearance can negatively impact self-image, contributing to feelings of inadequacy or unworthiness.

● **Superficial Validation:** Conversely, receiving matches primarily based on physical attractiveness may provide superficial validation but may not contribute to genuine self-worth or fulfillment. This cycle of seeking external validation through superficial criteria can perpetuate reliance on surface-level judgments.

4. Communication Dynamics:

- **Conversation Starters:** Superficial judgments may influence initial conversation dynamics, focusing on topics related to physical appearance or immediate attraction rather than exploring deeper interests or shared values. This can limit the scope of conversations and hinder the development of meaningful rapport.

- **Missed Opportunities:** Users may overlook potential connections with individuals who do not fit conventional beauty standards but possess qualities that align with their relationship preferences and emotional needs.

5. Overcoming Superficiality:

- **Promoting Authenticity:** Encouraging users to prioritize authenticity in profile representation can foster more meaningful connections. Highlighting personal interests, values, and experiences beyond physical appearance can attract like-minded individuals seeking genuine connections.

- **Enhancing Profile Depth:** Dating apps can introduce features that allow users to showcase diverse aspects of their personalities, such as multimedia content, detailed bios, or compatibility quizzes. These enhancements provide opportunities for users to engage more deeply and authentically with potential matches.

Conclusion

Superficial judgments on dating apps, driven by reliance on profile photos and brief bios, can hinder users' ability to assess compatibility beyond physical appearance. By promoting authenticity, encouraging profile depth, and emphasizing deeper connection-building, dating apps can support users in fostering meaningful relationships based on shared values, emotional compatibility, and mutual respect. Understanding the impact of superficial judgments is crucial for individuals navigating dating apps, empowering them to prioritize substantive connections that contribute to long-term relationship satisfaction and fulfillment.

Navigating Intentions in a Hookup-Centric Dating Environment

Navigating intentions on dating apps, particularly in environments where casual encounters dominate, requires clear communication and awareness of individual relationship goals and expectations. Here's a detailed exploration of how users can navigate intentions effectively:

1. Setting Clear Expectations:

- **Early Communication:** Clarifying intentions early in interactions is essential to establish mutual understanding. Users should openly communicate their relationship goals, whether seeking casual dating, a serious relationship, or something in between.

- **Honesty and Transparency:** Being honest about intentions avoids misunderstandings and ensures both parties are on the same page. This transparency fosters trust and reduces the likelihood of emotional mismatch or disappointment.

2. Identifying Compatibility:

- **Shared Values and Goals:** Discussing values, life goals, and expectations helps assess compatibility beyond physical attraction. Users can identify potential matches who align with their long-term relationship aspirations and emotional needs.

- **Mutual Respect:** Recognizing and respecting differences in relationship preferences ensures that interactions remain respectful and consensual. This mutual respect contributes to a positive dating experience, regardless of relationship outcomes.

3. Managing Ambiguity:

- **Navigating Mixed Signals:** In a hookup-centric environment, users may encounter mixed signals or ambiguous interactions. Clear communication allows individuals to navigate uncertainties and determine whether mutual interests align beyond physical attraction.
- **Avoiding Assumptions:** Clarifying intentions helps users avoid making assumptions about the nature of the relationship. Direct communication reduces the risk of misinterpreting gestures or actions as indicative of commitment or exclusivity.

4. Upholding Personal Boundaries:

- **Self-Awareness:** Understanding personal boundaries and comfort levels is crucial when navigating intentions on dating apps. Users should prioritize their emotional well-being and communicate boundaries to ensure respectful interactions.
- **Consent and Respect:** Respecting boundaries and seeking explicit consent in interactions reinforces a culture of respect and consent. Users can establish trust by prioritizing mutual comfort and ensuring that interactions are consensual.

5. Evaluating Relationship Progression:

- **Continuous Communication:** Ongoing dialogue about relationship dynamics allows users to evaluate the progression of their connections. Regular check-ins and discussions about emotional investment and relationship milestones help gauge mutual interest and commitment.
- **Reassessing Compatibility:** As connections evolve, users should reassess compatibility based on shared experiences, emotional connection, and alignment of relationship goals. Open communication facilitates discussions about relationship direction and future expectations.

Conclusion

Navigating intentions in a hookup-centric dating environment requires proactive communication, mutual respect, and awareness of individual preferences. By setting clear expectations early, identifying compatibility beyond physical attraction, managing ambiguity with open dialogue, upholding personal boundaries, and evaluating relationship progression, users can navigate dating apps with greater clarity and confidence. Understanding and communicating intentions fosters authentic connections based on mutual respect, emotional compatibility, and shared relationship goals, enhancing the potential for meaningful and fulfilling relationships in both casual and serious dating contexts.

Impact on Traditional Dating

Shift in Dating Norms Due to Dating Apps

Dating apps have significantly impacted traditional dating norms, reshaping the pace, expectations, and dynamics of modern relationships. Here's an in-depth exploration of how dating apps have facilitated this shift:

1. Accessibility and Choice:

- **Expanded Dating Pool:** Dating apps provide access to a vast and diverse pool of potential partners beyond traditional social circles. Users can connect with individuals based on shared interests, preferences, and geographical proximity, significantly broadening their dating options.

- **Increased Choice:** The abundance of profiles and matchmaking algorithms empower users to explore multiple potential matches simultaneously. This abundance of choice contrasts with traditional dating, where options were often limited to immediate social circles or introductions through friends and family.

2. Digital Interaction Dynamics:

- **Initial Interactions:** Dating apps prioritize digital interactions through profile browsing, swiping mechanisms, and messaging. These digital interactions replace or precede face-to-face encounters, influencing the initial stages of relationship development.

- **Communication Patterns:** Text-based communication on dating apps shapes conversational styles and communication norms. Users often engage in prolonged digital exchanges before transitioning to voice or video calls, altering the progression of relationship intimacy.

3. Shifting Relationship Expectations:

- **Pace of Relationships:** The immediacy and convenience of dating apps accelerate relationship dynamics, allowing users to initiate and dissolve connections quickly. This accelerated pace contrasts with traditional dating's gradual progression from acquaintance to commitment.

- **Casual Dating Norms:** Dating apps have normalized casual dating practices, where users may engage in non-committal interactions or short-term relationships. The prevalence of casual dating fosters diverse relationship expectations and experiences among app users.

4. Influence of Technology:

- **Algorithmic Matching:** Dating apps utilize algorithms to suggest potential matches based on user preferences, behaviors, and demographic data. Algorithmic matching influences relationship formation by prioritizing compatibility metrics and shared interests.

- **Visual Representation:** Profile photos and curated bios on dating apps shape initial impressions and attraction dynamics. Users may prioritize physical appearance or specific attributes when selecting potential matches, influencing relationship outcomes.

5. Social and Cultural Impact:

- **Acceptance of Online Dating:** The normalization of online dating through dating apps has reduced stigma surrounding digital matchmaking. Online dating is now widely accepted as a legitimate avenue for relationship formation, reflecting broader cultural shifts towards digital interaction and connectivity.

- **Generational Differences:** Younger generations, in particular, have embraced dating apps as primary avenues for meeting potential partners. These generational shifts highlight evolving attitudes towards technology-mediated relationships and digital intimacy.

6. Challenges and Adaptations:

- **Navigating Authenticity:** Users navigate authenticity amidst curated profiles and idealized self-presentations on dating apps. Balancing self-expression with digital impression management poses challenges in establishing genuine connections and mitigating misrepresentation.
- **Impact on Traditional Dating Norms:** Dating apps challenge traditional dating norms by prioritizing efficiency, choice, and digital interaction over traditional courting rituals and interpersonal dynamics.

Conclusion

Dating apps have ushered in a transformation of dating norms, influencing relationship dynamics, expectations, and the integration of technology into intimate interactions. The shift towards digital matchmaking reflects societal changes in communication, accessibility, and relationship formation preferences, shaping contemporary dating practices and fostering diverse relationship experiences among app users. Understanding these shifts provides insights into the evolving landscape of modern romance and the intersection of technology with interpersonal connections.

Diverse Preferences on Dating Apps

Dating apps, despite their association with hookup culture, cater to diverse preferences and relationship goals, including users seeking meaningful connections. Here's an in-depth exploration of how dating apps accommodate varied preferences:

1. Platform Diversity:

- **Range of Apps:** The dating app ecosystem includes a variety of platforms catering to different demographics, interests, and relationship goals. Some apps explicitly focus on casual dating, while others emphasize long-term relationships, marriage, or specific cultural or religious preferences.
- **Features and Filters:** Many dating apps incorporate features designed to facilitate serious dating. These may include detailed user profiles, compatibility assessments, and advanced filters for interests, values, and relationship expectations. These features help users navigate the app landscape according to their specific dating preferences.

2. User Intentions and Communication:

- **Profile Customization:** Users can customize their profiles on dating apps to reflect their personality, interests, and relationship goals. Detailed profiles provide insights beyond physical appearance, offering opportunities for users to express values, hobbies, and aspirations.
- **Communication Tools:** Platforms offer diverse communication tools beyond swiping and messaging, such as video calls, voice messages, or personality quizzes. These tools enable users to engage in meaningful interactions and assess compatibility before meeting in person.

3. Relationship-Oriented Features:

- **Compatibility Assessments:** Some apps use algorithms to assess compatibility based on user responses to personality quizzes, values assessments, or relationship questionnaires. These assessments aim to match users with compatible partners based on shared interests, values, and long-term relationship potential.
- **Long-Term Filters:** Advanced search filters allow users to specify preferences for potential matches, such as age range, location proximity, education level, and relationship status. These filters streamline the matchmaking process, aligning users with others who share similar relationship intentions.

4. Community and Support:

- **Community Engagement:** Dating apps may foster community engagement through forums, groups, or events focused on relationship advice, dating tips, or offline meetups. These features enhance user experience by providing social support and opportunities to connect beyond digital interactions.

- **Safety and Privacy:** Platforms prioritize safety measures, such as verification processes, moderation of inappropriate content, and user reporting systems. Ensuring user safety promotes trust and encourages users to engage more authentically in pursuit of meaningful connections.

5. Evolution of User Preferences:

- **Changing Attitudes:** As societal attitudes towards online dating evolve, more users prioritize meaningful connections over casual encounters. This shift influences app design and marketing strategies, encouraging platforms to innovate features that appeal to relationship-oriented users.

- **Success Stories:** Platforms highlight success stories of users who have found long-term relationships or marriage through their app. These narratives validate the efficacy of dating apps in facilitating serious dating and encourage users to pursue their relationship goals confidently.

Conclusion

Dating apps have evolved to accommodate diverse preferences, offering features and tools that cater to users seeking meaningful connections and long-term relationships. By prioritizing customization, compatibility assessments, and community engagement, these platforms empower users to navigate the digital dating landscape according to their individual dating goals and preferences. Understanding these diverse functionalities underscores the nuanced role of dating apps in modern romance, providing opportunities for both casual interactions and committed partnerships.

Balancing Choices on Dating Apps

Navigating dating apps involves striking a balance between exploring casual encounters and seeking meaningful, long-term relationships. Here's a detailed exploration of how users manage these choices:

1. Profile Evaluation:

- **Initial Impressions:** Users often make quick judgments based on profile photos, bios, and initial interactions. Balancing choices involves assessing whether a potential match aligns with their relationship goals—whether casual or serious—based on these limited cues.

- **Bio and Details:** Beyond photos, users scrutinize bios and additional profile details to gauge compatibility in terms of interests, values, and lifestyle choices. This evaluation helps users determine if there's potential for a deeper connection beyond physical attraction.

2. Communication Dynamics:

- **Messaging Style:** The manner in which users communicate—whether casual and flirtatious or thoughtful and introspective—can signal their intentions. Balancing choices entails adjusting communication style to match the desired relationship outcome, whether it's building rapport for a casual encounter or nurturing deeper connections.

- **Frequency and Depth:** Users manage communication frequency and depth to align with their dating preferences. For casual encounters, interactions may be lighter and more sporadic, while those seeking long-term relationships may prioritize meaningful conversations and deeper emotional engagement.

3. Values and Compatibility:

- **Shared Values:** Users navigating dating apps consider shared values and life goals when deciding whether to pursue a match further. Balancing choices involves identifying compatibility in areas such as family values, career aspirations, religion, or lifestyle preferences.

- **Compatibility Assessments:** Some apps offer compatibility assessments or personality quizzes to help users gauge potential matches based on shared interests and relationship expectations. This tool assists in balancing choices by providing data-driven insights into compatibility beyond initial impressions.

4. Intent Clarity:

● **Clear Communication:** To navigate between casual encounters and serious relationships, users communicate their intentions clearly and respectfully. Setting expectations early in interactions helps manage mutual understanding and avoids misunderstandings about relationship goals.

● **Flexibility and Adaptability:** Users may adjust their approach based on evolving preferences or experiences on the app. Balancing choices requires flexibility to explore different types of connections while remaining true to personal values and relationship aspirations.

5. Learning and Adaptation:

● **Feedback Loop:** Users learn from past interactions and adjust their approach to improve their chances of finding suitable matches. This iterative process involves refining search criteria, communication strategies, and overall app usage to better align with desired relationship outcomes.

6. Emotional Awareness:

● **Self-Awareness:** Users cultivate emotional awareness to navigate the emotional ups and downs of dating apps. Balancing choices involves recognizing and managing feelings of excitement, disappointment, or uncertainty that may arise from interactions and outcomes on the platform.

7. Personal Growth:

● **Reflection and Growth:** Navigating dating apps prompts users to reflect on their own desires, boundaries, and relationship readiness. Balancing choices encourages personal growth by fostering self-discovery and learning from dating experiences to refine relationship preferences over time.

Conclusion

Balancing choices on dating apps involves a nuanced approach that considers profile evaluation, communication dynamics, shared values, clarity of intentions, learning from experiences, and personal growth. By navigating between casual encounters and the pursuit of long-term relationships, users strategically manage their interactions and optimize their chances of finding meaningful connections that align with their relationship goals and aspirations. This process underscores the complexity and individuality of modern dating, where digital platforms offer both opportunities and challenges in the quest for romantic fulfillment.

Psychological Impact

Emotional Well-being and Dating Apps

The impact of dating apps, particularly in contexts dominated by hookup culture or challenges in finding serious relationships, can significantly influence users' emotional well-being. Here's a detailed exploration of these dynamics:

1. Hookup Culture and Emotional Impact:

● **Casual Encounters:** Dating apps facilitate quick, non-committal interactions that prioritize physical attraction and immediate gratification over emotional connection. Engaging in frequent casual encounters can lead to a sense of detachment and emotional emptiness, especially if these encounters lack depth or meaningful connection.

● **Loneliness and Isolation:** Despite the superficial validation of casual encounters, users may experience heightened feelings of loneliness or isolation. The transient nature of these interactions can exacerbate feelings of emotional disconnection from others, contributing to a sense of being unfulfilled or misunderstood.

● **Frustration and Disillusionment:** Users seeking meaningful relationships within hookup-centric environments may encounter frustration and disillusionment. The disparity between their desire for emotional intimacy and the prevalence of casual encounters can lead to feelings of disappointment or disillusionment with the dating process.

2. Challenges in Finding Serious Relationships:

● **Mismatched Expectations:** Users seeking serious relationships may struggle to find like-minded individuals amidst a sea of profiles prioritizing casual encounters. This mismatch in expectations can create frustration and uncertainty about the feasibility of finding a long-term partner on dating apps.

● **Emotional Investment:** The difficulty in forming lasting connections may discourage users from investing emotionally in new interactions. Fear of rejection or repeated disappointments can lead to guardedness and reluctance to open up to potential matches, hindering the development of meaningful relationships.

3. Impact on Self-Esteem:

● **Validation and Rejection:** The fluctuating nature of interactions on dating apps—ranging from validation through matches to rejection or indifference—can impact users' self-esteem. Repeated rejection or superficial acceptance based solely on physical appearance may lead to self-doubt or negative self-perception.

● **Comparison and Inadequacy:** Users may compare themselves unfavorably to others based on perceived success in dating app interactions. This comparison can amplify feelings of inadequacy or unworthiness, particularly if they perceive themselves as less desirable or successful in the dating pool.

4. Emotional Resilience and Coping Strategies:

● **Self-Awareness:** Building emotional resilience involves cultivating self-awareness about one's dating preferences, boundaries, and emotional triggers. Users can benefit from reflecting on their dating experiences and identifying patterns or behaviors that contribute to emotional distress.

● **Setting Boundaries:** Establishing clear boundaries in dating interactions helps protect emotional well-being. Users can prioritize connections that align with their values and relationship goals while respectfully declining interactions that do not meet their emotional needs.

5. Seeking Support:

● **Community and Resources:** Engaging with supportive communities or seeking resources on healthy dating practices can provide validation and guidance. Users can benefit from sharing experiences, seeking advice, or accessing professional support to navigate the emotional challenges of dating apps effectively.

Conclusion

Emotional well-being on dating apps is influenced by the prevalence of hookup culture, challenges in finding serious relationships, impact on self-esteem, and strategies for emotional resilience. By acknowledging these dynamics and proactively managing emotional responses, users can navigate dating apps in ways that prioritize their mental health and emotional fulfillment. Building self-awareness, setting boundaries, seeking support, and fostering meaningful connections are essential steps towards maintaining emotional well-being amidst the complexities of modern dating platforms.

Self-Esteem and Dating Apps

Self-esteem, or how individuals perceive and value themselves, is significantly influenced by their experiences and interactions on dating apps. Here's a detailed exploration of how dating apps can impact self-esteem:

1. Rejection and Self-Worth:

● **Impact of Rejection:** Users on dating apps often face rejection in various forms, such as not receiving matches, being unmatched, or conversations that do not progress. Repeated experiences of rejection can lead to feelings of inadequacy or unworthiness, affecting self-esteem. Individuals may internalize rejection as a reflection of their attractiveness, personality, or overall desirability.

● **Perceived Value:** The emphasis on profile photos and initial impressions can contribute to users feeling valued primarily for their physical appearance. This can create a superficial perception of self-worth, where individuals equate their attractiveness or external attributes with their overall value as a potential partner.

2. Validation and External Approval:

● **Superficial Validation:** Positive interactions, such as receiving matches or compliments on physical appearance, can provide temporary validation. However, this validation may be shallow and fleeting, especially if it does not translate into meaningful connections or relationships.

● **Dependency on Approval:** Users may develop a dependency on external validation from dating apps, seeking continual affirmation to bolster their self-esteem. The reliance on others' approval for validation can undermine intrinsic self-worth and confidence.

3. Comparisons and Self-Perception:

● **Comparison to Others:** The visible nature of dating app interactions can foster comparisons to other users based on perceived success or attractiveness. Users may compare themselves unfavorably to others who appear more successful or desirable, leading to negative self-comparisons and diminished self-esteem.

● **Impact on Self-Perception:** Negative experiences or comparisons can distort individuals' self-perception, reinforcing beliefs of inadequacy or unattractiveness. Over time, these perceptions may erode self-confidence and inhibit users from presenting their authentic selves on dating platforms.

4. Strategies for Maintaining Self-Esteem:

● **Self-Acceptance:** Building self-esteem involves cultivating self-acceptance and recognizing personal strengths and qualities beyond external validation. Users can benefit from focusing on intrinsic qualities, such as values, interests, and achievements, that contribute to their overall sense of self-worth.

● **Setting Realistic Expectations:** Managing expectations about dating outcomes on apps can reduce the impact of rejection or perceived failure. Users can approach interactions with openness and resilience, acknowledging that dating app dynamics do not define their value as individuals.

5. Seeking Support and Balance:

- **Social Support:** Engaging with supportive networks, friends, or communities can provide encouragement and perspective outside of dating app interactions. Sharing experiences and seeking empathy from others can help mitigate the emotional impact of dating challenges on self-esteem.
- **Balancing Offline Activities:** Allocating time for offline activities and hobbies that promote personal fulfillment and well-being can counteract the negative effects of dating app interactions. Balancing digital interactions with real-world experiences fosters a holistic approach to self-esteem and emotional health.

Conclusion

Self-esteem on dating apps fluctuates based on experiences of rejection, validation, comparisons with others, and perceptions of self-worth. By fostering self-acceptance, managing expectations, seeking social support, and maintaining offline activities, users can navigate dating apps in ways that promote positive self-esteem and emotional resilience. Recognizing intrinsic qualities and reducing dependency on external validation are essential steps towards cultivating a healthy self-perception amidst the complexities of online dating environments.

Cultural and Societal Influences

Generational Differences in Dating Attitudes and Dating Apps

Generational attitudes towards dating, shaped by technological advancements and evolving social norms, significantly influence how different age groups approach dating apps. Here's a detailed exploration of generational differences in attitudes towards hookup culture versus the pursuit of long-term relationships:

1. Technological Influence:

● **Digital Natives vs. Digital Immigrants:** Younger generations, often referred to as digital natives, have grown up with technology and are more accustomed to online interactions, including dating apps. They may be more comfortable with the immediacy and convenience of digital platforms for meeting potential partners.

● **Adaptation to Technology:** Older generations, considered digital immigrants, may approach dating apps with a different perspective, adapting to technology-driven dating norms later in life. They may have different expectations or reservations about online dating compared to younger cohorts.

2. Attitudes Towards Relationships:

● **Hookup Culture Among Younger Generations:** Dating apps have facilitated a rise in hookup culture among younger generations, where casual, non-committal encounters are prevalent. Features like swiping and instant messaging cater to quick, spontaneous interactions based on physical attraction.

● **Long-Term Relationship Pursuit:** While hookup culture is prominent, dating apps also cater to individuals seeking serious, long-term relationships. Some platforms offer features like detailed profiles, compatibility assessments, and relationship-oriented filters to facilitate meaningful connections.

3. Social Norms and Expectations:

● **Shift in Dating Norms:** Dating apps have contributed to a shift in traditional dating norms, where digital interactions influence the pace and expectations of relationships. Younger generations may prioritize flexibility, choice, and independence in their dating preferences.

● **Impact of Social Media:** Social media integration on dating apps allows users to showcase curated aspects of their lives, influencing how they present themselves and perceive potential matches. This curated presentation can impact dating dynamics and interpersonal expectations.

4. Communication Styles and Preferences:

● **Text-Based Communication:** Younger generations may prefer text-based communication on dating apps, valuing the convenience and control over responses. This mode of communication aligns with digital communication norms and enables users to manage interactions at their own pace.

● **Transition to Offline Interactions:** Despite digital interactions, both younger and older generations recognize the importance of transitioning from online to offline interactions to build deeper connections and assess compatibility beyond digital profiles.

5. Cultural and Societal Context:

● **Acceptance of Online Dating:** Over time, there has been a broader acceptance of online dating across generational divides. Younger generations may view dating apps as a natural extension of socializing, while older generations may approach them with initial skepticism or caution.

● **Evolution of Relationship Expectations:** Generational differences in relationship expectations may influence how users approach dating apps. Younger generations may prioritize flexibility and exploration, while older generations may seek stability and compatibility based on shared values and life experiences.

Conclusion

Generational attitudes towards dating apps reflect broader societal shifts in how relationships are formed and maintained. While hookup culture may be prevalent among younger generations on dating apps, platforms also accommodate diverse relationship preferences, including those seeking long-term commitment. Understanding these generational differences helps navigate the complexities of digital dating environments and adapt communication styles to foster meaningful connections across age groups. Whether embracing hookup culture or pursuing serious relationships, users leverage dating apps to meet personal relationship goals amidst evolving technological and cultural landscapes.

Social Validation in Dating Apps

Social validation plays a significant role in shaping user behavior and perceptions on dating apps, influencing both hookup culture and the pursuit of long-term relationships. Here's a detailed exploration of how social validation impacts users:

    1. Instant Feedback and Validation:

    ● **Immediate Gratification:** Dating apps provide immediate feedback through features like swiping and instant messaging. A right swipe that results in a match or positive responses to messages gives users instant validation of their desirability within the dating pool.

    ● **Reinforcement of Behavior:** Positive feedback reinforces behaviors that lead to matches or engaging conversations. This can include crafting appealing profiles, selecting attractive photos, or initiating conversations in a way that resonates with potential matches.

    2. Influence on Self-Perception:

    ● **Enhanced Self-Esteem:** Successful interactions on dating apps, such as receiving matches or positive responses, can boost users' self-esteem and confidence in their attractiveness. This positive reinforcement may encourage continued engagement with the app.

    ● **Impact of Rejection:** Conversely, experiences of rejection or lack of matches can negatively impact self-esteem, leading to feelings of inadequacy or questioning one's attractiveness. Users may adjust their approach or presentation based on these perceived responses.

    3. Alignment with Relationship Goals:

    ● **Hookup Culture:** In contexts where hookup culture prevails, social validation often emphasizes physical attractiveness and immediate appeal. Users may prioritize photos and initial interactions that cater to these preferences to maximize matches and validation.

    ● **Long-Term Relationships:** For users seeking serious relationships, social validation may focus more on compatibility and shared values rather than immediate physical attraction alone. Positive feedback on profiles or conversations that align with these goals reinforces their pursuit of meaningful connections.

    4. Psychological Impact:

    ● **Validation vs. Dependency:** While social validation can enhance self-esteem, excessive reliance on external validation from dating apps may lead to dependency on validation for self-worth. Users may continually seek validation through matches or interactions, potentially affecting emotional well-being.

    ● **Cognitive Bias:** Users may develop cognitive biases based on perceived validation or rejection on dating apps, influencing their self-perception and interactions both within and outside the app environment.

    5. Cultural and Societal Context:

- **Normalization of Online Dating:** Over time, the normalization of online dating has influenced how users perceive social validation on dating apps. It has become increasingly accepted as a legitimate way to meet potential partners, shaping societal norms around dating behaviors and expectations.
- **Impact on Offline Interactions:** Social validation received through dating apps may impact users' confidence and approach to offline dating interactions. Positive experiences can encourage users to engage more confidently in face-to-face settings, while negative experiences may lead to hesitation or caution.

Conclusion

Social validation on dating apps serves as a powerful motivator influencing user behavior, self-perception, and relationship goals. Whether reinforcing behaviors aligned with hookup culture or encouraging pursuits of long-term relationships, social validation shapes how users engage with dating apps and perceive their place within the dating landscape. Understanding these dynamics helps users navigate the complexities of digital dating environments while considering their individual relationship preferences and emotional well-being.

Chapter 8: Data Privacy Concerns

Dating apps have revolutionized the way people meet and interact, offering convenient platforms to connect with potential partners. However, alongside their popularity, these apps bring significant privacy and security concerns that users should be aware of.

Dating apps have transformed the landscape of modern dating, providing users with easy access to a vast pool of potential matches at their fingertips. These platforms leverage technology to facilitate connections based on shared interests, proximity, and personal preferences. While the convenience of swiping and matching has streamlined the dating process, it also raises critical issues related to privacy and security.

Data Privacy Concerns

1. Collection and Usage of Personal Information: Dating apps typically require users to create profiles containing personal details such as photos, age, location, and interests. While this information helps in matching users with compatible partners, it also raises concerns about the extent of data collected and how it is used:

- **Extent of Data Collection:** Users often provide extensive personal information, including relationship preferences and even sensitive data such as sexual orientation or religious beliefs.

- **Data Security Measures:** Questions arise regarding the security measures in place to protect this data from unauthorized access or breaches. The vulnerability of personal information on dating apps can lead to identity theft or exploitation if not properly safeguarded.

2. User Consent and Transparency: Ensuring users are fully informed about how their data is collected, stored, and shared is crucial for maintaining trust:

- **Transparency in Privacy Policies:** Many users may not thoroughly review privacy policies or understand the implications of data sharing practices. Clear, accessible privacy policies are essential to inform users about how their information will be utilized.

- **Consent and Control:** Users should have control over what information they share and with whom. Concerns arise when data is shared with third parties or used for purposes beyond matchmaking without explicit consent.

Safety Issues

1. Catfishing and Fake Profiles: One of the most significant risks on dating apps is the creation of fake profiles with deceptive intentions:

- **Risk of Catfishing:** Fake profiles mislead users by presenting false identities, photos, or information. This practice can lead to emotional manipulation, financial scams, or other forms of exploitation.

- **Verification Processes:** Effective verification mechanisms are critical to authenticate users and mitigate the creation of fake profiles. However, some apps may lack robust verification procedures, making it easier for malicious actors to deceive genuine users.

2. Harassment and Abuse: Online platforms can become breeding grounds for harassment or abusive behavior, impacting users' safety and well-being:

- **Online Harassment:** Users, particularly women, may encounter unwanted advances, explicit messages, or harassment from other users. This behavior can create a hostile environment and deter users from engaging further on the platform.

- **Safety Features:** Dating apps should implement robust reporting and blocking features to empower users to report harassment and block abusive accounts swiftly.

3. Physical Safety Concerns: Meeting someone in person whom you've met online carries inherent risks, including physical safety concerns:

● **Meeting Strangers:** Users should exercise caution when arranging face-to-face meetings with matches from dating apps. Safety tips, such as meeting in public places and informing a trusted friend or family member about plans, can mitigate potential risks.

● **User Education:** Apps can play a role in educating users about safe dating practices and providing guidance on how to navigate potential risks associated with offline interactions.

Conclusion

While dating apps offer unprecedented opportunities to meet new people and explore potential relationships, they also require users to navigate complex privacy and security landscapes. Addressing these concerns involves enhancing data privacy practices, implementing effective security measures, and promoting safe online behaviors. By prioritizing user safety and transparency, dating apps can foster a trustworthy environment conducive to meaningful connections while mitigating risks associated with privacy breaches and abusive behavior.

Extent Of Data Collection

The extent of data collection on dating apps involves gathering a wide array of personal information from users to facilitate matchmaking and enhance user experience. This process is crucial for algorithms to suggest potential matches based on shared interests, location, demographics, and preferences. Here's a detailed look at the extent of data collection on dating apps:

Types of Personal Information Collected

1. Basic Profile Information:

- **Name and Age:** Users typically provide their real names and birthdates.

- **Photos:** Profile photos are essential for making a first impression and are often required during signup.

- **Location:** Geographical data is used to suggest matches within a certain radius.

2. Demographic Information:

- **Gender and Sexual Orientation:** Users may specify their gender identity and sexual orientation to receive relevant match suggestions.

- **Ethnicity and Language:** Some apps may collect information about ethnicity or preferred languages for cultural compatibility.

3. Relationship Preferences:

- **Desired Relationship Type:** Users indicate whether they are seeking casual dating, a serious relationship, friendship, or other types of connections.

- **Preferences in a Partner:** Criteria such as age range, physical attributes, and lifestyle preferences help tailor match suggestions.

4. Personal Interests and Hobbies:

- **Hobbies and Interests:** Users often list hobbies, interests, and activities to find like-minded individuals.

5. Bio and Personal Description:

- **Self-Description:** Users may write a bio to introduce themselves, share personal anecdotes, or highlight their values and beliefs.

6. Sensitive Information:

- **Religious Beliefs:** Some apps allow users to disclose their religious beliefs or preferences for partners with specific religious backgrounds.

- **Political Views:** Preferences or affiliations in politics may be disclosed to gauge compatibility.

Rationale for Data Collection

1. Enhanced Matching Algorithms:

○ By collecting diverse data points, dating apps can employ sophisticated algorithms to generate personalized match recommendations. These algorithms analyze user preferences, behaviors, and demographic data to predict compatibility and increase the likelihood of successful matches.

2. User Experience Customization:

○ Personalized experiences, such as tailored notifications or content recommendations, can be provided based on user data. This customization aims to improve user engagement and satisfaction with the app.

3. Advertising and Monetization:

○ Some apps may use collected data for targeted advertising purposes, allowing advertisers to reach specific demographics or interests. This data-driven approach can contribute to the app's revenue model.

Concerns and Privacy Considerations

1. **Data Security:** Collecting and storing extensive personal information raises concerns about data security and privacy breaches. Apps must implement robust security measures to protect user data from unauthorized access or cyberattacks.
2. **Transparency and Consent:** Users should be informed about how their data will be used, shared, and stored through clear privacy policies. Providing users with control over their data and obtaining explicit consent for data processing are essential for building trust.
3. **Sensitive Data Handling:** Given the sensitivity of information such as sexual orientation or religious beliefs, apps must handle this data with utmost care to prevent discrimination or misuse.
4. **Regulatory Compliance:** Compliance with data protection regulations, such as GDPR in Europe or CCPA in California, is critical to safeguarding user rights and maintaining legal compliance in data handling practices.

In conclusion, while extensive data collection on dating apps serves to enhance user experience and facilitate meaningful connections, it also necessitates careful consideration of privacy implications and regulatory requirements to protect user privacy and maintain trust in the platform.

Data Security Measures

Data security measures on dating apps are crucial to protect users' personal information from unauthorized access, breaches, and potential exploitation. Here's a detailed exploration of the security measures typically implemented by dating apps:

Encryption Protocols

1. **Data Encryption:**

   ○ Dating apps employ encryption protocols such as Transport Layer Security (TLS) to encrypt data transmitted between users' devices and the app's servers. This ensures that sensitive information, including usernames, passwords, and messages, is securely transmitted and protected from interception by malicious actors.

2. **Storage Encryption:**

   ○ Personal data stored on servers is often encrypted at rest. This means that even if unauthorized access occurs, the encrypted data is unintelligible without the decryption keys held by the app's administrators.

Authentication and Access Control

1. **User Authentication:**

   ○ Secure authentication mechanisms, such as multi-factor authentication (MFA) or biometric authentication (e.g., fingerprint or facial recognition), help verify users' identities during login processes. This prevents unauthorized access even if login credentials are compromised.

2. **Access Control Policies:**

   ○ Role-based access control (RBAC) ensures that only authorized personnel within the app's organization have access to users' personal data based on their roles and responsibilities. This minimizes the risk of internal breaches or data misuse.

Secure Development Practices

1. **Secure Coding Practices:**

   ○ Dating apps adhere to secure coding standards and practices to mitigate common vulnerabilities, such as SQL injection, cross-site scripting (XSS), and insecure deserialization. Regular code reviews and vulnerability assessments are conducted to identify and address potential security flaws.

2. **Penetration Testing:**

   ○ Regular penetration testing, conducted by cybersecurity professionals, assesses the app's infrastructure and applications for vulnerabilities. This proactive approach helps identify and remediate security weaknesses before they can be exploited by malicious actors.

Data Minimization and Anonymization

1. Data Minimization:

○ Dating apps collect and retain only necessary personal information required for matchmaking and app functionality. Unnecessary data is minimized to reduce the potential impact of a data breach.

2. Anonymization Techniques:

○ To protect user privacy, some apps anonymize or pseudonymize personal data whenever possible. This ensures that even if data is accessed without authorization, individuals cannot be readily identified.

Incident Response and Monitoring

1. Incident Response Plan:

○ Dating apps have established incident response plans that outline procedures for detecting, responding to, and mitigating security incidents, such as data breaches or unauthorized access. Rapid response is crucial to minimize the impact on users and mitigate further risks.

2. Continuous Monitoring:

○ Continuous monitoring of app activity, network traffic, and user interactions helps detect suspicious behavior or unauthorized access attempts in real-time. Intrusion detection systems (IDS) and security information and event management (SIEM) tools are often employed for this purpose.

Privacy Policies and User Education

1. Transparent Privacy Policies:

○ Dating apps provide clear and transparent privacy policies that outline how users' personal data is collected, used, shared, and protected. Users are informed about their rights regarding data access, correction, and deletion.

2. User Education:

○ Educating users about best practices for securing their accounts, recognizing phishing attempts, and reporting suspicious activity is essential. Apps may provide tips on creating strong passwords, enabling security features, and being cautious about sharing personal information.

In conclusion, robust data security measures on dating apps are essential to safeguard users' personal information from unauthorized access, breaches, and potential exploitation. By implementing encryption protocols, secure authentication methods, secure development practices, data minimization strategies, incident response plans, and transparent privacy policies, dating apps can enhance user trust and protect user privacy in an increasingly digital dating landscape.

Transparency in privacy policies

Transparency in privacy policies is crucial for ensuring that users understand how their personal information is collected, used, and protected by dating apps. Here's a detailed exploration of why clear and accessible privacy policies are essential:

Importance of Transparency

1. Informed Consent:

○ Clear privacy policies enable users to make informed decisions about whether to use the app and what information to share. By understanding how their data will be used, users can consent to the terms with greater awareness.

2. Trust and Confidence:

○ Transparent privacy policies build trust between the app provider and users. When users feel confident that their data is handled responsibly and securely, they are more likely to engage with the app and share accurate information.

Components of Transparent Privacy Policies

1. Information Collection:

○ Policies should clearly state what types of personal information are collected from users, such as names, photos, email addresses, location data, and preferences. This helps users understand the scope of data sharing.

2. Purpose of Data Use:

○ Apps should explain how collected data will be used, such as for matchmaking, analytics, personalized recommendations, or marketing purposes. Users should be aware of all potential uses to make informed decisions.

3. Data Sharing Practices:

○ Policies should disclose whether and how users' data may be shared with third parties, such as advertising partners, service providers, or affiliated companies. This includes information on whether data is anonymized or pseudonymized before sharing.

4. Security Measures:

○ Details about the security measures in place to protect user data should be clearly outlined. This includes encryption protocols, access controls, and incident response procedures to reassure users about data protection.

5. User Rights and Control:

○ Policies should inform users about their rights regarding their personal data, such as the right to access, correct, or delete information. Clear instructions on how users can exercise these rights should be provided.

6. Updates and Changes:

○ App providers should explain how they will notify users of changes to the privacy policy and when consent may be required for new data practices. Users should be able to easily access previous versions of the policy.

Accessibility and Plain Language

1. Easy Accessibility:

○ Privacy policies should be prominently displayed within the app interface and on the app's website. Links to the policy should be accessible from registration screens and user profiles for easy reference.

2. Plain Language:

○ Policies should be written in clear, non-technical language that is easy for the average user to understand. Avoiding jargon and complex legal terms helps ensure that users comprehend their rights and responsibilities.

User Education and Awareness

1. Promoting Understanding:

○ App providers can enhance user awareness through pop-up notifications, educational materials, or FAQs that summarize key points of the privacy policy. This encourages users to review the policy thoroughly before agreeing to terms.

2. Support and Contact Information:

○ Contact information for inquiries or concerns about privacy practices should be readily available. Providing customer support channels reinforces transparency and demonstrates commitment to addressing user questions.

Compliance and Accountability

1. Regulatory Compliance:

○ Privacy policies should align with applicable data protection laws and regulations, such as GDPR in Europe or CCPA in California. Adhering to legal requirements reinforces trust and ensures accountability for data handling practices.

2. Auditing and Certification:

○ Some apps may undergo independent audits or obtain certifications to demonstrate compliance with industry standards for data privacy and security. This external validation further enhances transparency and user trust.

In summary, transparent privacy policies are essential for fostering user trust, promoting informed consent, and ensuring that users understand how their personal information is handled by dating apps. By providing clear, accessible, and comprehensive information about data practices, app providers can empower users to make informed decisions and protect their privacy effectively.

Consent and control

Consent and control over personal information are critical aspects of user privacy on dating apps. Here's a detailed explanation of why these elements are important and how they should be managed:

Importance of Consent

1. User Autonomy:

o Consent empowers users to make informed decisions about sharing their personal information. It acknowledges their autonomy and right to control what data is collected, how it's used, and who has access to it.

2. Trust and Transparency:

o Transparent consent processes build trust between users and app providers. When users understand and agree to how their data will be handled, they are more likely to trust the app and engage with it confidently.

Elements of Consent

1. Informed Consent:

o Users should be provided with clear and accessible information about what personal data will be collected, the purposes for which it will be used, and any potential sharing with third parties. This ensures that consent is informed and not based on vague or misleading information.

2. Explicit Consent:

o For sensitive data, such as sexual orientation or religious beliefs, explicit consent should be obtained from users. Apps should clearly explain why such information is needed and how it will be used to justify requesting this data.

3. Granular Consent Options:

o Users should have granular control over the types of data they share and the permissions granted to the app. This may include options to selectively share certain information or to opt-out of data uses that are not essential for basic app functionality.

Control Over Data Sharing

1. Third-Party Sharing:

o Users should be notified and given the choice to consent or opt-out before their data is shared with third parties, such as advertisers or analytics providers. Clear explanations should be provided about why data is shared and what protections are in place.

2. Purpose Limitation:

○ Data should only be used for the specific purposes for which consent was given. If an app intends to use data for additional purposes beyond matchmaking (e.g., targeted advertising), separate consent should be obtained from users.

Ensuring Effective Consent Mechanisms

1. User Interface Design:

○ Consent mechanisms should be integrated into the app interface in a clear and accessible manner. This includes using pop-up notifications, checkboxes, or consent screens that are easy to understand and navigate.

2. Revocability of Consent:

○ Users should have the ability to withdraw their consent at any time and easily revoke permissions granted for data processing. Apps should provide straightforward methods for users to manage their privacy settings and preferences.

Privacy by Design and Default

1. Default Privacy Settings:

○ Apps should implement privacy settings that prioritize user privacy by default. This means minimizing data collection to what is necessary for app functionality and allowing users to opt-in to additional features or data uses.

2. Data Minimization:

○ Only collect and retain data that is necessary for the intended purposes. Minimizing data collection reduces the risk of misuse or exposure in the event of a data breach.

Compliance and Accountability

1. Legal and Regulatory Compliance:

○ App providers should adhere to relevant data protection laws and regulations, such as GDPR in Europe or CCPA in California. Compliance frameworks ensure that consent practices align with legal requirements and industry standards.

2. Auditing and Monitoring:

○ Regular audits and monitoring of data practices help ensure that consent mechanisms are effective and that user preferences are respected. App providers should be accountable for honoring user choices regarding their personal information.

In conclusion, ensuring robust consent and control mechanisms on dating apps is essential for respecting user privacy, building trust, and promoting responsible data handling practices. By empowering users with informed consent and granular control over their data, apps can enhance user confidence and foster a safer and more transparent digital dating experience.

Risk of Catfishing

Catfishing poses significant risks to users of dating apps, impacting both emotional well-being and personal safety. Here's a detailed explanation of the risks associated with catfishing:

Understanding Catfishing

1. Definition:

○ Catfishing refers to the creation of fake profiles on dating apps or social media platforms, where individuals misrepresent themselves by using false identities, photos, or information. These profiles are designed to deceive and manipulate unsuspecting users.

2. Motivations:

○ Catfishers may have various motivations, including seeking attention, emotional gratification, financial gain through scams, or even revenge. They exploit the trust and vulnerability of others for personal advantage.

Risks and Consequences

1. Emotional Manipulation:

○ Victims of catfishing often develop emotional connections with the fake persona, believing they are interacting with a genuine person. When the deception is revealed, victims experience profound emotional distress, betrayal, and loss.

2. Financial Scams:

○ Catfishers may engage in financial scams by deceiving victims into sending money or sharing sensitive financial information under false pretenses. This can lead to financial loss and exploitation.

3. Identity Theft:

○ In some cases, catfishers may use stolen photos or personal information to impersonate someone else. This can result in identity theft, where victims' identities are compromised and used for fraudulent activities.

4. Privacy Violations:

○ Catfishing violates users' privacy by manipulating their personal information and using it for deceptive purposes without consent. Victims may feel exposed and vulnerable upon discovering their information has been used dishonestly.

5. Impact on Trust:

○ Being deceived through catfishing undermines users' trust in online interactions and dating platforms. It can make them more cautious and skeptical in future online relationships, affecting their ability to form genuine connections.

Prevention and Mitigation

1. Verification and Authentication:

○ Dating apps can implement verification measures, such as photo verification or linking profiles to social media accounts, to confirm users' identities and deter catfishing.

2. Education and Awareness:

○ Educating users about the signs of catfishing, such as suspicious behavior, inconsistencies in stories, or reluctance to meet in person, can help them recognize and avoid fraudulent profiles.

3. Reporting and Response Mechanisms:

○ Apps should provide clear mechanisms for users to report suspicious profiles or behavior. Prompt responses and investigations by app administrators can mitigate the impact of catfishing incidents and protect other users.

4. Privacy Settings and Control:

○ Empowering users with robust privacy settings and control over their profile visibility and interactions can help reduce vulnerability to catfishing and unauthorized use of personal information.

Legal and Ethical Considerations

1. Legal Consequences:

○ Catfishing may violate laws related to fraud, impersonation, or privacy rights, depending on jurisdiction. App providers have a responsibility to enforce terms of service and protect users from fraudulent activities.

2. Ethical Guidelines:

○ Upholding ethical standards in data handling and user interactions is crucial for maintaining trust and safety on dating platforms. Apps should prioritize user safety and well-being in their operational practices.

In conclusion, catfishing poses multifaceted risks to users of dating apps, ranging from emotional manipulation to financial exploitation and identity theft. Effective prevention strategies, user education, and responsive support mechanisms are essential in mitigating these risks and promoting a safer online dating environment.

Verification Processes

Effective verification processes on dating apps are crucial for ensuring user safety, maintaining trust, and reducing the prevalence of fake profiles. Here's a detailed explanation of verification processes and their importance:

Importance of Verification Processes

1. Authenticity Assurance:

○ Verification processes aim to confirm that users are who they claim to be. By verifying identities, apps can increase confidence among users that they are interacting with genuine individuals, thus fostering a safer environment for online dating.

2. Reducing Fake Profiles:

○ One of the primary purposes of verification is to reduce the prevalence of fake profiles or catfishing. Fake profiles mislead users and can lead to emotional manipulation, financial scams, or privacy violations. Robust verification helps mitigate these risks.

3. Enhancing Trust:

○ Verified profiles contribute to a higher level of trust between users. When individuals know that others on the platform have undergone verification, they are more likely to engage in meaningful interactions and pursue genuine relationships.

Types of Verification Processes

1. Photo Verification:

○ Apps may require users to verify their identity by submitting a photo that matches a specific pose or gesture. This method ensures that the person in the profile photos is the same as the one creating the account.

2. Social Media Linking:

○ Linking profiles to social media accounts, such as Facebook or Instagram, can provide additional verification. This allows apps to cross-reference user information and confirm the authenticity of profiles.

3. Phone Number Verification:

○ Verifying a phone number through SMS or voice call verification can confirm that the user has access to the phone number associated with their account. It adds an extra layer of security against fake accounts.

4. Identity Document Verification:

○ Some apps may request users to upload a government-issued ID, such as a driver's license or passport. This method verifies the user's legal identity and is more secure but requires handling sensitive personal information responsibly.

Challenges and Limitations

1. User Privacy Concerns:

○ Collecting personal data for verification purposes raises privacy concerns among users. Apps must handle and store this information securely, adhering to data protection regulations and ensuring user consent.

2. Effectiveness and Accessibility:

○ Verification processes need to strike a balance between effectiveness and user convenience. Overly complex or intrusive verification methods may deter users from completing the process, impacting user acquisition and retention.

3. Resource Intensity:

○ Implementing and maintaining robust verification systems requires significant resources and ongoing monitoring. Some smaller or newer apps may struggle to invest in comprehensive verification measures.

Best Practices

1. Transparency:

○ Apps should clearly communicate their verification processes to users, including what information will be verified and how it will be used. Transparent policies build trust and encourage users to participate in verification.

2. User Education:

○ Educating users about the importance of verification and how it enhances their safety can encourage compliance with verification requirements. Clear explanations of the benefits of verified profiles can also increase user confidence.

3. Continuous Improvement:

○ Regularly updating and refining verification processes based on user feedback and emerging security threats ensures that apps remain effective in combating fake profiles and maintaining user trust.

In summary, effective verification processes on dating apps play a crucial role in mitigating risks associated with fake profiles, enhancing user trust, and promoting a safer online dating experience. By implementing transparent, user-friendly verification methods, apps can foster a community where users feel secure and confident in their interactions.

Online Harassment

Online harassment on dating apps, especially targeting women, is a serious issue that can significantly impact users' experiences and perceptions of safety. Here's a detailed explanation of online harassment on dating apps:

Types of Online Harassment

1. Unwanted Advances:

○ Users may receive persistent messages or requests for dates despite indicating disinterest or not responding. This can create feelings of discomfort and intrusion into personal boundaries.

2. Explicit Messages:

○ Some users may receive unsolicited explicit messages or photos, which are inappropriate and offensive. This type of harassment can be particularly distressing and intimidating.

3. Stalking and Monitoring:

○ In extreme cases, individuals may be stalked or monitored by other users who attempt to track their online activity or whereabouts. This behavior is invasive and poses serious safety concerns.

4. Verbal Abuse and Insults:

○ Harassment may include verbal abuse, insults, or derogatory comments directed at a user based on their appearance, ethnicity, gender identity, or other personal attributes. Such behavior contributes to a hostile environment.

Impact on Users

1. Emotional Distress:

○ Constant exposure to harassment can lead to emotional distress, anxiety, and feelings of vulnerability. Users may feel unsafe and hesitant to continue using the app or engage with new matches.

2. Deterioration of Trust:

○ Experiencing harassment undermines trust in the platform's ability to provide a safe environment. Users may question the efficacy of reporting tools or the app's commitment to addressing harassment.

3. Decreased Engagement:

○ Harassment can deter users from actively participating in the app, limiting their interactions and potentially reducing their chances of finding meaningful connections. This impacts overall user satisfaction and retention.

Challenges in Addressing Online Harassment

1. Underreporting:

○ Many users may choose not to report instances of harassment due to fear of retaliation, lack of confidence in the app's response, or concerns about further victimization.

2. Moderation and Response Time:

○ Apps must have effective moderation systems in place to promptly address reports of harassment. Delays or inadequate responses can exacerbate the impact on affected users and contribute to a negative reputation for the app.

3. Cultural and Social Norms:

○ Harassment on dating apps often reflects broader societal issues, including gender stereotypes and norms around online behavior. Addressing these issues requires a multifaceted approach that goes beyond app features alone.

Strategies to Address Online Harassment

1. Clear Community Guidelines:

○ Establishing clear and comprehensive community guidelines that explicitly prohibit harassment and outline consequences for violators can set expectations for user behavior.

2. Robust Reporting Mechanisms:

○ Implementing easy-to-use reporting tools that allow users to flag harassment incidents swiftly. Apps should prioritize anonymity and protection for users who report harassment.

3. Educational Initiatives:

○ Providing users with resources on respectful online communication, consent, and boundaries can help foster a culture of respect and accountability within the app community.

4. Supportive Resources:

○ Offering support services, such as access to counselors or moderators trained in handling harassment cases, can provide immediate assistance to affected users and demonstrate a commitment to their safety.

Conclusion

Addressing online harassment on dating apps requires proactive measures to protect users, promote respectful interactions, and maintain a positive user experience. By prioritizing safety features, fostering a supportive community culture, and continuously refining moderation practices, apps can mitigate the impact of harassment and create a safer environment for all users.

Safety Features

Safety features are essential components of dating apps that aim to protect users from harassment and create a safer online environment. Here's a detailed explanation of key safety features that dating apps should implement:

Robust Reporting Mechanisms

1. Reporting Tools:

○ Dating apps should provide easy-to-access reporting tools that allow users to flag inappropriate behavior, harassment, or suspicious accounts. These tools should be prominently displayed within the app interface, such as on user profiles or within chat conversations.

2. Anonymous Reporting:

○ Users should have the option to report incidents anonymously to protect their privacy and safety. Anonymity encourages more users to report harassment without fear of retaliation or exposure.

3. Comprehensive Reporting Categories:

○ Apps should offer multiple reporting categories to cover various forms of harassment, including unwanted advances, explicit messages, stalking, and hate speech. Clear guidelines should accompany each category to assist users in understanding what constitutes reportable behavior.

4. Immediate Response and Action:

○ Upon receiving a report, dating apps should prioritize prompt review and action. This may involve suspending or permanently banning accounts found to be engaging in harassment, as well as notifying affected users of the outcome.

Blocking and Privacy Controls

1. Blocking Functionality:

○ Users should have the ability to block other users directly from their profiles or chat conversations. Blocking prevents further communication and interaction with unwanted individuals, providing immediate relief from harassment.

2. Mutual Blocking:

○ Implementing a mutual blocking feature allows both parties in a conversation to block each other simultaneously. This ensures equitable control over interactions and enhances user autonomy.

3. Privacy Settings:

○ Apps should offer robust privacy settings that allow users to control who can view their profile, send messages, or see their activity on the platform. This includes options to restrict visibility to specific age groups, locations, or user preferences.

Safety Education and Resources

1. Educational Resources:

○ Providing users with educational materials on safe online dating practices, recognizing signs of harassment, and understanding consent is crucial. These resources empower users to navigate the app responsibly and recognize potential risks.

2. Support Services:

○ Access to support services, such as customer support teams trained in handling harassment cases or resources for counseling, can provide immediate assistance to users experiencing harassment. These services should be easily accessible within the app.

Proactive Monitoring and Moderation

1. Content Moderation:

○ Dating apps should employ proactive content moderation strategies to detect and remove inappropriate content or accounts violating community guidelines. This may involve automated tools combined with human moderation to ensure swift action.

2. User Verification:

○ Implementing robust user verification processes, such as photo verification or linking social media accounts, can reduce the prevalence of fake profiles and malicious behavior. Verified accounts may also enjoy enhanced trust within the community.

Collaboration and Transparency

1. Collaboration with Law Enforcement:

○ In cases involving serious threats or criminal behavior, dating apps should collaborate with law enforcement authorities to address safety concerns and protect users from potential harm.

2. Transparency:

○ Apps should maintain transparency regarding their safety features, data handling practices, and response protocols for handling harassment reports. Clear communication fosters user trust and confidence in the platform's commitment to safety.

Conclusion

By implementing robust reporting and blocking features, providing comprehensive privacy controls, offering safety education and support resources, and maintaining proactive moderation practices, dating apps can significantly enhance user safety and mitigate the risks associated with online harassment. These features empower users to navigate the app with confidence, fostering a safer and more inclusive digital dating experience.

Meeting Strangers

Meeting strangers from dating apps in person introduces potential risks that users should approach with caution. Here's a detailed explanation of safety considerations and tips for users:

Understanding the Risks

1. **Anonymity and Unknown Intentions:**

    ○ Meeting someone in person whom you've only interacted with online carries inherent risks due to the anonymity and the limited information available about their true intentions.

2. **Safety Concerns:**

    ○ Users should be aware of common safety concerns such as catfishing (where someone pretends to be someone else online), potential scams, and risks of physical harm or assault.

3. **Emotional Risks:**

    ○ Beyond physical safety, there are emotional risks involved, including disappointment if the person does not match their online persona or if the interaction does not meet expectations.

Safety Tips for Meeting Strangers

1. **Public Meeting Places:**

    ○ Always meet in public places such as cafes, restaurants, or parks where there are other people around. Avoid secluded or private locations for initial meetings.

2. **Inform Others:**

    ○ Inform a trusted friend or family member about your plans, including where and when you plan to meet your date. Share your date's profile information and keep your phone charged and easily accessible.

3. **Trust Your Instincts:**

    ○ Trust your instincts and prioritize your comfort and safety. If you feel uneasy or uncomfortable during the interaction, it's okay to end the meeting early or leave the situation.

4. **Arrange Your Transportation:**

    ○ Use your own transportation to and from the meeting place. Avoid accepting rides from your date until you feel comfortable and trust them.

5. **Limit Alcohol Consumption:**

    ○ Limit alcohol consumption to maintain clear judgment and awareness of your surroundings. Avoid leaving your drink unattended.

6. **Verify Identity:**

○ Before meeting in person, consider video chatting or requesting additional photos to verify the identity of your match. This can help confirm their authenticity and build trust.

7. **Set Boundaries:**

○ Establish clear boundaries and communicate your expectations before meeting. Respect each other's comfort levels and personal space throughout the interaction.

Post-Meeting Considerations

1. **Feedback and Communication:**

○ After the meeting, communicate with a friend or family member about your experience. Share any concerns or positive aspects of the meeting to gain perspective and support.

2. **Stay Connected:**

○ Stay connected with trusted individuals during and after the meeting. Let someone know when you arrive safely home.

3. **Report Concerns:**

○ If you experience any form of harassment, misconduct, or suspicious behavior during or after the meeting, report it to the dating app's support team and consider contacting local authorities if necessary.

Conclusion

Meeting strangers from dating apps can be an exciting opportunity to connect with new people, but it's essential to prioritize safety and take precautions to minimize risks. By following these safety tips and exercising caution, users can enhance their personal safety and enjoy a more positive dating experience both online and offline.

User education

User education plays a crucial role in promoting safe dating practices and mitigating risks associated with offline interactions facilitated by dating apps. Here's a detailed explanation of how apps can contribute to user education:

Importance of User Education

1. **Awareness of Risks:**

   ○ Many users may not be fully aware of the potential risks involved in meeting strangers from dating apps. Educating users about these risks helps them make informed decisions and take appropriate precautions.

   2. **Empowerment:**

   ○ Education empowers users to recognize warning signs of suspicious behavior, scams, or potential dangers during online interactions and face-to-face meetings.

   3. **Building Trust:**

   ○ By providing transparent information and safety guidelines, dating apps can build trust with their user base, fostering a safer and more supportive community environment.

Components of User Education

1. **Safety Guidelines:**

   ○ Dating apps should offer comprehensive safety guidelines that cover both online and offline interactions. These guidelines should include tips on profile security, safe messaging practices, and precautions for meeting in person.

   2. **Video Tutorials and FAQs:**

   ○ Incorporating video tutorials or frequently asked questions (FAQs) sections within the app can educate users on how to use safety features effectively and what to expect when meeting someone offline.

   3. **Blog Articles and Resources:**

   ○ Apps can publish blog articles or provide resources within the app that address topics such as recognizing red flags in online interactions, setting boundaries, and understanding consent.

   4. **Interactive Features:**

   ○ Implementing interactive features such as quizzes or scenarios can engage users in learning about safe dating practices and testing their knowledge in real-world scenarios.

Promoting Responsible Behavior

1. **Consent and Respect:**

○ Emphasize the importance of consent and respectful communication in all interactions. Encourage users to seek explicit consent before sharing personal information or engaging in physical contact.

2. **Reporting Mechanisms:**

○ Educate users on how to use reporting and blocking features effectively. Prompt responses to reports of harassment or misconduct demonstrate a commitment to user safety.

3. **Community Guidelines:**

○ Clearly outline community guidelines that define acceptable behavior and consequences for violations. Regularly update these guidelines to address emerging issues and feedback from users.

Collaboration with Experts

1. Partnerships with Organizations:

○ Collaborate with dating safety organizations, counselors, or law enforcement agencies to develop educational content and strategies tailored to the app's user base.

2. Feedback and Improvement:

○ Solicit feedback from users on their experiences with safety features and educational resources. Use this feedback to continuously improve and update educational initiatives.

Conclusion

User education on safe dating practices is essential for fostering a positive and secure environment on dating apps. By equipping users with knowledge, tools, and resources to navigate potential risks, apps can empower individuals to make informed decisions and build meaningful connections while prioritizing their safety and well-being.

Chapter 9: Authenticity and honesty

Authenticity and honesty are crucial factors in the dynamics of dating apps, where users often navigate a landscape shaped by curated personas and the potential for misrepresentation.

Curated Personas

1. Idealized Self-Presentation:

○ Dating apps encourage users to present themselves in a favorable light to attract potential matches. This often leads to the curation of profiles that highlight the best aspects of a person's life, interests, and appearance.

○ Users may selectively choose photos, hobbies, and personal details that portray an idealized version of themselves, aiming to make a strong first impression.

2. Filtering Information:

○ Profiles may omit less flattering aspects or present a narrow view of a user's personality. This selective sharing can create a skewed perception of reality, where only positive attributes are emphasized.

3. Impact on Perceptions:

○ The prevalence of curated personas can contribute to unrealistic expectations and perceptions among users. Matches may perceive each other based on these idealized images rather than the complex realities of their lives.

Honesty in Profiles

1. Misrepresentation:

○ Despite efforts to showcase authenticity, misrepresentation in dating profiles is common. This can range from minor exaggerations of interests or physical attributes to more significant fabrications about career, relationship status, or lifestyle.

○ Misrepresentation may stem from a desire to appear more attractive or compatible with potential matches, or from insecurity about one's true self.

2. Motivations for Dishonesty:

○ Users may engage in dishonesty due to societal pressures to conform to certain ideals of attractiveness or success. Fear of rejection or the competitive nature of dating apps can also drive individuals to embellish their profiles.

3. Consequences of Misrepresentation:

○ Dishonesty in profiles can undermine trust and lead to disappointment when users discover discrepancies between online personas and real-life interactions. This can hinder the development of genuine connections based on mutual understanding and trust.

Addressing Authenticity and Honesty

1. Encouraging Genuine Connections:

○ Dating apps can promote authenticity by encouraging users to present themselves honestly and openly. Emphasizing the value of genuine connections over superficial impressions can foster more meaningful interactions.

2. Verification and Validation:

○ Implementing verification processes, such as photo verification or linking profiles to social media accounts, can enhance the authenticity of profiles. This helps users feel more confident in the identities of their potential matches.

3. Educational Resources:

○ Providing guidance on creating honest profiles and navigating the complexities of online dating can educate users on the importance of authenticity. Tips on how to showcase genuine interests and values can support users in forming more compatible connections.

4. Community Standards:

○ Enforcing community standards that discourage dishonest behavior and misrepresentation can cultivate a more trustworthy and respectful dating environment. Clear guidelines and penalties for violating these standards can uphold integrity within the app.

Conclusion

Authenticity and honesty are foundational to building meaningful relationships on dating apps. By addressing the challenges of curated personas and promoting truthful self-representation, apps can enhance user satisfaction, trust, and the potential for genuine connections based on mutual respect and understanding.

Curated Personas

Idealized Self-Presentation

Idealized self-presentation on dating apps involves users strategically crafting their profiles to showcase their most attractive qualities and present themselves in a positive light. This practice is influenced by the platform's emphasis on visual appeal and the competitive nature of online dating. Here's a detailed exploration of how idealized self-presentation unfolds:

Motivations and Strategies

1. **Attractiveness and Appeal:**

   ○ Users understand that first impressions matter significantly on dating apps. As a result, they carefully select photos that highlight their best physical features, often choosing flattering angles, outfits, or settings.

   ○ The aim is to catch the eye of potential matches quickly and positively. Studies show that profile pictures significantly impact initial attraction and interest.

2. **Highlighting Achievements and Interests:**

   ○ Beyond photos, users curate their profiles to emphasize accomplishments, hobbies, and interests that reflect well on them. This might include mentioning prestigious educational backgrounds, exciting travel experiences, or engaging in activities that suggest a well-rounded personality.

   ○ By showcasing these aspects, users aim to convey qualities like ambition, sociability, and cultural sophistication, which they believe are attractive to potential partners.

3. **Selective Sharing of Personal Details:**

   ○ Users often omit or downplay less flattering aspects of their lives or personalities. This can include aspects like past relationships, career setbacks, or personal challenges.

   ○ By focusing on positive aspects, users attempt to create a narrative that positions them as desirable and capable of forming a fulfilling relationship.

Challenges and Considerations

1. **Authenticity vs. Idealization:**

   ○ While idealized self-presentation can enhance attractiveness initially, it may lead to challenges later on. Users may struggle to maintain consistency between their curated online persona and their real-life self.

   ○ This discrepancy can create disappointment or distrust when potential matches discover discrepancies between the online profile and offline interactions.

2. Impact on Self-Esteem:

○ The pressure to present an idealized version of oneself can contribute to self-esteem issues. Users may feel inadequate if they perceive themselves as falling short of the idealized standards they see in others' profiles.

○ Additionally, comparing oneself to others' curated profiles can foster feelings of insecurity or dissatisfaction with one's own life and achievements.

3. Ethical Considerations:

○ There are ethical implications to consider regarding honesty and transparency in online interactions. While embellishing profiles is common, misrepresentation or deception can harm trust and the integrity of the dating experience.

○ Platforms and users alike may benefit from promoting more genuine interactions that prioritize authenticity and mutual understanding.

Promoting Authentic Connections

1. Encouraging Balanced Representation:

○ Dating apps can play a role in promoting authenticity by encouraging users to present themselves honestly while highlighting a balanced view of their lives. This can include showcasing strengths alongside vulnerabilities, which can foster deeper connections based on genuine understanding.

2. User Education and Awareness:

○ Providing guidance on creating authentic profiles and navigating the complexities of online dating can empower users to approach the platform with realistic expectations. Tips on portraying oneself accurately while still emphasizing positive qualities can support users in forming more meaningful connections.

3. Building Trust and Respect:

○ Enforcing community standards that discourage dishonest behavior and promote respectful interactions can contribute to a safer and more trustworthy dating environment. Clear guidelines on profile authenticity and penalties for misleading information can uphold integrity within the app.

In summary, idealized self-presentation on dating apps is a common practice driven by the desire to attract potential matches. However, it raises important considerations about authenticity, self-esteem, and ethical conduct. Balancing the portrayal of one's best qualities with transparency and honesty can contribute to more meaningful and fulfilling connections in the digital dating landscape.

Filtering Information

Filtering information on dating app profiles involves users intentionally choosing which aspects of themselves to highlight while omitting or downplaying less favorable traits or experiences. Here's a detailed exploration of how this selective sharing can impact perceptions and interactions:

Motivations Behind Filtering Information

1. Creating a Positive Impression:

○ Users aim to present themselves in the best possible light to attract potential matches. This often means showcasing achievements, hobbies, and personality traits that reflect positively on them.

○ By filtering out less flattering details, users seek to create an initial impression that is attractive and appealing, hoping to increase their chances of receiving interest and engagement from others.

2. Managing Perceptions:

○ Selective sharing helps users manage how they are perceived by others. They may choose to highlight aspects of their lives that align with societal norms of success, attractiveness, or desirability.

○ This can include showcasing professional accomplishments, exciting hobbies, travel experiences, or physical appearance, which they believe will make them more appealing to potential matches.

3. Minimizing Vulnerability:

○ Omitting negative or sensitive information can serve to protect users from potential judgment, rejection, or misunderstanding. For instance, users may avoid disclosing past relationship issues, personal challenges, or aspects of their personality that they perceive as less attractive.

Implications of Filtering Information

1. Perception of Authenticity:

○ While filtering information can enhance initial attraction, it can also lead to questions about authenticity and trustworthiness over time. Potential matches may wonder if the curated profile accurately reflects the user's true self or if it presents an idealized version.

○ This discrepancy between online presentation and real-life interaction can create challenges in building genuine connections based on mutual understanding and acceptance.

2. Impact on Relationship Development:

○ The selective sharing of information may hinder the development of deeper connections and intimacy. When users prioritize presenting only positive attributes, they may miss opportunities to share vulnerabilities or deeper aspects of their personalities that are crucial for building trust and emotional closeness.

○ This can contribute to relationships that are based more on surface-level attraction or shared interests rather than on a deeper understanding of each other's values and life experiences.

3. Ethical Considerations:

○ There are ethical implications to consider regarding transparency and honesty in online interactions. While it's natural to want to present oneself in a favorable light, deliberate misrepresentation or omitting important details can undermine trust and lead to disappointment or disillusionment.

○ Dating apps and users alike can benefit from promoting more genuine interactions that prioritize authenticity and mutual respect.

Promoting Balanced Representation

1. Encouraging Authenticity:

○ Dating apps can play a role in promoting authenticity by encouraging users to present themselves honestly while still highlighting their positive qualities. This can create a more realistic and inclusive environment where users feel comfortable being themselves.

○ Providing guidelines or prompts that encourage users to share a balanced view of their lives, including strengths and vulnerabilities, can facilitate more meaningful connections.

2. User Education:

○ Educating users on the importance of authenticity and the potential consequences of filtering information excessively can empower them to navigate dating apps with integrity. Tips on how to portray oneself accurately while still emphasizing positive qualities can support users in forming genuine connections.

3. Building Trust and Understanding:

○ Establishing clear community standards that discourage deceptive practices and promote respectful interactions can contribute to a safer and more trustworthy dating environment. Encouraging open communication and mutual understanding can foster relationships built on trust and acceptance.

In summary, filtering information on dating app profiles is a common strategy aimed at creating a positive impression and managing perceptions. However, it raises important considerations about authenticity, trust, and ethical conduct. Balancing the portrayal of one's best qualities with transparency and honesty can contribute to more meaningful and fulfilling connections in the digital dating landscape.

Impact on Perceptions

The impact of curated personas on dating app perceptions is significant, influencing how users perceive themselves and others within the digital dating landscape. Here's a detailed exploration of how these curated personas shape perceptions and interactions:

Creation of Idealized Images

1. Idealized Self-Presentation:

○ Users often curate their profiles to present an idealized version of themselves, emphasizing attractive qualities, achievements, and interests that they believe will enhance their appeal.

○ This can include carefully selected photos, descriptions of exciting activities, and positive personality traits, aimed at making a strong first impression.

2. **Managing Perceptions:**

○ Curated personas are crafted to manage how users are perceived by potential matches. By highlighting their best attributes and achievements, users seek to attract interest and validation.

○ This selective presentation aims to create an initial impression that aligns with societal norms of success, attractiveness, and desirability, often omitting aspects that may be perceived as less favorable.

Impact on User Perceptions

1. **Unrealistic Expectations:**

○ When users encounter heavily curated profiles, they may develop unrealistic expectations about potential matches. They might expect that the person they see online represents their entire personality and lifestyle accurately.

○ This can lead to disappointment or frustration when real-life interactions reveal discrepancies between the curated online persona and the complexities of the individual's real-life personality, interests, or life circumstances.

2. **Comparison and Judgment:**

○ The prevalence of curated personas can foster a culture of comparison among users. Individuals may compare themselves unfavorably to the idealized images presented by others, feeling inadequate or insecure about their own lives.

○ This can perpetuate a cycle where users feel pressured to maintain or enhance their own curated personas to compete for attention or validation within the dating app community.

3. **Impact on Self-Esteem:**

○ For users presenting curated personas, there may be pressure to live up to the idealized image they have created. This can contribute to anxiety or stress about maintaining appearances and receiving validation from others.

○ Conversely, encountering idealized profiles from others may lead to feelings of inadequacy or self-doubt if users perceive themselves as falling short of the standards set by these profiles.

Ethical and Psychological Considerations

1. Authenticity vs. Misrepresentation:

   ○ There are ethical considerations regarding the balance between presenting oneself in a positive light and misrepresenting one's true identity. Deliberate misrepresentation or excessive curation can undermine trust and authenticity in online interactions.

   ○ Dating apps and users alike can benefit from promoting more genuine interactions that prioritize honesty and transparency, fostering relationships based on mutual understanding and acceptance.

   2. Navigating Realism in Online Dating:

   ○ Encouraging users to present a balanced view of themselves, including strengths and vulnerabilities, can contribute to more realistic expectations and healthier interactions.

   ○ Educating users about the importance of authenticity and the potential consequences of heavily curated personas can promote a more inclusive and understanding dating environment.

Promoting Realistic Interactions

1. Encouraging Open Communication:

   ○ Dating apps can play a role in promoting open communication and genuine connections by encouraging users to share authentic aspects of themselves while still highlighting positive qualities.

   ○ Providing prompts or guidelines that facilitate meaningful self-expression can empower users to build connections based on shared values and interests rather than solely on curated images.

   2. Building Mutual Understanding:

   ○ Establishing community standards that discourage deceptive practices and prioritize respectful interactions can contribute to a safer and more trustworthy dating environment.

   ○ Promoting empathy and understanding among users can foster relationships built on mutual respect and appreciation for each other's unique identities and experiences.

In summary, the prevalence of curated personas on dating apps can shape perceptions and expectations among users, influencing how individuals present themselves and how they perceive others. Balancing the portrayal of one's best qualities with authenticity and transparency is essential for promoting realistic interactions and fostering genuine connections in the digital dating landscape.

Honesty in Profiles

Misrepresentation

Misrepresentation in dating profiles is a prevalent issue in the online dating landscape, influenced by various factors ranging from self-perception to social pressures. Here's a detailed exploration of why misrepresentation occurs and its implications:

Reasons for Misrepresentation

1. **Desire for Attraction and Validation:**

   ○ Users may embellish or exaggerate aspects of their profile to appear more attractive or appealing to potential matches. This can include enhancing physical appearance through selective photos or embellishing interests and achievements.

   ○ The goal is often to increase the likelihood of receiving positive attention and validation from others, which can boost self-esteem and reinforce a sense of desirability.

2. **Insecurity and Self-Presentation:**

   ○ Individuals may misrepresent themselves due to insecurities about their true selves or fear of rejection based on perceived shortcomings.

   ○ This can lead to presenting a more idealized version of oneself that may not accurately reflect their personality, lifestyle, or values.

3. **Social Norms and Expectations:**

   ○ Social pressures and cultural norms regarding attractiveness, success, or lifestyle can influence users to present themselves in ways that conform to these ideals.

   ○ For example, users may feel compelled to exaggerate their career achievements or interests to align with perceived societal expectations of success or compatibility.

Types of Misrepresentation

1. **Exaggerated Interests and Hobbies:**

   ○ Users may inflate their interests or hobbies to create a more appealing profile. For instance, someone might claim to enjoy hiking or traveling extensively when these activities are infrequent or unfamiliar.

   ○ This type of misrepresentation aims to attract individuals who share similar interests but may create false expectations in potential matches.

2. **Selective Presentation of Photos:**

○ Choosing flattering or outdated photos can mislead others about one's current appearance. Photos may be edited or filtered to enhance attractiveness, potentially leading to disappointment or distrust when meeting in person.

3. Fabrication of Career or Financial Status:

○ Some users may embellish their career achievements or financial stability to convey a more affluent or successful lifestyle.

○ This can be motivated by a desire to attract partners who value financial security or professional success, but it risks creating a disparity between online persona and reality.

4. Relationship Status and Intentions:

○ Misrepresentation about relationship status, such as hiding a current relationship or marital status, can deceive potential matches and lead to ethical concerns and emotional harm.

Implications of Misrepresentation

1. Trust Issues and Disappointment:

○ Discovering discrepancies between online personas and real-life identities can erode trust and lead to disappointment or frustration among users.

○ This can damage relationships before they have a chance to develop, undermining the foundation of trust essential for meaningful connections.

2. Ethical Concerns:

○ Deliberate misrepresentation raises ethical concerns about honesty and integrity in online interactions. It can harm the credibility of dating platforms and contribute to a culture of distrust among users.

3. Impact on Self-Esteem:

○ Individuals who engage in misrepresentation may experience guilt or anxiety about their deception, impacting their own self-esteem and sense of authenticity.

○ Conversely, those who discover they have been deceived may feel deceived and question their own judgment or ability to trust others.

4. Legal and Safety Risks:

○ In extreme cases, misrepresentation can pose legal risks, such as fraud or identity theft, particularly if personal or financial information is misrepresented or exploited.

Addressing Misrepresentation

1. **Promoting Authenticity:**

   ○ Dating platforms can encourage users to present themselves authentically by emphasizing the value of honesty and transparency in profiles.

   ○ Educating users about the long-term benefits of genuine connections built on mutual respect and understanding can foster a more positive dating culture.

   2. **Verification and Validation:**

   ○ Implementing robust verification processes, such as photo verification or linking profiles to social media accounts, can help authenticate users and reduce the prevalence of fake profiles and misrepresentation.

   ○ This can enhance trust and confidence among users in the authenticity of profiles they encounter.

   3. **Education and Awareness:**

   ○ Providing resources and guidelines on ethical online dating practices can empower users to navigate dating apps responsibly.

   ○ This includes understanding the potential consequences of misrepresentation and promoting respectful communication and behavior in digital interactions.

In conclusion, while misrepresentation in dating profiles is common and driven by various motivations, promoting authenticity and transparency is crucial for fostering genuine connections and a positive online dating experience. Addressing the underlying reasons for misrepresentation and implementing measures to authenticate profiles can contribute to building a more trustworthy and respectful digital dating environment.

Motivations for Dishonesty

Dishonesty in dating profiles on apps and websites often stems from a variety of motivations, influenced by societal norms, personal insecurities, and the dynamics of online interactions. Here's a detailed exploration of the motivations behind dishonesty:

Societal Pressures and Idealized Standards

1. **Conforming to Attractive Ideals:**

   ○ **Motivation:** Society often places a premium on physical attractiveness, success, and lifestyle. Users may feel pressured to present themselves in ways that align with these ideals to attract more matches.

   ○ **Example:** Individuals may exaggerate their physical appearance through selective photos or editing, or they might embellish their interests and hobbies to appear more culturally or socially desirable.

   2. **Perceived Social Expectations:**

○ **Motivation:** There is a perceived expectation to conform to certain standards of success or lifestyle portrayed as desirable by society.

○ **Example:** Users might fabricate details about their career, financial status, or lifestyle to create a more appealing profile that they believe will attract matches who share or value these traits.

Fear of Rejection and Insecurity

1. Fear of Negative Evaluation:

○ **Motivation:** Users may fear rejection based on perceived shortcomings or inadequacies. This fear can drive them to present a more idealized version of themselves to minimize the risk of being overlooked or rejected.

○ **Example:** Someone insecure about their job might exaggerate their career achievements to appear more successful and attractive to potential matches.

2. Competitive Nature of Dating Apps:

○ **Motivation:** Dating apps create a competitive environment where users often compare themselves to others and strive to stand out among numerous profiles.

○ **Example:** Users may feel compelled to embellish their profiles or use more flattering photos to increase their chances of receiving matches and positive attention in a crowded dating pool.

Online Interaction Dynamics

1. Anonymity and Lack of Accountability:

○ **Motivation:** The digital nature of dating apps can reduce the perceived consequences of dishonesty since users may not immediately face the repercussions of misrepresentation.

○ **Example:** Individuals may feel emboldened to misrepresent themselves knowing that they are interacting through a screen, where they feel less accountable for their actions compared to face-to-face interactions.

2. Seeking Validation and Attention:

○ **Motivation:** Users may seek validation and attention from others, which can lead them to present a more idealized or exaggerated version of themselves to elicit positive feedback.

○ **Example:** Someone insecure about their physical appearance might use highly edited photos to garner compliments and boost their self-esteem through external validation.

Social and Cultural Influences

1. Cultural Norms and Expectations:

○ **Motivation:** Cultural norms around dating, relationships, and social status can influence how individuals perceive themselves and others on dating platforms.

○ **Example:** In cultures where certain traits or characteristics are highly valued in potential partners (e.g., financial stability, educational achievements), users may be more inclined to embellish these aspects of their profiles to fit societal expectations.

Conclusion

Understanding the motivations behind dishonesty in dating profiles reveals complex interactions between personal insecurities, societal pressures, and the dynamics of digital communication. While users may engage in misrepresentation to enhance their chances of success or protect themselves from rejection, fostering a culture of authenticity and transparency can promote healthier and more meaningful connections on dating apps. Addressing these underlying motivations through education, platform features, and cultural shifts can contribute to a more positive and respectful online dating experience for all users.

Consequences of Misrepresentation

Misrepresentation in dating profiles, where individuals present themselves inaccurately or selectively, can have significant consequences that affect both individuals and the dating community as a whole. Here's a detailed exploration of the consequences of misrepresentation:

Undermining Trust and Authenticity

1. Trust Issues:

○ **Impact:** Misrepresentation erodes trust between users when discrepancies between online profiles and real-life interactions are discovered.

○ **Example:** Someone who misrepresented their interests or lifestyle may struggle to build trust once their true self is revealed, leading to skepticism and reluctance to engage in further interactions.

2. Authenticity Concerns:

○ **Impact:** Users may become wary of authenticity on dating platforms, questioning the sincerity of others' profiles and interactions.

○ **Example:** Individuals who encounter misrepresentation may doubt the genuineness of potential matches, making it challenging to establish genuine connections based on mutual honesty and understanding.

Disappointment and Emotional Impact

1. Emotional Disappointment:

○ **Impact:** Discovering misrepresentation can lead to disappointment and emotional distress, especially when users invest time and emotions in developing connections based on false premises.

○ **Example:** A user who believed they shared common interests with a match may feel let down upon realizing those interests were misrepresented, undermining their initial excitement and potential for a meaningful relationship.

2. Negative Self-Perception:

○ **Impact:** Individuals who experience misrepresentation may question their judgment or attractiveness, leading to lowered self-esteem.

○ **Example:** Someone repeatedly encountering misrepresented profiles might internalize negative beliefs about their ability to discern genuine connections, affecting their confidence in future interactions.

Implications for Dating Culture

1. Cultural Norms and Expectations:

○ **Impact:** Misrepresentation can perpetuate a culture where dishonesty is normalized, undermining efforts to foster authenticity and transparency.

○ **Example:** Continued misrepresentation may contribute to a cycle of skepticism and cynicism among users, hindering the development of a positive and trustworthy dating environment.

2. Community Impact:

○ **Impact:** The prevalence of misrepresentation can harm the dating community's reputation and user satisfaction.

○ **Example:** Platforms known for high levels of misrepresentation may struggle to attract and retain users seeking genuine connections, affecting overall community engagement and satisfaction.

Legal and Ethical Considerations

1. Legal Issues:

○ **Impact:** In some cases, severe misrepresentation or fraud on dating apps can have legal implications, particularly if financial scams or identity theft are involved.

○ **Example:** Instances of deliberate deception for financial gain or malicious intent may lead to legal action, highlighting the importance of platforms implementing stringent policies and security measures.

Conclusion

Misrepresentation in dating profiles can have wide-ranging consequences that extend beyond individual experiences to impact trust, authenticity, and community dynamics. Addressing these issues requires a collective effort from dating platforms, users, and broader societal

Addressing Authenticity and Honesty

Encouraging Genuine Connections

Encouraging genuine connections on dating apps involves creating an environment where users feel inclined to be authentic and open in their interactions. Here's a detailed look at how dating apps can promote authenticity and foster meaningful connections:

1. Authentic Profile Creation:

● **Encouragement:** Dating apps can prompt users to create detailed profiles that reflect their true personalities, interests, and values. Emphasizing the importance of authenticity in profiles can steer users away from presenting idealized versions of themselves.

   ● **Example:** Platforms could provide tips on how to write a bio that showcases genuine interests and aspirations rather than focusing solely on physical appearance or material success. They could also encourage users to upload a variety of photos that represent different aspects of their lives, rather than just their most attractive shots.

2. Promoting Honest Communication:

● **Encouragement:** Apps can encourage users to engage in open and honest conversations right from the start. This can be done through prompts that suggest asking deeper questions about shared interests, values, and life goals rather than just exchanging pleasantries.

   ● **Example:** Implementing conversation starters that focus on meaningful topics can help users break the ice and establish a more genuine connection. This approach shifts the focus from superficial small talk to discussions that can lead to a deeper understanding of each other.

3. Verification and Trust-building:

● **Verification:** Robust verification processes can help authenticate users and reduce the presence of fake profiles. This builds trust among users, making them more comfortable with sharing genuine information and engaging in meaningful conversations.

   ● **Example:** Apps might introduce verification badges or procedures that confirm users' identities through photo verification or social media integration. This reassures users that they are interacting with real people, enhancing their confidence in the platform.

4. Community Guidelines and Support:

● **Guidelines:** Clearly defined community guidelines that prohibit harassment, discrimination, and dishonest behavior set a standard for respectful interactions. Enforcing these guidelines ensures a safer and more welcoming environment for users seeking genuine connections.

   ● **Example:** Platforms could provide easy access to reporting and blocking features to empower users to address inappropriate behavior promptly. They could also offer real-time support or moderation to handle any issues that arise, reinforcing a commitment to user safety and well-being.

5. Educational Resources:

● **Education:** Providing educational content on the benefits of authenticity and genuine connections can encourage users to prioritize honesty in their interactions.
    ● **Example:** Apps might offer articles, videos, or blog posts that share success stories of couples who found meaningful relationships through authentic profiles and conversations. Highlighting these stories can inspire users and demonstrate the positive outcomes of being genuine.

6. Feedback and Improvement:

● **User Feedback:** Regularly seeking feedback from users about their experiences and preferences can help dating apps tailor their features to better support genuine connections.
    ● **Example:** Platforms could conduct surveys or host focus groups to gather insights into what encourages users to engage authentically. Using this feedback, apps can continuously refine their algorithms and features to promote more meaningful interactions.

Conclusion

Encouraging genuine connections on dating apps requires a concerted effort to prioritize authenticity and foster an environment where users feel safe and encouraged to be themselves. By promoting honest profile creation, supporting open communication, implementing robust verification processes, upholding community guidelines, providing educational resources, and soliciting user feedback, dating platforms can help users forge meaningful relationships based on mutual understanding and respect. This approach not only enhances user satisfaction but also contributes to a more fulfilling and positive online dating experience for all participants.

Verification and Validation

Implementing verification and validation processes on dating apps is crucial for enhancing trust and authenticity among users. Here's a detailed exploration of how these processes work and their impact:

1. Types of Verification Processes:

● **Photo Verification:** This involves users submitting a photo of themselves that matches their profile photos. Apps may use facial recognition technology or manual review by moderators to confirm the authenticity of the submitted photos.
    ● **Social Media Integration:** Linking profiles to social media accounts, such as Facebook or Instagram, can provide additional validation. Users may opt to display their social media handles on their dating profiles to showcase more aspects of their lives and confirm their identity.
    ● **Phone Number Verification:** Verifying a user's phone number through SMS or voice call confirmation adds another layer of authentication. This helps ensure that the phone number provided matches the user's identity and is not associated with multiple accounts.

2. Benefits of Verification Processes:

● **Enhanced Trust:** When users know that profiles have been verified through reliable methods, they are more likely to trust that the people they are interacting with are genuine and not using fake identities.

● **Reduced Fake Profiles:** Verification processes deter individuals from creating fake profiles or impersonating others, as they increase the likelihood of being identified and removed from the platform.

● **Safer Environment:** By confirming the identity of users, dating apps create a safer environment where users can feel more comfortable sharing personal information and engaging in conversations.

3. Implementation Challenges:

● **User Privacy Concerns:** Some users may be hesitant to provide personal information for verification due to privacy concerns. It's essential for apps to clearly communicate how user data will be used and protected.

● **Technical Limitations:** Implementing effective verification processes requires robust technical infrastructure and resources. Apps must ensure that their methods are reliable and resistant to manipulation.

● **User Experience:** Verification processes should be seamless and user-friendly to encourage compliance. Complicated or time-consuming procedures may deter users from completing the verification.

4. Best Practices:

● **Clear Communication:** Apps should clearly explain their verification methods and how they contribute to user safety and authenticity. Transparent communication builds user confidence and encourages participation.

● **Optional Verification:** Providing optional verification methods allows users to choose how much information they want to disclose while still offering the benefits of verified profiles to those who opt in.

● **Continuous Improvement:** Regularly updating and refining verification processes based on user feedback and technological advancements ensures they remain effective and relevant.

5. Impact on User Experience:

● **Increased Confidence:** Verified profiles give users confidence that they are interacting with real people, which can lead to more meaningful connections and higher engagement on the platform.

● **Improved Matchmaking:** Authentic profiles enable more accurate matchmaking algorithms, enhancing the likelihood of compatible matches and reducing disappointment from mismatches.

Conclusion

Verification and validation processes play a crucial role in maintaining the integrity of dating app platforms. By implementing reliable methods such as photo verification, social media integration, and phone number verification, apps can enhance user trust, reduce fake profiles, and create a safer and more authentic environment for users to connect and build relationships. These processes not only benefit individual users by increasing their confidence in the platform but also contribute to a positive overall user experience.

Educational Resources

Educational resources provided by dating apps can significantly enhance users' understanding of creating honest profiles and navigating the nuances of online dating. Here's a detailed exploration of how these resources can support authenticity and foster more compatible connections:

Importance of Educational Resources:

1. Understanding Authenticity:

○ **Guidance on Honesty:** Educational materials can emphasize the importance of honesty in profiles, encouraging users to present themselves truthfully rather than creating idealized versions. Tips may include highlighting genuine interests, hobbies, and personality traits that accurately reflect who they are.

○ **Impact of Authenticity:** Users who understand the value of authenticity are more likely to attract compatible matches who appreciate them for their true selves. This can lead to more meaningful connections based on shared values and interests.

2. Navigating Online Dating Complexity:

○ **Profile Optimization:** Resources can provide tips on how to optimize profiles to reflect personality and preferences effectively. This includes suggestions on choosing profile photos that are genuine and representative, rather than overly edited or misleading.

○ **Communication Skills:** Guidance on initiating conversations, maintaining engaging dialogue, and showing genuine interest can help users build rapport and trust with potential matches. Effective communication fosters connections beyond superficial attraction.

Components of Educational Resources:

1. Articles and Guides:

○ **Written Content:** Articles or blog posts can delve into topics such as the psychology of attraction, building trust online, and strategies for authentic self-presentation. These resources can educate users on the underlying principles of successful online dating.

○ **Case Studies:** Real-life examples and success stories can illustrate how authenticity in profiles and interactions has led to meaningful relationships, inspiring users to prioritize honesty.

2. Video Tutorials and Webinars:

○ **Visual Learning:** Video tutorials or webinars can offer step-by-step guidance on creating profiles, choosing photos, and engaging in meaningful conversations. These formats cater to different learning preferences and provide practical demonstrations.

○ **Expert Insights:** Inviting relationship experts or psychologists to discuss topics like building trust, managing expectations, and fostering connections can offer valuable insights to users navigating the complexities of online dating.

3. **Interactive Tools:**

○ **Profile Assessments:** Tools that assess profile completeness, authenticity, and attractiveness based on genuine attributes can guide users in optimizing their profiles for better matches.

○ **Compatibility Tests:** Interactive quizzes or compatibility tests can help users identify and articulate their values, preferences, and relationship goals, facilitating more informed matchmaking.

Implementation and Effectiveness:

1. **User Accessibility:**

○ **Integration within App:** Educational resources should be easily accessible within the dating app interface, preferably integrated into the profile creation process and search functionalities.

○ **Notifications and Reminders:** Apps can send notifications or reminders to users encouraging them to explore educational resources periodically, ensuring ongoing engagement and learning.

2. **Feedback Mechanisms:**

○ **User Feedback:** Soliciting feedback from users on the usefulness and relevance of educational resources allows apps to continuously improve content and address user needs.

○ **Analytics and Metrics:** Tracking user engagement with educational content can provide insights into its effectiveness in promoting authenticity and improving user experience.

Conclusion:

Educational resources play a pivotal role in promoting authenticity and enhancing user experience on dating apps. By providing guidance on creating honest profiles, navigating online dating complexities, and fostering genuine connections, apps can empower users to approach digital dating with confidence and integrity. These resources not only educate users on best practices but also contribute to a more supportive and fulfilling online dating environment conducive to meaningful relationships.

Community Standards

Enforcing community standards within dating apps is crucial for fostering a trustworthy and respectful environment that promotes genuine interactions. Here's a detailed exploration of how community standards can be implemented and their impact:

Importance of Community Standards:

1. Promoting Trust and Safety:

○ **Discouraging Misrepresentation:** Clear community standards discourage users from creating fake profiles, using misleading photos, or providing false information about themselves. This helps maintain trust among users and reduces the likelihood of deceptive practices.

○ **Protecting Users:** Standards aimed at preventing harassment, inappropriate behavior, and other forms of misconduct ensure that users feel safe and respected while using the app. This protection is essential for maintaining a positive user experience and preventing harm.

2. Upholding App Integrity:

○ **Enhancing Credibility:** Apps that enforce and uphold strict community standards demonstrate a commitment to integrity and user well-being. This enhances their reputation as a reliable platform for finding meaningful connections.

○ **Building User Confidence:** When users trust that the app actively addresses misconduct and dishonesty, they are more likely to engage authentically and invest in building relationships through the platform.

Components of Community Standards:

1. Clear Guidelines:

○ **Policy Statements:** Detailed policies should outline acceptable and unacceptable behaviors, including guidelines on profile authenticity, respectful communication, and appropriate conduct during interactions.

○ **Examples and Scenarios:** Providing specific examples of prohibited behavior helps users understand what constitutes a violation of community standards. This clarity reduces ambiguity and facilitates compliance.

2. Enforcement Measures:

○ **Reporting Mechanisms:** Apps should offer easy-to-use reporting tools that allow users to flag inappropriate content or behavior. Prompt response to reports ensures that issues are addressed swiftly.

○ **Penalties for Violations:** Establishing consequences for violating community standards, such as temporary account suspension or permanent bans, reinforces the importance of adhering to guidelines.

Implementation and Effectiveness:

1. Education and Communication:

○ **User Awareness:** Apps should educate users about community standards through onboarding processes, in-app notifications, and educational resources. Clear communication helps set expectations from the outset.

○ **Updates and Reminders:** Regular updates and reminders about community standards keep users informed of any changes or clarifications. This ongoing communication reinforces the app's commitment to maintaining a respectful environment.

2. **Monitoring and Feedback:**

○ **Moderation Teams:** Dedicated moderation teams or automated systems can monitor user activity to detect and address violations of community standards proactively. Timely intervention prevents misconduct from escalating.

○ **User Feedback:** Soliciting feedback from users on their experiences with community standards allows apps to continuously refine policies and enforcement strategies based on real-world interactions.

Impact on User Experience:

1. **Enhanced User Trust:** When users perceive that the app prioritizes their safety and well-being through robust community standards, they are more likely to engage authentically and invest in meaningful connections.
2. **Reduced Misconduct:** Enforcing clear guidelines reduces instances of harassment, deception, and other negative behaviors that undermine user confidence and satisfaction.
3. **Positive App Reputation:** A reputation for maintaining high community standards can attract new users and retain existing ones, contributing to the long-term success and growth of the dating app.

Conclusion:

Community standards play a vital role in shaping the culture and integrity of dating apps. By establishing clear guidelines, enforcing rules consistently, and promoting user education, apps can create a safer and more respectful environment conducive to genuine connections. Upholding community standards not only protects users from harm but also strengthens trust in the platform, fostering a positive and rewarding online dating experience for all participants.

Chapter 10: The Impact on Social Skills

Dating apps have revolutionized how people meet and interact in the modern dating landscape. These platforms offer convenience and accessibility, allowing users to connect with potential partners based on shared interests and preferences. However, alongside their benefits, dating apps also influence users' social skills and can exacerbate social anxiety in various ways. This discussion delves into the impact of dating apps on social skills development and the challenges individuals may face, particularly concerning social anxiety.

Impact on Social Skills

Decline in Social Skills:

Dating apps primarily facilitate communication through text-based messages and profiles, reducing opportunities for face-to-face interactions. This shift away from traditional forms of socializing can lead to a decline in certain social skills:

- **Limited Face-to-Face Interaction:** The reliance on digital communication may diminish individuals' ability to engage in spontaneous conversations, read non-verbal cues, and develop interpersonal skills crucial for real-world interactions.

- **Surface-Level Interactions:** Interactions on dating apps often prioritize superficial aspects such as profile photos and brief bios over deeper conversations that foster genuine connections. Users may become accustomed to shallow interactions that emphasize initial attraction rather than meaningful engagement.

- **Dependency on Digital Communication:** Continuous use of dating apps can foster a preference for text-based communication over face-to-face interactions. This preference may limit users' ability to navigate complex social dynamics, handle conflicts, or express emotions effectively in offline settings.

- **Impact on Confidence:** Reduced exposure to face-to-face interactions may erode individuals' confidence in social settings. Without regular practice in real-world conversations, users may feel less comfortable initiating or sustaining meaningful interactions offline.

Overcoming Social Anxiety:

Dating apps can pose unique challenges for individuals with social anxiety, exacerbating existing fears and uncertainties:

- **Pressure to Perform:** Online dating platforms can heighten the pressure to make a positive impression through curated profiles and messages. This pressure can intensify feelings of self-doubt or fear of rejection when transitioning from virtual to real-life interactions.

- **Miscommunication Concerns:** Individuals with social anxiety may struggle with interpreting social cues or accurately conveying their intentions in text-based conversations. The ambiguity inherent in digital communication can amplify anxiety about how one is perceived or understood by potential matches.

- **Gradual Exposure:** Overcoming social anxiety often involves gradual exposure to social situations. Dating apps can provide a controlled environment for practicing communication skills and building confidence in initiating and maintaining connections, albeit primarily online.

- **Seeking Support:** Users facing social anxiety can benefit from seeking professional support or utilizing dating apps that offer features to facilitate genuine connections, such as video calls or group activities. These features can help bridge the gap between online interactions and real-life encounters, providing opportunities for gradual social integration.

Conclusion

While dating apps offer unprecedented convenience in meeting potential partners, they also impact users' social skills and can amplify social anxiety. Addressing these challenges involves promoting balanced interactions that support both online engagement and offline social skills development. Integrating features that encourage authentic communication and providing resources for managing social anxiety can contribute to a more positive and enriching dating experience. By fostering a mindful approach to digital interactions, dating apps can empower users to navigate social challenges effectively while fostering meaningful connections in both virtual and real-world settings.

Decline in Social Skills

Limited Face-to-Face Interaction: Impact of Digital Communication on Social Skills

In the digital age, dating apps have significantly altered how people initiate and maintain relationships. One notable consequence of this shift is the reduced frequency of face-to-face interactions, which traditionally play a vital role in developing interpersonal skills. Here's how the reliance on digital communication affects individuals:

1. **Diminished Spontaneity:**

   ○ **Online Interaction Dynamics:** Dating apps facilitate communication primarily through text-based messages, which are often composed and edited before sending. This controlled environment contrasts sharply with face-to-face interactions, where spontaneity and quick thinking are essential.

   ○ **Impact on Spontaneous Conversations:** Users accustomed to composing thoughtful messages may find it challenging to engage in spontaneous conversations offline. The ability to think on one's feet and respond in real-time may diminish with less practice in face-to-face settings.

2. **Reading Non-Verbal Cues:**

   ○ **Importance of Non-Verbal Communication:** In face-to-face interactions, non-verbal cues such as facial expressions, body language, and tone of voice convey essential information about emotions, intentions, and attitudes.

   ○ **Absence in Digital Communication:** Text-based messaging lacks these non-verbal cues, making it harder for individuals to accurately interpret the emotions or reactions of their conversation partners. This can lead to misunderstandings or miscommunications that may not occur in face-to-face interactions where non-verbal cues provide additional context.

3. **Development of Interpersonal Skills:**

   ○ **Crucial Skills for Real-World Interactions:** Interpersonal skills, including active listening, empathy, and conflict resolution, are honed through regular face-to-face interactions. These skills are essential for building meaningful relationships and navigating social dynamics effectively.

   ○ **Impact of Reduced Practice:** With less exposure to face-to-face interactions, individuals may experience a decline in their ability to develop and maintain interpersonal skills. This can affect their confidence in social situations and their capacity to form genuine connections outside of digital platforms.

4. **Social Confidence and Comfort:**

   ○ **Building Comfort in Social Settings:** Face-to-face interactions allow individuals to gradually build confidence and comfort in various social settings. Over time, this exposure helps reduce social anxiety and facilitates smoother interactions with diverse individuals.

   ○ **Risk of Social Withdrawal:** Heavy reliance on digital communication, particularly through dating apps, may lead some individuals to withdraw from face-to-face interactions altogether. This withdrawal can reinforce social anxiety and further limit opportunities for developing social skills in real-world settings.

Conclusion

The shift towards digital communication through dating apps offers convenience and accessibility but also poses challenges to the development of interpersonal skills crucial for offline interactions. Addressing these challenges involves finding a balance between digital and face-to-face interactions, promoting opportunities for practicing spontaneity, reading non-verbal cues, and honing interpersonal skills. By recognizing the impact of limited face-to-face interaction, individuals can take proactive steps to maintain and enhance their social skills, ensuring meaningful connections both online and offline.

Surface-Level Interactions on Dating Apps

Dating apps have revolutionized how people connect, but they often prioritize superficial aspects over deeper, more meaningful interactions. This emphasis on surface-level characteristics can impact users in several ways:

1. **Profile-Based Judgments:**

   o **Focus on Visual Appeal:** Dating apps typically present users with profiles that include photos and short bios. This format encourages users to make snap judgments based on physical appearance and brief descriptions.

   o **Superficial Initial Impressions:** Users may prioritize attractive photos or common interests highlighted in bios, often leading to interactions that are based more on initial attraction than on deeper compatibility or shared values.

2. **Limited Conversation Depth:**

   o **Convenience and Efficiency:** The design of dating apps often encourages quick interactions and rapid decision-making through features like swiping or instant messaging.

   o **Lack of Incentive for Deep Conversations:** Users may engage in brief exchanges that focus on small talk or surface-level topics. This can discourage deeper conversations that require time and effort to develop.

3. **Emphasis on Quantity Over Quality:**

   o **High Volume of Interactions:** The ease of swiping and matching on dating apps can lead to a high volume of interactions for users.

   o **Impact on Engagement:** Users may prioritize quantity (e.g., the number of matches or messages) over the quality of each interaction. This can result in a cycle of shallow connections that do not progress beyond initial introductions.

4. **Challenges in Building Meaningful Connections:**

○ **Barriers to Genuine Connection:** Surface-level interactions may hinder the development of genuine connections based on shared values, beliefs, or long-term goals.

○ **Risk of Misalignment:** Users may find it challenging to gauge compatibility beyond physical attraction or superficial interests, potentially leading to mismatches or misunderstandings in relationships.

5. **Psychological Effects:**

○ **Validation and Self-Worth:** Users may experience validation or disappointment based on the quantity or quality of their matches and interactions.

○ **Long-Term Satisfaction:** While dating apps offer convenience and accessibility, reliance on surface-level interactions may contribute to feelings of dissatisfaction or a lack of fulfillment in relationships that lack depth.

Conclusion

Surface-level interactions on dating apps can shape users' experiences by emphasizing initial attraction and efficiency in matching. While these platforms offer convenience and accessibility, they may also present challenges in fostering genuine connections that go beyond superficial impressions. Encouraging users to engage in more meaningful conversations and prioritize compatibility over immediate attraction can support the development of deeper and more fulfilling relationships on dating apps.

Dependency on Digital Communication in Dating Apps

Dating apps have transformed how people initiate and maintain relationships, often leading to a dependency on digital communication. This dependency can impact users in several ways:

1. **Preference for Text-Based Communication:**

○ **Convenience and Accessibility:** Dating apps offer a platform where users can communicate via text messages at any time and from any location, providing convenience and immediate accessibility.

○ **Control Over Communication:** Users have control over the timing and content of their responses, allowing them to carefully craft messages and manage the pace of interactions.

2. **Limitations of Text-Based Communication:**

○ **Absence of Non-Verbal Cues:** Unlike face-to-face interactions, text-based communication lacks non-verbal cues such as facial expressions, body language, and tone of voice. This can make it challenging to accurately interpret emotions or intentions conveyed through messages.

○ **Potential for Miscommunication:** The absence of non-verbal cues can lead to misunderstandings or misinterpretations in text-based conversations. Users may struggle to convey or understand emotions effectively, which can hinder the development of meaningful connections.

3. **Impact on Social Skills:**

○ **Decline in Face-to-Face Interaction Skills:** Continuous reliance on digital communication may diminish individuals' ability to engage in spontaneous face-to-face conversations, read social cues, or develop interpersonal skills crucial for real-world interactions.

○ **Handling Complex Social Dynamics:** Users accustomed to text-based communication may find it challenging to navigate complex social dynamics, such as managing conflicts, expressing empathy, or negotiating in-person interactions.

4. Emotional Expression and Connection:

○ **Delayed Emotional Connection:** Text-based communication may delay the development of emotional connection and intimacy compared to face-to-face interactions. Users may find it easier to express emotions or vulnerability through written messages rather than in-person interactions.

5. Dependency and Adaptation:

○ **Preference Reinforcement:** Continuous use of dating apps reinforces the preference for text-based communication over face-to-face interactions. This dependency may shape users' social behavior and communication patterns, affecting how they approach offline relationships and interactions.

6. Psychological Impact:

○ **Self-Esteem and Confidence:** Dependency on digital communication may impact users' self-esteem and confidence in face-to-face settings. Users may feel more comfortable expressing themselves through text rather than in-person, leading to potential challenges in building authentic connections offline.

Conclusion

Dependency on digital communication through dating apps offers convenience and control but can also limit users' ability to navigate offline social dynamics effectively. Balancing text-based interactions with face-to-face communication can help users develop well-rounded social skills and foster deeper emotional connections in both online and offline relationships. Recognizing the strengths and limitations of digital communication is essential for promoting healthy and fulfilling interactions on dating apps and beyond.

Impact on Confidence Due to Reduced Face-to-Face Interactions

Dating apps, which predominantly facilitate digital communication, can impact users' confidence in face-to-face social settings in several ways:

1. Limited Practice in Real-World Conversations:

○ **Skill Development:** Face-to-face interactions are essential for developing and honing social skills, including initiating conversations, reading non-verbal cues, and maintaining engaging dialogues. Regular practice in these areas helps individuals feel more comfortable and confident in social settings.

○ **Lack of Exposure:** Users heavily reliant on dating apps may have fewer opportunities for face-to-face interactions, leading to reduced exposure to real-world social dynamics and scenarios.

2. Social Anxiety and Confidence Issues:

○ **Exacerbation of Social Anxiety:** Dependence on digital communication can exacerbate existing social anxiety or create apprehension about face-to-face interactions. Users may feel more comfortable expressing themselves through written messages rather than in-person conversations, which can perpetuate feelings of social discomfort.

○ **Fear of Rejection:** Limited exposure to face-to-face interactions may increase the fear of rejection or failure in social settings. Users may hesitate to initiate conversations or engage in social activities due to concerns about their social skills or perceived inadequacies.

3. Impact on Self-Perception and Identity:

○ **Self-Esteem:** Reduced confidence in face-to-face interactions can affect users' self-esteem and self-perception. They may question their social abilities or feel insecure about their communication skills, especially if they primarily rely on digital communication for social interactions.

○ **Authenticity:** Face-to-face interactions allow individuals to convey their personality, emotions, and authenticity more effectively. Over-reliance on dating apps' text-based communication may hinder the development of authentic self-expression and genuine connections.

4. Dependency on Digital Communication:

○ **Preference Reinforcement:** Continuous use of dating apps reinforces a preference for digital communication over face-to-face interactions. This dependency can further diminish users' confidence in offline social settings, as they may rely on familiar digital platforms rather than engaging in real-world social interactions.

5. Strategies for Building Confidence:

○ **Gradual Exposure:** Encouraging gradual exposure to face-to-face interactions can help users build confidence over time. Starting with small social interactions and gradually increasing exposure can alleviate anxiety and boost confidence.

○ **Skill Development:** Engaging in activities that promote social skills development, such as joining clubs or attending social events, can provide valuable practice and enhance confidence in real-world interactions.

○ **Positive Reinforcement:** Celebrating small successes and acknowledging personal growth in face-to-face interactions can bolster self-confidence and encourage further engagement in offline social settings.

Conclusion

While dating apps offer convenience and accessibility in connecting people, they can inadvertently contribute to reduced confidence in face-to-face interactions. Recognizing the importance of balanced social interactions and actively practicing real-world communication skills are essential steps in maintaining and enhancing confidence in offline social settings. By acknowledging these challenges and proactively addressing them, users can cultivate healthier and more fulfilling social relationships both online and offline.

Overcoming Social Anxiety

Pressure to Perform on Online Dating Platforms

Online dating platforms introduce unique pressures that can impact users' emotional well-being and interactions, particularly when transitioning from virtual to real-life scenarios:

1. **Curated Profiles and Impressions:**

   ○ **Idealized Presentations:** Users often curate their profiles to showcase their best attributes, interests, and photos. This curated presentation aims to attract potential matches and create a positive first impression.

   ○ **Pressure for Perfection:** The desire to present oneself in the best light can create pressure to appear flawless or exceptionally attractive. Users may feel compelled to exaggerate positive traits or downplay less favorable aspects to maximize their appeal.

2. **Heightened Expectations and Self-Doubt:**

   ○ **Expectation Management:** As users engage in virtual interactions, they may develop expectations about their matches based on curated profiles and initial messages. These expectations can create pressure to meet or exceed perceived standards during subsequent face-to-face meetings.

   ○ **Fear of Disappointment:** The discrepancy between online personas and real-life interactions can lead to self-doubt or fear of rejection. Users may worry about not living up to the expectations set by their online presence, fearing disappointment or disinterest from their matches.

3. **Transitioning to Real-Life Interactions:**

   ○ **Anxiety and Nervousness:** Moving from virtual interactions to real-life meetings can heighten anxiety and nervousness. Users may experience uncertainty about how their matches will perceive them in person, especially if their online interactions were predominantly text-based.

   ○ **Authenticity Concerns:** The pressure to maintain a positive impression can affect authenticity during face-to-face meetings. Users may feel inclined to continue projecting their curated persona rather than presenting their genuine selves, potentially hindering the development of authentic connections.

4. **Impact on Self-Esteem and Emotional Well-Being:**

   ○ **Self-Esteem Challenges:** The pressure to perform and make a positive impression can impact users' self-esteem. Rejection or perceived failure to meet expectations may reinforce feelings of inadequacy or unworthiness.

   ○ **Emotional Rollercoaster:** Users may experience emotional highs and lows throughout the dating process, from excitement and anticipation to disappointment or frustration. These fluctuations can affect overall emotional well-being and confidence in navigating future interactions.

5. **Strategies for Managing Pressure:**

○ **Authenticity and Transparency:** Encouraging genuine self-presentation can alleviate pressure and promote more authentic connections. Being honest about interests, values, and expectations from the outset can foster mutual understanding and reduce anxiety about meeting expectations.

○ **Mindfulness and Self-Reflection:** Practicing mindfulness techniques and self-reflection can help users manage feelings of self-doubt or anxiety. Recognizing and challenging unrealistic expectations or negative self-talk can promote a healthier mindset.

○ **Open Communication:** Establishing open communication with matches about fears or concerns related to meeting in person can facilitate mutual support and understanding. Discussing expectations and navigating potential challenges together can build trust and reduce pressure.

Conclusion

The pressure to perform on online dating platforms stems from curated profiles, heightened expectations, and the transition to real-life interactions. This pressure can impact users' self-esteem, emotional well-being, and authenticity in forming connections. By promoting honesty, managing expectations, and fostering open communication, users can navigate the challenges of online dating more confidently and authentically.

Miscommunication Concerns in Online Dating

Online dating platforms, primarily reliant on text-based communication, present challenges for individuals with social anxiety, particularly in interpreting social cues and expressing intentions accurately:

1. **Interpreting Social Cues:**

○ **Ambiguity in Text:** Text-based conversations lack non-verbal cues such as facial expressions, tone of voice, and body language, which are crucial for understanding context and emotions in face-to-face interactions.

○ **Difficulty Deciphering Intentions:** Without visual and auditory cues, individuals may struggle to accurately gauge the intentions, emotions, or underlying meaning behind their matches' messages. This ambiguity can lead to misinterpretations or misunderstandings.

2. **Anxiety Amplification:**

○ **Fear of Misunderstanding:** Individuals with social anxiety may fear being misunderstood or misinterpreted due to the inherent ambiguity in digital communication. Uncertainty about how their messages are perceived can intensify anxiety about forming a positive impression or maintaining a conversation.

○ **Overanalyzing Responses:** Socially anxious individuals may overanalyze messages, searching for hidden meanings or signs of rejection. This tendency can further exacerbate anxiety and self-doubt about their ability to communicate effectively.

3. **Expressing Intentions Clearly:**

○ **Fear of Rejection:** Social anxiety can hinder individuals from expressing their intentions or feelings clearly in fear of rejection or negative judgment. This fear may prevent them from initiating conversations or sharing personal information, impacting their ability to form meaningful connections.

○ **Difficulty Initiating Conversations:** Initiating and sustaining conversations can be challenging for individuals with social anxiety, especially when unsure about how their messages will be received. This hesitation can lead to missed opportunities for connection or interaction.

4. **Strategies for Managing Miscommunication:**

○ **Clarity in Communication:** Encouraging clear and concise communication can help mitigate miscommunication and reduce anxiety. Using straightforward language, asking clarifying questions, and expressing intentions openly can enhance mutual understanding.

○ **Utilizing Emojis and Tone Indicators:** Incorporating emojis, punctuation marks, or tone indicators (e.g., sarcasm tags) can clarify emotions and intentions in text-based messages. These visual cues can help bridge the gap left by the absence of non-verbal communication.

○ **Seeking Feedback:** Seeking feedback from trusted friends or peers on message content or communication style can provide reassurance and perspective. Constructive feedback can also help individuals refine their communication skills and build confidence over time.

5. **Professional Support:** Individuals experiencing significant challenges with miscommunication or anxiety may benefit from professional support, such as therapy or counseling. Cognitive-behavioral techniques can help address negative thought patterns, improve communication skills, and manage anxiety related to online dating interactions.

Conclusion

Miscommunication concerns in online dating, exacerbated by the absence of non-verbal cues and social anxiety, can impact individuals' ability to interpret intentions and express themselves clearly. By promoting clear communication, utilizing supportive strategies, and seeking appropriate support, individuals can navigate online dating interactions more effectively and confidently, despite the challenges posed by social anxiety.

Gradual Exposure and Social Anxiety in Online Dating

Individuals with social anxiety often face challenges in social interactions, including those facilitated by dating apps. Here's how gradual exposure through dating apps can help:

1. **Controlled Environment:**

○ **Safe Space for Practice:** Dating apps offer a controlled environment where individuals can engage in social interactions at their own pace and comfort level. This controlled setting can reduce the overwhelming nature of face-to-face interactions, providing a sense of safety and security.

2. **Building Communication Skills:**

○ **Practice in Communication:** Engaging with potential matches on dating apps allows individuals to practice initiating conversations, expressing interests, and maintaining dialogues. This practice can help build confidence in communication skills, which is crucial for overcoming social anxiety.

○ **Experimenting with Approaches:** Users can experiment with different communication approaches, such as initiating conversations, asking questions, or sharing personal anecdotes. This experimentation fosters a learning process where individuals can discover what works best for them in social interactions.

3. **Managing Anxiety Levels:**

○ **Reduced Immediate Pressure:** Unlike face-to-face interactions, online conversations on dating apps often involve less immediate pressure to respond or perform socially. This reduced pressure can alleviate anxiety symptoms, allowing individuals to focus on developing connections at their own pace.

○ **Control Over Interaction:** Users have control over when and how they engage with others on dating apps. This control empowers individuals to manage anxiety triggers, such as fear of rejection or negative judgment, by gradually exposing themselves to social interactions.

4. **Positive Reinforcement:**

○ **Building Positive Experiences:** Successful interactions and positive responses from matches can serve as reinforcement for individuals overcoming social anxiety. These experiences contribute to a sense of achievement and validation, boosting self-esteem and motivation to continue engaging socially.

5. **Challenges and Growth:**

○ **Navigating Rejections:** While dating apps offer opportunities for positive interactions, they also present challenges such as rejections or mismatches. Navigating these challenges can help individuals develop resilience and coping strategies, essential for managing anxiety in various social contexts.

○ **Progression Towards Offline Interactions:** Gradual exposure through dating apps can eventually lead to increased comfort with offline social interactions. As individuals build confidence and communication skills online, they may feel more prepared to transfer these skills to face-to-face settings.

Conclusion

Dating apps provide a valuable platform for individuals with social anxiety to engage in gradual exposure to social interactions. By offering a controlled environment for practicing communication skills, managing anxiety levels, and building positive experiences, dating apps support individuals in overcoming social anxiety barriers. With consistent practice and supportive strategies, users can develop confidence in social interactions both online and offline, contributing to personal growth and enhanced social well-being.

Seeking Support for Social Anxiety on Dating Apps

Individuals facing social anxiety often seek strategies and support systems to navigate social interactions, including those facilitated by dating apps. Here's how seeking support can be beneficial:

1. Professional Guidance:

○ **Therapeutic Support:** Seeking guidance from mental health professionals, such as therapists or counselors, can provide tailored strategies for managing social anxiety. Therapists can offer techniques like cognitive-behavioral therapy (CBT) to challenge negative thoughts, exposure therapy to gradually confront fears, and social skills training to enhance communication abilities.

2. Choosing Supportive Platforms:

○ **Feature-Rich Apps:** Opting for dating apps that prioritize features facilitating genuine connections can enhance the social experience for individuals with social anxiety. Platforms offering video calls, virtual events, or group activities provide opportunities for users to interact in ways that mirror real-life social dynamics while maintaining a level of comfort.

3. Benefits of Feature-Rich Apps:

○ **Video Calls:** Apps that integrate video calls allow users to engage in face-to-face interactions without the pressure of meeting in person immediately. This feature enables individuals to practice social skills, observe non-verbal cues, and build rapport with potential matches in a controlled setting.

○ **Group Activities:** Some platforms organize virtual group activities or events, such as games or discussions, fostering a sense of community and easing social anxiety by reducing the focus on one-on-one interactions. Participating in group settings can enhance social skills and provide opportunities for shared interests to emerge naturally.

4. Gradual Integration:

○ **Transitioning to Offline Interactions:** Supportive dating apps can facilitate a gradual transition from online interactions to offline meetings. By offering features that encourage meaningful connections and realistic social scenarios, these platforms help users build confidence in navigating real-life social settings.

5. Personal Growth and Confidence:

○ **Building Social Skills:** Engaging with supportive platforms encourages users to practice communication skills, manage anxiety triggers, and develop resilience in handling social challenges. Positive interactions and feedback contribute to personal growth, boosting self-esteem and enhancing overall social well-being.

6. Community and Understanding:

○ **Shared Experiences:** Being part of a community of users who understand and empathize with social anxiety can provide validation and support. Platforms that foster a supportive environment promote mutual understanding, reducing feelings of isolation and stigma associated with anxiety disorders.

Conclusion

Seeking support while using dating apps can significantly benefit individuals with social anxiety. Whether through professional guidance, choosing feature-rich platforms, or participating in community activities, users can enhance their social skills, manage anxiety effectively, and foster genuine connections. By leveraging supportive resources and platforms, individuals can navigate dating app interactions with confidence, paving the way for meaningful relationships and improved social well-being.

Chapter 11: Cultural and Societal Impacts of Dating Apps

Dating apps have brought about significant changes in cultural and societal norms, influencing relationship dynamics and expectations globally. This impact varies across cultures, shaping both individual behaviors and broader societal attitudes towards dating and relationships.

Changing Relationship Norms

1. **Shift in Dating Practices:**

   ○ **Casualization of Relationships:** Dating apps have popularized casual dating and non-committal interactions. They provide platforms where individuals can explore multiple relationships simultaneously, challenging traditional norms that prioritize monogamy and long-term commitment.

   ○ **Speed and Convenience:** The convenience and accessibility of dating apps have accelerated the pace of relationships. Users can initiate and terminate connections quickly, leading to shorter courtship periods and faster transitions between dating stages.

2. **Reevaluation of Relationship Expectations:**

   ○ **Focus on Compatibility:** Apps emphasize matching based on shared interests, values, and preferences, shifting the focus from traditional factors like social status or family approval. This encourages individuals to prioritize compatibility and personal fulfillment in relationships.

   ○ **Diverse Relationship Models:** Dating apps accommodate diverse relationship models, including polyamory, open relationships, and LGBTQ+ partnerships. They provide a platform for individuals to explore and express their unique relationship preferences beyond societal norms.

3. **Impact on Gender Dynamics:**

   ○ **Empowerment and Agency:** Dating apps have empowered individuals, particularly women, by providing greater control over their dating lives. Women can initiate conversations, set boundaries, and assert preferences without traditional gender roles dictating their actions.

   ○ **Challenges to Gender Stereotypes:** Platforms that promote inclusivity and respect for diverse gender identities challenge traditional gender stereotypes. They encourage users to embrace authenticity and acceptance in relationships, fostering more equitable dating practices.

Cultural Differences in Dating App Usage

1. **Adoption and Popularity:**

   ○ **Regional Preferences:** Dating app usage varies significantly across cultures and regions. In some cultures, there may be greater societal acceptance and adoption of digital dating platforms as mainstream avenues for meeting potential partners. In contrast, other cultures may prioritize traditional matchmaking methods or face cultural barriers to embracing online dating.

2. **Impact on Social Norms:**

○ **Generation Gaps:** Younger generations, influenced by digital connectivity and globalized media, tend to adopt dating apps more readily than older generations. This adoption can lead to generational gaps in dating behaviors and relationship expectations within societies.

○ **Cultural Adaptation:** Dating apps must navigate cultural sensitivities and norms to successfully penetrate new markets. Platforms often tailor their features, advertising, and user guidelines to align with cultural values and expectations, fostering acceptance and usability among diverse populations.

3. **Challenges and Opportunities:**

○ **Social Stigma:** In some cultures, there may be social stigma attached to online dating, particularly for women or LGBTQ+ individuals. Dating apps can challenge these stigmas by promoting inclusivity, privacy, and safety measures that protect user identities and preferences.

○ **Cultural Resilience:** Successful integration of dating apps into diverse cultural contexts requires sensitivity to local customs, values, and relationship traditions. Platforms that respect and adapt to cultural nuances can bridge cultural divides and facilitate meaningful connections across borders.

Conclusion

Dating apps are reshaping cultural and societal norms by influencing relationship practices, challenging gender dynamics, and adapting to diverse cultural contexts. They provide opportunities for individuals to explore new relationship models, assert personal agency, and navigate globalized dating landscapes. As these platforms continue to evolve, their impact on cultural attitudes towards relationships will likely shape future social norms and expectations worldwide.

Shift in Dating Practices

Casualization of Relationships

The advent of dating apps has significantly altered how people approach relationships. These platforms have popularized casual dating and non-committal interactions, providing an environment where individuals can explore multiple relationships simultaneously. This trend challenges traditional norms that have long prioritized monogamy and long-term commitment.

1. Ease of Access and Abundance of Choices

● **Swipe Culture:** Dating apps like Tinder, Bumble, and others have introduced a 'swipe' feature, making it easy for users to quickly browse through potential matches. This mechanism encourages users to make rapid decisions based on limited information, often leading to superficial connections focused on immediate attraction rather than deeper compatibility.

● **Infinite Options:** The vast pool of potential matches available on dating apps creates a sense of abundance. Users may feel less inclined to commit to a single partner when they know that many other options are just a swipe away. This abundance can foster a mentality of continuous searching for the 'perfect' match, rather than settling into a committed relationship.

2. Changing Attitudes Towards Commitment

● **Decreased Pressure for Long-Term Commitment:** With casual dating becoming more normalized, there is less societal pressure to commit to long-term relationships early on. People can take their time to explore different partners and experiences before deciding to settle down, if they choose to do so at all.

● **Normalization of Non-Monogamy:** Dating apps have provided a platform for exploring various forms of non-monogamous relationships, such as open relationships and polyamory. This exposure has contributed to the acceptance and normalization of these alternative relationship models, further challenging traditional monogamous norms.

3. Focus on Immediate Gratification

● **Instant Connectivity:** Dating apps offer instant communication, allowing users to connect and engage with potential matches quickly. This instant gratification can lead to a focus on short-term interactions and experiences rather than investing time in building long-term relationships.

● **Hookup Culture:** Many dating apps are associated with hookup culture, where the primary goal is casual sexual encounters rather than emotional intimacy or long-term commitment. This culture is particularly prevalent among younger users who may prioritize physical attraction and sexual experiences over deeper emotional connections.

4. Impact on Relationship Dynamics

- **Reduced Emotional Investment:** The casual nature of interactions on dating apps can lead to reduced emotional investment in any single relationship. When users engage in multiple casual relationships simultaneously, they may be less likely to develop deep emotional bonds with any one partner.
- **Temporary and Transitional Relationships:** Many relationships formed through dating apps are seen as temporary or transitional, serving as a way to pass time or fulfill short-term needs. This perspective can make it difficult for users to transition from casual dating to serious, committed relationships.

5. Challenges to Traditional Norms

- **Rejection of Traditional Timelines:** Traditional relationship timelines, such as dating for a specific period before getting engaged or married, are increasingly being rejected. People are more open to exploring different relationship trajectories that do not conform to conventional expectations.
- **Flexibility and Personal Autonomy:** Dating apps empower individuals to define their own relationship goals and timelines. This flexibility allows people to prioritize personal autonomy and self-discovery over adhering to societal expectations regarding relationships and commitment.

Conclusion

The casualization of relationships facilitated by dating apps represents a significant shift in modern dating culture. By providing platforms that encourage casual dating and non-committal interactions, these apps challenge traditional norms of monogamy and long-term commitment. While this trend offers greater flexibility and autonomy for individuals, it also presents challenges in forming deep, meaningful connections. As dating apps continue to evolve, their impact on relationship dynamics and societal norms will likely remain a topic of ongoing discussion and analysis.

Speed and Convenience

Dating apps have revolutionized the way people meet and interact, offering unprecedented speed and convenience in initiating and managing relationships. This technological advancement has significantly accelerated the pace of relationships, leading to shorter courtship periods and quicker transitions between different stages of dating.

1. Immediate Access to Potential Matches

- **24/7 Availability:** Dating apps are accessible at any time, allowing users to browse profiles and initiate connections whenever they have a moment, be it during a commute, a lunch break, or late at night. This constant availability means that the process of meeting new people is no longer limited to specific social events or activities.
- **Geographical Flexibility:** Users can connect with people in their immediate vicinity or broaden their search to include potential matches in different cities or countries. This flexibility increases the pool of potential partners, making it easier to find someone who meets specific preferences and criteria.

2. Efficient Matching Algorithms

● **Algorithm-Based Recommendations:** Modern dating apps use sophisticated algorithms to suggest matches based on users' preferences, behaviors, and shared interests. These algorithms streamline the search process, saving users time and effort in finding compatible partners.

● **Enhanced Filtering Options:** Users can filter potential matches based on various criteria such as age, location, interests, and lifestyle choices. These filters further refine the search, allowing users to quickly identify and connect with individuals who align with their dating goals.

3. Rapid Communication

● **Instant Messaging:** Dating apps provide instant messaging features, enabling users to initiate conversations immediately after matching. This instant communication reduces the traditional waiting period associated with meeting someone through conventional means.

● **Multimedia Messaging:** The ability to share photos, videos, and voice messages within the app enhances communication and allows users to build a rapport quickly. This multimedia interaction can create a sense of familiarity and intimacy, accelerating the relationship-building process.

4. Shorter Courtship Periods

● **Quick Decision-Making:** The swiping mechanism encourages users to make rapid decisions based on limited information, often leading to quick matches and immediate conversations. This fast-paced interaction can result in shorter courtship periods as users quickly determine their interest and compatibility.

● **Efficient Planning:** The convenience of scheduling dates through messaging apps means that users can arrange to meet in person within a short timeframe after connecting online. This efficiency speeds up the transition from online interaction to face-to-face meetings.

5. Accelerated Relationship Stages

● **Rapid Escalation:** The convenience of constant communication and easy access to potential matches can lead to rapid escalation of relationships. Users may progress through traditional dating stages—such as getting to know each other, developing emotional intimacy, and becoming physically involved—more quickly than in traditional dating scenarios.

● **Frequent Transitions:** The ease of initiating and terminating connections on dating apps means that users may experience frequent transitions between relationships. This dynamic can lead to shorter durations for individual relationships and a higher turnover of partners.

6. Impact on Relationship Dynamics

● **Superficial Interactions:** The speed and convenience of dating apps can sometimes result in more superficial interactions, where users prioritize quick connections over developing deeper emotional bonds. This focus on immediacy can affect the quality and depth of relationships.

● **Reduced Investment:** The fast-paced nature of app-based dating can lead to reduced emotional investment in any single relationship. Knowing that new potential matches are readily available may discourage users from putting in the effort required to nurture and sustain long-term relationships.

Conclusion

The speed and convenience offered by dating apps have profoundly impacted modern dating culture. These platforms have accelerated the pace of relationships, enabling users to initiate and terminate connections quickly and efficiently. While this rapid interaction offers numerous benefits, such as increased access to potential partners and efficient communication, it also presents challenges in fostering deep, meaningful connections. As dating apps continue to evolve, understanding their impact on relationship dynamics will be crucial for navigating the complexities of contemporary dating.

Reevaluation of Relationship Expectations

Focus on Compatibility

Dating apps have significantly shifted the dynamics of how relationships are formed by emphasizing compatibility over traditional factors such as social status, family approval, or economic background. This modern approach encourages individuals to prioritize shared interests, values, and personal fulfillment when seeking potential partners, fostering more meaningful and satisfying relationships.

1. Algorithm-Based Matching

- **Personalized Recommendations:** Dating apps utilize sophisticated algorithms that analyze users' profiles, preferences, and behaviors to suggest matches with high compatibility. These algorithms consider factors such as interests, hobbies, lifestyle choices, and personality traits to create personalized recommendations.
  - **Data-Driven Insights:** By leveraging large datasets, dating apps can identify patterns and preferences that may not be immediately apparent to users. This data-driven approach helps in finding matches that align closely with individual values and expectations.

2. Detailed Profiles

- **Comprehensive Information:** Users are encouraged to create detailed profiles that include information about their interests, values, and preferences. This comprehensive self-representation allows potential matches to assess compatibility beyond surface-level attributes.
  - **Emphasis on Values and Interests:** Profiles often feature sections dedicated to personal beliefs, long-term goals, and specific interests, which help users identify potential partners who share similar values and aspirations.

3. Compatibility Questions and Tests

- **Personality Assessments:** Some dating apps incorporate personality tests and questionnaires to gauge users' compatibility on a deeper level. These assessments evaluate traits such as communication style, emotional intelligence, and conflict resolution skills.
  - **Match Scores:** Based on the results of compatibility tests, apps provide match scores or compatibility percentages that indicate how well users might get along. This feature helps users prioritize potential matches with higher compatibility.

4. Focus on Shared Interests

- **Interest-Based Matching:** Many dating apps allow users to filter potential matches based on shared interests and activities. This focus on common hobbies and passions facilitates connections grounded in mutual enjoyment and shared experiences.
  - **Event and Activity Suggestions:** Some apps suggest events or activities that align with users' interests, encouraging them to meet in settings where they can bond over shared passions. This approach enhances the likelihood of developing meaningful connections.

5. Value-Driven Connections

- **Alignment of Beliefs and Goals:** Apps often prioritize matching individuals with similar values and long-term goals, such as career aspirations, family planning, and lifestyle choices. This alignment helps ensure that partners are compatible in key areas that affect relationship longevity and satisfaction.
  - **Open Communication:** Emphasizing values and preferences from the outset encourages open and honest communication about important topics. This transparency helps users establish a strong foundation for their relationships.

6. Reduced Influence of Traditional Factors

- **Independence from Social Status:** Unlike traditional dating scenarios, where social status or family approval might play a significant role, dating apps empower users to make independent choices based on personal compatibility. This shift allows individuals to prioritize their own happiness and fulfillment.
  - **Egalitarian Approach:** Dating apps promote an egalitarian approach to relationship formation, where the focus is on individual compatibility rather than external factors. This democratization of dating opens up opportunities for diverse and inclusive relationships.

7. Personal Fulfillment

- **Prioritizing Happiness:** By focusing on compatibility, dating apps encourage users to seek relationships that contribute to their personal happiness and well-being. This emphasis on fulfillment fosters healthier and more satisfying partnerships.
  - **Long-Term Satisfaction:** Relationships formed on the basis of shared values and interests are more likely to be enduring and fulfilling. Compatibility-driven connections help partners navigate challenges and grow together, enhancing long-term relationship satisfaction.

Conclusion

The focus on compatibility in dating apps represents a significant evolution in the way relationships are formed. By prioritizing shared interests, values, and personal fulfillment, these platforms enable individuals to forge deeper and more meaningful connections. This approach reduces the influence of traditional factors like social status or family approval, empowering users to prioritize their own happiness and well-being. As dating apps continue to refine their algorithms and features, the emphasis on compatibility will likely remain a central pillar in fostering successful and fulfilling relationships.

Diverse Relationship Models on Dating Apps

Dating apps have revolutionized the way individuals seek and form relationships, providing platforms that accommodate a wide variety of relationship models beyond traditional monogamy. These platforms offer inclusive features that support polyamory, open relationships, and LGBTQ+ partnerships, allowing users to explore and express their unique preferences in a way that aligns with their personal values and desires. Here's a detailed exploration of how dating apps support diverse relationship models:

1. Polyamory and Open Relationships

Profile Customization and Preferences

● **Relationship Status Options:** Many dating apps offer users the ability to specify their relationship status and intentions clearly. Options include "open relationship," "polyamorous," and "seeking multiple partners," allowing users to openly communicate their preferences from the start.

● **Customizable Search Filters:** Users can utilize filters to search for others with similar relationship preferences, making it easier to find compatible matches who are interested in polyamorous or open relationships.

Community Features

● **Groups and Forums:** Some apps provide community features such as groups and forums where users can discuss topics related to polyamory and open relationships. These spaces offer support, advice, and opportunities to connect with like-minded individuals.

● **Events and Meetups:** Dating apps may organize or promote events and meetups specifically for people interested in non-monogamous relationships, facilitating in-person connections within the polyamorous community.

Educational Resources

● **Information on Ethical Non-Monogamy:** Apps often include resources and articles about ethical non-monogamy, helping users understand the principles and practices involved. This education promotes healthy and consensual polyamorous relationships.

● **Guides on Communication and Boundaries:** Effective communication and setting boundaries are crucial in non-monogamous relationships. Dating apps may provide guides and tools to help users navigate these aspects successfully.

2. LGBTQ+ Partnerships

Inclusivity in Profile Options

● **Gender Identity and Sexual Orientation:** Dating apps are increasingly inclusive, allowing users to specify their gender identity and sexual orientation with a wide range of options beyond the binary choices. This inclusivity ensures that LGBTQ+ individuals can accurately represent themselves.

● **Preferred Pronouns:** Many platforms allow users to display their preferred pronouns, fostering respect and proper recognition of each individual's gender identity.

Safe Spaces for Connection

● **LGBTQ+ Specific Apps:** There are dating apps specifically designed for LGBTQ+ individuals, providing a safe and supportive environment tailored to the community's unique needs and experiences.

● **Inclusive Matching Algorithms:** General dating apps are also evolving to include inclusive matching algorithms that consider various gender identities and sexual orientations, ensuring that LGBTQ+ users receive relevant and respectful matches.

Community and Support

● **Resources for Coming Out and Support:** Apps may offer resources for users who are navigating their sexuality or gender identity, including coming out guides and mental health support.

● **Events and Social Gatherings:** Just as with polyamory, apps may promote LGBTQ+ friendly events and gatherings, both virtual and in-person, to help users connect in safe and affirming environments.

3. Expressing Unique Relationship Preferences

Personalized Profiles

- **Detailed Descriptions:** Users are encouraged to create detailed profiles where they can express their unique relationship preferences, interests, and values. This level of detail helps in finding truly compatible matches.
- **Bio Prompts and Tags:** Many apps offer bio prompts and tags that allow users to highlight specific aspects of their personalities or relationship desires, such as "open to polyamory," "seeking long-term partnership," or "interested in kink."

Transparency and Honesty

- **Encouraging Open Communication:** Dating apps promote transparency by encouraging users to be honest about their relationship intentions and preferences from the outset. This openness helps in forming connections based on mutual understanding and respect.
- **Match Questions and Compatibility Scores:** Some platforms include questions related to relationship models and preferences, generating compatibility scores that reflect users' alignment on these important issues.

Supportive Environment

- **Positive Reinforcement:** By fostering a supportive environment, dating apps help users feel confident and secure in expressing their unique relationship preferences without fear of judgment or discrimination.
- **Community Guidelines:** Strict community guidelines ensure that all users, regardless of their relationship preferences, are treated with respect and dignity. These guidelines help maintain a positive and inclusive atmosphere on the platform.

Conclusion

Dating apps have significantly expanded the possibilities for forming diverse and meaningful relationships by accommodating various relationship models. They provide platforms where individuals can explore polyamory, open relationships, and LGBTQ+ partnerships openly and safely. Through inclusive features, educational resources, and community support, dating apps empower users to express their unique relationship preferences and connect with others who share their values. This evolution in dating technology reflects a broader societal shift towards acceptance and inclusivity, allowing individuals to pursue fulfilling relationships that align with their true selves.

Impact on Gender Dynamics

Empowerment and Agency Through Dating Apps

Dating apps have significantly transformed the landscape of modern dating by empowering individuals to take control of their romantic lives. This empowerment is particularly notable among women, who traditionally have faced gender roles that limited their agency in dating. Here's a detailed exploration of how dating apps empower women and enhance their sense of agency:

1. Initiating Conversations

Breaking Traditional Gender Roles
- **Historical Context:** Traditionally, dating norms have often placed the onus on men to initiate conversations and make the first move. This dynamic can limit women's active participation in their romantic pursuits.
- **App Features:** Many dating apps, such as Bumble, specifically empower women by allowing them to initiate conversations. On Bumble, for instance, only women can send the first message in heterosexual matches, encouraging them to take charge of their interactions.

Confidence and Autonomy
- **Active Participation:** By initiating conversations, women can directly engage with potential matches who genuinely interest them, fostering a sense of autonomy and control over their dating lives.
- **Building Confidence:** The ability to make the first move can boost women's confidence and self-assurance, reducing the hesitation or fear of rejection often associated with traditional dating approaches.

2. Setting Boundaries

Control Over Interactions
- **Boundary Setting:** Dating apps empower women to set clear boundaries regarding their interactions. Features such as blocking, reporting, and filtering messages allow users to manage unwanted advances and ensure respectful communication.
- **Consent and Comfort:** Women can establish their comfort levels regarding topics of conversation, timing of replies, and progression of interactions, reinforcing the importance of consent and mutual respect in the dating process.

Safety and Security
- **Enhanced Safety Measures:** Many dating apps include safety features that allow users to report harassment, inappropriate behavior, or any concerns they may have. These features ensure that women can maintain control over their interactions and protect themselves from potential risks.
- **Verification Processes:** Some apps implement verification processes to reduce the likelihood of encountering fake profiles or deceptive individuals, enhancing users' overall sense of security.

3. Asserting Preferences

Personalized Profiles

- **Detailed Preferences:** Women can create detailed profiles that specify their preferences regarding potential partners, relationship goals, and personal values. This clarity helps attract matches who align with their expectations and desires.
- **Filter and Search Options:** Dating apps offer advanced filter and search options, allowing women to narrow down potential matches based on specific criteria such as interests, lifestyle, and values. This customization ensures that their dating experience is tailored to their unique preferences.

Empowered Decision-Making

- **Informed Choices:** With access to extensive profile information and communication tools, women can make informed decisions about who they engage with, avoiding connections that don't meet their standards or expectations.
- **Rejecting Stereotypes:** By asserting their preferences and taking control of their dating choices, women can reject societal stereotypes that often dictate whom they should date, instead focusing on what genuinely matters to them.

4. Balancing Power Dynamics

Equitable Interactions

- **Shared Responsibility:** Dating apps promote a more balanced power dynamic by enabling both parties to contribute equally to initiating and maintaining conversations. This shared responsibility fosters mutual respect and equality in interactions.
- **Empowerment Through Equality:** By leveling the playing field, dating apps empower women to engage in relationships where their voices are heard, their preferences are respected, and their autonomy is upheld.

Challenging Traditional Norms

- **Redefining Dating Norms:** The shift towards greater female agency on dating apps challenges traditional norms that often limited women's roles in dating. This redefinition encourages more egalitarian relationships where both partners contribute equally.
- **Social Change:** As more women embrace their empowerment through dating apps, societal perceptions of gender roles in dating evolve, promoting broader acceptance of women's agency and independence.

5. Creating Supportive Communities

Women-Centric Platforms

- **Female-Friendly Environments:** Some dating apps are designed specifically with women's safety and empowerment in mind, providing environments that prioritize respectful interactions and user well-being.
- **Support Networks:** These platforms often foster supportive communities where women can share experiences, seek advice, and connect with others who understand their challenges and aspirations.

Educational Resources

- **Empowerment Through Education:** Many dating apps offer resources and tips on navigating the dating world, including advice on setting boundaries, recognizing red flags, and building healthy relationships. These educational tools further empower women by providing them with knowledge and strategies for successful dating.

Conclusion

Dating apps have played a crucial role in empowering women by providing them with greater control over their dating lives. By enabling women to initiate conversations, set boundaries, and assert their preferences, these platforms challenge traditional gender roles and promote more equitable interactions. Through personalized profiles, enhanced safety features, and supportive communities, dating apps empower women to navigate the dating landscape with confidence and autonomy. This empowerment fosters not only personal growth but also broader social change, as societal norms continue to evolve towards greater gender equality and respect.

Challenges to Gender Stereotypes: Inclusivity and Respect in Dating Apps

Dating apps have the potential to be powerful tools in challenging and reshaping traditional gender stereotypes by promoting inclusivity and respect for diverse gender identities. By encouraging users to embrace authenticity and acceptance, these platforms can foster more equitable and progressive dating practices. Here is a detailed exploration of how dating apps challenge gender stereotypes and promote inclusivity:

1. Inclusivity in Gender Options

Beyond Binary Genders
- **Expanded Gender Categories:** Many dating apps have moved beyond the traditional binary gender options of male and female. They now offer a wide range of gender identities, such as non-binary, genderqueer, and genderfluid, allowing users to accurately represent their identities.
- **Personal Pronouns:** Users can specify their preferred pronouns, which promotes respect for their gender identity and encourages others to use the correct pronouns in interactions.

Visibility and Representation
- **Normalizing Diversity:** By including diverse gender options, dating apps normalize the presence of non-binary and gender-nonconforming individuals. This visibility helps to break down societal stereotypes and misconceptions about gender.
- **Community Support:** Platforms that celebrate gender diversity provide support and validation for users who may feel marginalized in other social contexts. This inclusivity fosters a sense of belonging and acceptance.

2. Encouraging Authentic Self-Expression

Authentic Profiles
- **Detailed Self-Descriptions:** Dating apps encourage users to create profiles that reflect their true selves, including their gender identity, interests, and values. This authenticity helps users find more compatible matches and builds a foundation for genuine connections.
- **Embracing Uniqueness:** By allowing users to express their individuality, dating apps challenge the notion that people must conform to traditional gender roles or stereotypes to be desirable.

Acceptance of Differences
- **Diverse Relationship Models:** Dating apps that support diverse relationship models, including polyamory and open relationships, challenge the traditional norms of monogamy and heteronormativity. This inclusivity promotes acceptance of different ways of forming and maintaining relationships.

● **Open Dialogue:** Platforms that encourage open dialogue about gender and relationships foster understanding and respect among users, helping to break down stereotypes and promote empathy.

3. Promoting Respect and Equality

Anti-Discrimination Policies
● **Zero Tolerance for Harassment:** Many dating apps have implemented strict policies against harassment, discrimination, and hate speech. These policies protect users from gender-based harassment and create a safer environment for everyone.
● **Reporting and Moderation:** Effective reporting mechanisms and active moderation ensure that discriminatory behavior is promptly addressed, reinforcing the platform's commitment to respect and equality.
Education and Awareness
● **Resources on Gender Identity:** Dating apps can provide educational resources on gender identity, helping users understand and respect the experiences of transgender and non-binary individuals. This awareness promotes a more inclusive and respectful dating culture.
● **Campaigns and Initiatives:** Platforms may run campaigns or initiatives that celebrate diversity and challenge gender stereotypes. These efforts raise awareness and encourage users to adopt more inclusive attitudes and behaviors.

4. Empowering Marginalized Genders

Supportive Communities
● **Safe Spaces:** Dating apps that cater specifically to LGBTQ+ communities provide safe spaces for users to explore relationships without fear of judgment or discrimination. These platforms empower marginalized genders by offering a supportive and understanding environment.
● **Community Building:** Features like forums, events, and social groups within dating apps help users connect with others who share similar experiences and challenges, fostering a sense of solidarity and empowerment.
Amplifying Voices
● **User Stories:** Sharing user stories and experiences related to gender identity and relationships can amplify the voices of marginalized individuals. This visibility helps to challenge stereotypes and educate the broader user base about diverse perspectives.
● **Influencers and Advocates:** Collaborating with influencers and advocates from diverse gender backgrounds can help raise awareness and promote acceptance within the dating app community.

5. Challenging Traditional Dating Norms

Reimagining Roles
● **Equal Participation:** Dating apps that encourage all users to initiate conversations, regardless of gender, challenge the traditional norm that men should make the first move. This promotes gender equality and empowers everyone to take control of their dating experiences.
● **Breaking Stereotypes:** By facilitating connections based on shared interests and values rather than traditional gender roles, dating apps help users see beyond stereotypes and appreciate the unique qualities of each individual.
Redefining Success

- **Focus on Compatibility:** Emphasizing compatibility and mutual respect over superficial attributes helps redefine what it means to be successful in dating. This shift encourages users to seek meaningful connections based on genuine understanding and acceptance.
- **Valuing Diversity:** Highlighting the importance of diversity and inclusivity in successful relationships challenges the notion that conformity to traditional gender roles is necessary for happiness and fulfillment.

Conclusion

Dating apps are at the forefront of challenging traditional gender stereotypes by promoting inclusivity and respect for diverse gender identities. By offering expanded gender options, encouraging authentic self-expression, and implementing anti-discrimination policies, these platforms create a more equitable and accepting dating environment. They empower marginalized genders, challenge traditional dating norms, and promote genuine connections based on mutual respect and understanding. As dating apps continue to evolve, their commitment to inclusivity and equality can help reshape societal attitudes towards gender and relationships, fostering a more inclusive and respectful world.

Adoption and Popularity

Regional Preferences in Dating App Usage

The adoption and use of dating apps vary significantly across different cultures and regions. These variations are influenced by societal norms, cultural values, technological infrastructure, and the level of acceptance of digital dating platforms. Here is a detailed exploration of how dating app usage differs regionally and the factors that contribute to these differences.

1. Societal Acceptance and Mainstream Adoption

Western Countries

- **High Adoption Rates:** In many Western countries, dating apps are widely accepted and have become mainstream tools for meeting potential partners. This acceptance is driven by the cultural norm of individualism and the emphasis on personal choice in romantic relationships.
- **Integration into Daily Life:** Dating apps in these regions are integrated into daily life, with people using them casually to expand their social circles, date, and find long-term partners. The convenience and accessibility of these platforms align with the fast-paced lifestyles of urban populations.

Eastern Countries

- **Growing Acceptance:** In many Eastern countries, the acceptance and use of dating apps are growing, particularly among younger generations who are more open to adopting new technologies. However, traditional values and societal expectations still play a significant role in shaping attitudes toward online dating.
- **Balancing Tradition and Modernity:** In countries like Japan, South Korea, and China, there is a balance between traditional matchmaking methods and the use of dating apps. While arranged marriages and family introductions are still common, dating apps provide an alternative for those seeking more autonomy in their romantic choices.

2. Cultural Values and Norms

Conservative Societies

- **Privacy and Discretion:** In conservative societies, where dating and relationships may be more private or restricted, dating apps are used discreetly. Users may prefer platforms that offer strong privacy features to protect their identities and maintain discretion.
- **Cultural Barriers:** Cultural barriers, such as stigma associated with online dating or societal disapproval of casual relationships, can limit the adoption of dating apps. In these regions, people may face challenges in openly using such platforms due to fear of judgment or backlash.

Liberal Societies

- **Openness to Digital Dating:** In more liberal societies, there is a greater openness to digital dating, and dating apps are seen as an extension of social interaction. The emphasis on personal freedom and individual rights supports the widespread use of these platforms.
- **Diverse Relationship Models:** These societies are often more accepting of diverse relationship models, including casual dating, polyamory, and same-sex relationships. Dating apps in these regions cater to a wide range of preferences and orientations.

3. Technological Infrastructure

Developed Countries
- **Advanced Technology:** In developed countries with advanced technological infrastructure, high-speed internet and widespread smartphone usage facilitate the adoption of dating apps. These regions have the resources to support sophisticated app features, enhancing user experience.
- **Innovation and Development:** The availability of technology encourages the development and innovation of new dating apps, leading to a competitive market with diverse options for users.

Developing Countries
- **Access Challenges:** In developing countries, limited access to the internet and smartphones can restrict the use of dating apps. Economic barriers and lack of technological infrastructure can pose significant challenges to widespread adoption.
- **Rising Adoption:** Despite these challenges, the increasing availability of affordable smartphones and internet services is driving the growth of dating app usage in these regions. As technology becomes more accessible, the adoption rates are expected to rise.

4. Traditional Matchmaking Methods

Cultural Significance
- **Role of Family and Community:** In many cultures, family and community play a central role in matchmaking. Arranged marriages, family introductions, and community events are traditional methods for finding partners, often prioritized over digital platforms.
- **Preserving Traditions:** Cultural practices and traditions hold significant importance in many regions. People may prefer traditional matchmaking methods to preserve cultural heritage and align with societal expectations.

Blending Traditions with Technology
- **Hybrid Approaches:** Some regions blend traditional methods with modern technology. For example, dating apps may incorporate features that allow family involvement or facilitate introductions within community networks. This hybrid approach respects cultural values while embracing technological advancements.
- **Cultural Customization:** Dating apps that cater to specific cultural preferences and traditions can find success in these regions. By customizing features and marketing strategies to align with cultural norms, these apps can better meet the needs of their target audience.

5. Unique Impacts of Dating App Usage

Western Influence
- **Global Trends:** The popularity of Western dating apps like Tinder, Bumble, and OkCupid has influenced dating cultures worldwide. These platforms introduce Western dating norms and practices, such as casual dating and swiping mechanisms, to diverse regions.
- **Adapting to Local Contexts:** Western dating apps often adapt their features to suit local contexts. For instance, they may introduce language options, cultural references, and region-specific marketing campaigns to appeal to local users.

Local Innovations

- **Regional Apps:** Local dating apps that cater specifically to regional preferences and cultural values have emerged. These apps often understand and address the unique needs of their users, offering features and experiences that resonate with local traditions.
- **Community Building:** Regional dating apps can foster a sense of community by connecting users with similar cultural backgrounds and values. They create spaces for users to explore relationships within their cultural contexts, promoting a sense of belonging and understanding.

Conclusion

The usage of dating apps varies significantly across cultures and regions, shaped by societal norms, cultural values, technological infrastructure, and traditional matchmaking methods. While some regions readily embrace digital dating platforms, others face cultural barriers or prioritize traditional methods. Understanding these regional preferences is crucial for dating app developers and users alike, as it highlights the importance of cultural sensitivity and adaptability in promoting successful and meaningful connections. As technology continues to evolve, the integration of traditional values with modern dating practices will shape the future of relationships globally.

Impact on Social Norms

Generation Gaps in Dating App Usage

Dating app usage exhibits significant generational differences, driven by varying levels of digital literacy, attitudes towards technology, and societal influences. Younger generations, who have grown up with digital connectivity and globalized media, are more likely to adopt dating apps compared to older generations. This divergence in adoption and attitudes can create noticeable generational gaps in dating behaviors and relationship expectations within societies. Here's a detailed exploration of these generational differences and their implications.

1. Digital Literacy and Comfort with Technology

Younger Generations
- **Native Users of Technology:** Millennials (born 1981-1996) and Generation Z (born 1997-2012) are often referred to as digital natives. They have grown up in an environment where digital technology is ubiquitous, making them more comfortable and proficient in using smartphones, social media, and dating apps.
- **Seamless Integration:** For these younger generations, integrating dating apps into their social lives feels natural. They are adept at navigating app interfaces, utilizing features, and leveraging technology to expand their social and romantic networks.

Older Generations
- **Digital Immigrants:** Baby Boomers (born 1946-1964) and Generation X (born 1965-1980) did not grow up with digital technology. They had to adapt to technological advancements later in life, often resulting in a steeper learning curve and less intuitive use of dating apps.
- **Traditional Preferences:** Older generations may prefer traditional methods of meeting potential partners, such as through mutual friends, family introductions, or community events. They may be more hesitant to embrace online dating due to unfamiliarity or distrust of digital platforms.

2. Attitudes Towards Online Dating

Younger Generations
- **Acceptance and Normalization:** Younger generations generally view online dating as a normal and acceptable way to meet people. The stigma that once surrounded online dating has diminished significantly, with many young adults considering dating apps as their primary method for finding romantic partners.
- **Casual Dating Culture:** The ease of access and the casual nature of many dating apps align with the dating behaviors of younger generations, who may be more open to exploring casual relationships, hookups, and short-term dating.

Older Generations
- **Skepticism and Caution:** Older individuals may approach online dating with more skepticism and caution. Concerns about privacy, safety, and the authenticity of online profiles can deter them from fully engaging with dating apps.
- **Focus on Long-Term Relationships:** Older generations may prioritize long-term relationships and commitment over casual dating. They might find the fast-paced and often superficial nature of dating apps misaligned with their relationship goals.

3. Impact of Globalized Media

Younger Generations

- **Exposure to Global Trends:** Access to globalized media exposes younger generations to diverse dating norms and practices. Influences from Western culture, popularized by movies, TV shows, and social media, have normalized the use of dating apps and modern dating behaviors.
- **Diverse Relationship Models:** Younger generations are more likely to encounter and accept diverse relationship models, such as polyamory, open relationships, and LGBTQ+ partnerships, often facilitated by inclusive dating apps.

Older Generations

- **Traditional Media Influences:** Older generations may be more influenced by traditional media, which often emphasizes conventional relationship norms and values. Their exposure to global dating trends might be limited compared to younger generations.
- **Cultural Retention:** While some older individuals may adopt dating apps, they often retain traditional values and expectations in their relationships, seeking stability and commitment over experimentation.

4. Generational Gaps in Dating Behaviors

Younger Generations

- **Embracing Change:** Younger generations are more adaptable and willing to experiment with different dating formats and relationship structures. They are more likely to embrace change and redefine traditional dating norms.
- **Quick Adaptation:** These generations quickly adapt to new dating app features, trends, and updates, making them more agile in navigating the evolving landscape of digital dating.

Older Generations

- **Conservatism in Dating:** Older generations may adhere more closely to conservative dating practices, valuing courtship, stability, and familial approval. Their dating behaviors often reflect a slower, more deliberate approach to forming relationships.
- **Resistance to Change:** There may be resistance to changing long-established dating practices, leading to a slower adoption of new dating technologies and methods.

5. Implications of Generational Gaps

Intergenerational Understanding

- **Bridging the Gap:** Intergenerational dialogue and understanding can help bridge the gap between differing dating behaviors and expectations. Younger individuals can assist older generations in navigating dating apps, while older generations can offer wisdom and perspective on long-term relationship building.
- **Mutual Respect:** Recognizing and respecting the different approaches and values of each generation can foster mutual respect and reduce generational conflicts related to dating and relationships.

Evolving Dating Platforms

- **Catering to All Ages:** Dating app developers can create platforms that cater to the needs of all age groups, offering features that appeal to both younger and older users. Inclusive design, user-friendly interfaces, and robust safety measures can enhance the experience for all.
- **Educational Resources:** Providing educational resources on the use of dating apps and the importance of digital literacy can empower older generations to engage confidently with these platforms.

Conclusion

Generational gaps in dating app usage highlight the differences in digital literacy, attitudes towards technology, and societal influences between younger and older generations. While younger generations readily adopt dating apps and embrace modern dating behaviors, older generations may approach these platforms with caution and a preference for traditional methods. Understanding these generational differences is crucial for fostering intergenerational dialogue, mutual respect, and inclusive dating environments that cater to diverse needs and expectations. As dating apps continue to evolve, bridging the generational divide will be key to promoting meaningful connections and enhancing the dating experiences of users across all age groups.

Cultural Adaptation in Dating Apps: Navigating Sensitivities and Norms

As dating apps expand into new markets, they must navigate cultural sensitivities and norms to gain acceptance and usability among diverse populations. This process, known as cultural adaptation, involves tailoring features, advertising, and user guidelines to align with local values and expectations. Here's a detailed exploration of how dating apps achieve cultural adaptation and the various factors they consider.

1. Understanding Local Cultural Values

Cultural Research and Sensitivity
- **In-depth Research:** Successful cultural adaptation begins with thorough research into the cultural, social, and religious values of the target market. Understanding these values helps app developers design features and content that resonate with local users.
- **Sensitivity to Norms:** Cultural sensitivities around dating, gender roles, family expectations, and privacy vary widely. Apps must be sensitive to these norms to avoid offending potential users and to foster a respectful and inclusive environment.

Respecting Social Norms
- **Conservative Societies:** In more conservative societies, dating apps might need to implement features that allow for discreet interactions. For example, offering options to blur profile pictures or providing more stringent privacy settings can help users feel secure.
- **Gender Dynamics:** Understanding gender dynamics is crucial. In some cultures, it may be necessary to allow women more control over who can view their profiles or initiate conversations, addressing concerns around safety and autonomy.

2. Tailoring Features and Functionality

Localized Features
- **Language Customization:** Offering the app in local languages is fundamental. Beyond simple translation, localization ensures that idiomatic expressions and cultural references make sense to the target audience.
- **Customizable Search Filters:** Including filters that cater to specific cultural or religious practices can enhance the user experience. For example, options to filter matches based on religious beliefs, dietary preferences, or cultural practices can be valuable in multicultural settings.

Privacy and Safety Measures

- **Enhanced Privacy Settings:** In cultures where public dating is stigmatized, apps may offer enhanced privacy settings, such as the ability to hide profiles from specific contacts or regions.
- **Verification Features:** Robust verification features can build trust among users by reducing the prevalence of fake profiles. This is particularly important in markets where online dating is met with skepticism.

3. Culturally Relevant Advertising

Marketing Strategies
- **Localized Advertising Campaigns:** Advertisements should reflect local culture, using familiar symbols, scenarios, and language. Campaigns might feature local celebrities or influencers to build credibility and relatability.
- **Cultural Sensitivity in Messaging:** Marketing messages should be crafted to respect local values and norms. This might involve emphasizing family-oriented narratives or the app's role in facilitating meaningful, long-term relationships in markets where casual dating is less accepted.

Collaborations and Partnerships
- **Local Partnerships:** Collaborating with local organizations, influencers, or media outlets can help apps gain trust and credibility. These partnerships can also provide valuable insights into local preferences and behaviors.
- **Community Engagement:** Engaging with local communities through events, sponsorships, or content creation can build a positive brand image and foster user loyalty.

4. User Guidelines and Support

Culturally Informed User Guidelines
- **Clear Conduct Guidelines:** Establishing clear guidelines that reflect local cultural norms can help maintain a respectful and safe user environment. These guidelines should address acceptable behavior, communication etiquette, and privacy practices.
- **Reporting and Moderation:** Effective reporting and moderation systems are essential to address harassment or inappropriate behavior swiftly. In culturally sensitive markets, apps might need to provide additional support to users facing social or familial pressure.

Localized Customer Support
- **Accessible Support Channels:** Offering customer support in local languages and through familiar channels (e.g., popular messaging apps) can enhance user satisfaction. Providing culturally sensitive support ensures users feel understood and respected.
- **Education and Resources:** Educating users about online safety, privacy, and respectful interactions is crucial. This can include in-app tutorials, FAQs, or partnerships with local organizations focused on digital literacy and safety.

5. Case Studies of Cultural Adaptation

Example 1: Bumble in India
- **Localized Features:** Bumble introduced features like "Religion" and "Caste" filters to cater to the specific needs of Indian users. The app also emphasized safety features such as "Women Make the First Move" to align with cultural dynamics.
- **Culturally Relevant Campaigns:** Bumble's marketing campaigns in India featured prominent Bollywood actresses and focused on themes of empowerment and modern relationships, resonating with the local audience.

Example 2: Tinder in Japan
- **Privacy and Discretion:** Recognizing the need for discretion in Japan's conservative dating culture, Tinder implemented features that allowed users to hide their profiles from specific contacts.
- **Localized Content:** Tinder's marketing efforts in Japan included collaborations with local influencers and campaigns that highlighted cultural practices, such as group dating.

Conclusion

Cultural adaptation is a critical process for dating apps seeking to enter and thrive in new markets. By understanding and respecting local cultural values, tailoring features and functionality, creating culturally relevant advertising, and providing localized support, dating apps can foster acceptance and usability among diverse populations. This approach not only enhances user experience but also builds trust and credibility, ultimately contributing to the app's success in various cultural contexts.

Challenges and Opportunities

Social Stigma: Challenging Norms with Inclusivity, Privacy, and Safety Measures

Dating apps, while widely accepted in many parts of the world, often face significant social stigma in certain cultures. This stigma can be particularly pronounced for women and LGBTQ+ individuals, who may encounter societal disapproval or discrimination for using online dating platforms. However, dating apps have the potential to challenge and change these stigmas by promoting inclusivity, privacy, and safety measures. Here's a detailed exploration of these dynamics and the steps dating apps can take to address them.

1. Understanding Social Stigma in Different Cultures

Cultural Sensitivities

- **Gender Norms:** In many cultures, traditional gender norms dictate that women should not actively seek out romantic relationships. Women using dating apps may be viewed as contravening these norms, leading to social backlash or judgment.
- **LGBTQ+ Discrimination:** LGBTQ+ individuals often face heightened scrutiny and discrimination. In regions where non-heteronormative relationships are stigmatized or even criminalized, using dating apps can be particularly risky.

Privacy Concerns

- **Fear of Exposure:** Fear of exposure is a significant concern. Users worry about being recognized on dating apps, which could lead to social ostracism, professional repercussions, or familial conflicts.

2. Promoting Inclusivity

Inclusive Marketing and Messaging

- **Representation Matters:** Dating apps can promote inclusivity by featuring diverse users in their marketing campaigns. This includes showcasing people of different genders, sexual orientations, ethnicities, and body types to reflect the diversity of their user base.
- **Empowerment Narratives:** Campaigns that focus on empowerment and autonomy can help shift cultural narratives. Highlighting stories of individuals finding meaningful connections or love through the app can normalize online dating and challenge stigmas.

Support for LGBTQ+ Communities

- **LGBTQ+ Specific Features:** Offering features specifically designed for LGBTQ+ users, such as gender identity and sexual orientation options, can make these communities feel seen and supported.
- **Partnerships with LGBTQ+ Organizations:** Collaborating with local LGBTQ+ organizations can enhance credibility and provide resources for users. This partnership can also help in understanding the unique challenges faced by LGBTQ+ individuals in different cultural contexts.

3. Enhancing Privacy Measures

Anonymity and Discretion

- **Profile Privacy Settings:** Implementing robust privacy settings allows users to control who can see their profiles. Features like "incognito mode" or the ability to hide profiles from contacts can help protect users' identities.
- **Discreet App Icons:** In regions where social stigma is high, apps can offer discreet icons and names that don't immediately identify them as dating platforms, thus providing an extra layer of privacy.

Secure Communication

- **End-to-End Encryption:** Ensuring that messages are end-to-end encrypted protects users' conversations from being intercepted or exposed.
- **Temporary Chat Features:** Features that allow messages or photos to disappear after a certain time can enhance privacy and reduce the risk of sensitive information being leaked.

4. Implementing Safety Measures

User Verification and Reporting

- **Verification Processes:** Implementing robust verification processes helps ensure that users are interacting with real individuals. This can involve photo verification, linking to social media accounts, or other methods that confirm identity.
- **Report and Block Features:** Easy-to-use report and block features empower users to take action against harassment, abuse, or inappropriate behavior. Swift and effective moderation is crucial to maintaining a safe environment.

Educational Resources and Support

- **Safety Tips:** Providing in-app safety tips and resources can educate users on best practices for protecting their privacy and security. This includes advice on meeting in public places, informing friends or family about dates, and recognizing red flags.
- **Mental Health Support:** Access to mental health resources or partnerships with counseling services can offer support to users dealing with the stress or anxiety related to online dating and societal pressures.

5. Challenging Social Norms and Reducing Stigma

Community Building and Advocacy

- **Online Communities:** Creating online communities within the app where users can share experiences, advice, and support can foster a sense of belonging and reduce feelings of isolation.
- **Advocacy Campaigns:** Engaging in advocacy campaigns that promote the acceptance of online dating can help shift societal perceptions. This includes public endorsements by influencers, celebrities, or respected community leaders.

Feedback and Adaptation

- **User Feedback:** Regularly gathering feedback from users helps apps understand the evolving needs and concerns of their communities. This feedback can guide the development of new features or policies that better address privacy, safety, and inclusivity.
- **Cultural Adaptation:** Continuously adapting the app to align with cultural norms while pushing for progressive changes is essential. This involves a balance between respecting cultural sensitivities and advocating for the rights and safety of all users.

Conclusion

Dating apps have the potential to challenge and change social stigmas by promoting inclusivity, enhancing privacy, and implementing robust safety measures. By understanding the unique cultural contexts and addressing the concerns of women and LGBTQ+ individuals, these platforms can create a more inclusive and supportive environment. Through thoughtful design, sensitive marketing, and strong community support, dating apps can play a crucial role in reshaping societal norms and fostering acceptance for diverse forms of romantic relationships.

Cultural Resilience in Dating Apps: Bridging Divides and Facilitating Connections

Dating apps, while global in reach, encounter diverse cultural landscapes that shape user behaviors, expectations, and acceptance. Achieving cultural resilience involves understanding and respecting local customs, values, and relationship traditions. By adapting features and policies to align with cultural nuances, dating apps can bridge divides and foster meaningful connections across borders. Here's a detailed exploration of how cultural resilience is crucial for dating apps:

1. Understanding Local Customs and Values

Respect for Tradition

- **Cultural Sensitivity:** Different cultures have varying attitudes towards relationships, marriage, and dating practices. For example, some cultures prioritize arranged marriages or courtship rituals, while others emphasize individual choice and autonomy.
- **Religious Considerations:** Religious beliefs often influence relationship norms and behaviors. Dating apps must navigate sensitivities related to dating outside one's faith or cultural expectations regarding modesty and gender roles.

Social Etiquette

- **Communication Styles:** Cultural differences in communication styles impact how users interact on dating apps. Some cultures value indirect communication and subtlety, while others prioritize directness and clarity.
- **Social Taboos:** Topics such as sexuality, marriage, and family dynamics may be sensitive or taboo in certain cultures. Apps must navigate these topics respectfully to avoid cultural insensitivity.

2. Adapting Features to Cultural Nuances

Localized Features

- **Language Support:** Providing multilingual support allows users to navigate the app in their preferred language, enhancing accessibility and user experience.
- **Customized Filters:** Offering filters based on cultural preferences, such as dietary practices, religious observances, or regional interests, helps users find matches aligned with their cultural values.

Privacy and Identity Protection

- **Anonymity Options:** In regions with strong social stigma around dating, apps can offer features like discreet app icons or profile visibility controls to protect users' privacy and identity.
- **Data Security:** Ensuring robust data security measures is crucial to safeguarding users' personal information, especially in regions where data privacy laws may be less stringent.

3. Building Trust Through Transparency

Clear Policies and Guidelines
- **Privacy Policies:** Transparent and accessible privacy policies inform users about how their data will be used and protected. This transparency builds trust and reassures users concerned about privacy breaches or misuse of personal information.
- **Community Guidelines:** Clearly defined community guidelines outline expected behaviors and consequences for violating norms, promoting a respectful and safe dating environment.

4. Supporting Cultural Inclusivity

Representation and Diversity
- **Inclusive Marketing:** Featuring diverse representations in marketing campaigns, including people of different ethnicities, religions, and sexual orientations, demonstrates commitment to inclusivity.
- **Community Engagement:** Engaging with local communities through partnerships, events, or initiatives fosters trust and understanding, demonstrating a commitment to respecting and supporting cultural diversity.

5. Navigating Regulatory and Legal Frameworks

Compliance with Local Laws
- **Legal Compliance:** Adhering to local laws and regulations regarding data privacy, consumer protection, and online communication is essential. This ensures apps operate within legal boundaries and maintain trust with users and regulatory authorities.
- **Cultural Sensitivity Training:** Providing cultural sensitivity training to staff and moderators helps ensure that app policies and practices align with cultural norms and sensitivities.

Conclusion

Cultural resilience in dating apps involves adapting to and respecting diverse cultural contexts to facilitate meaningful connections. By understanding local customs, values, and relationship traditions, apps can bridge cultural divides and build trust among users from different backgrounds. Through localized features, transparent policies, and inclusive practices, dating apps can promote cultural inclusivity and contribute to cross-cultural understanding in the realm of modern relationships.

Chapter 12: The Business of Dating Apps: Monetization and User Retention Strategies

Dating apps have revolutionized how people connect romantically, but they are also robust business ventures that employ various strategies to monetize their platforms and retain users. Here's a detailed analysis of the monetization strategies and user retention tactics employed by dating apps:

Monetization Strategies

1. Subscription Models

- **Premium Features:** Many dating apps offer tiered subscription models that unlock premium features such as unlimited swipes, advanced search filters, and ad-free experiences.
- **Subscription Plans:** Apps typically offer monthly, quarterly, or annual subscription plans, with discounts for longer commitments to encourage retention.

2. In-App Purchases

- **Virtual Currency:** Some apps use virtual currencies or tokens that users can purchase to unlock additional features or boost visibility in search results.
- **Gifts and Boosts:** Users may buy virtual gifts or boosts that enhance their profile visibility or send virtual gifts to other users, generating revenue for the app.

3. Advertising Revenue

- **Display Ads:** Dating apps often display targeted ads based on user demographics and preferences. These ads can be a significant source of revenue, especially for free-to-use apps.
- **Sponsored Content:** Apps may collaborate with brands for sponsored content or partnerships, integrating promotional campaigns that resonate with their user base.

4. Freemium Model

- **Basic vs. Premium:** Many dating apps operate on a freemium model, offering basic functionalities for free while charging for premium features or ad-free experiences to generate revenue.

5. Partnerships and Affiliations

- **Affiliate Marketing:** Apps may earn commissions through affiliate marketing by promoting third-party services or products relevant to their user base, such as matchmaking services or relationship counseling.

User Retention Strategies

1. Engagement Features

- **Interactive Features:** Dating apps introduce interactive features like quizzes, games, or icebreakers to encourage user engagement and interaction beyond swiping profiles.
- **Messaging Tools:** Robust messaging tools with multimedia support and voice messaging can enhance communication and keep users engaged on the platform.

2. Personalization and Algorithms

- **Matching Algorithms:** Advanced algorithms analyze user data and behavior to suggest highly compatible matches, improving user satisfaction and retention.
- **Personalized Recommendations:** Apps provide personalized recommendations based on user preferences and previous interactions, increasing the likelihood of meaningful connections.

3. Safety and Security

- **Trust and Safety Features:** Implementing robust safety measures, such as profile verification, reporting systems for inappropriate behavior, and data encryption, enhances user trust and retention.
- **Moderation and Support:** Prompt and effective moderation of content and user support services help maintain a safe and respectful community environment.

4. Retention Campaigns

- **Push Notifications:** Apps use targeted push notifications to re-engage users with new matches, messages, or special promotions, reminding them to return to the platform.
- **Incentives and Rewards:** Offering incentives such as free boosts, premium trials, or discounts on subscriptions can incentivize users to remain active on the app.

5. Continuous Innovation

- **Feature Updates:** Regular updates and feature enhancements based on user feedback and technological advancements keep the app competitive and appealing to users.
- **Adapting to Trends:** Staying abreast of dating trends and cultural shifts allows apps to adapt their offerings and stay relevant in a dynamic market.

Conclusion

Dating apps leverage a variety of monetization strategies, including subscriptions, in-app purchases, advertising, and partnerships, to generate revenue while employing sophisticated user retention tactics. By prioritizing user engagement, personalization, safety, and continuous innovation, dating apps can foster a loyal user base and sustain growth in a competitive industry. Balancing monetization with user experience remains crucial to maintaining trust and longevity in the ever-evolving landscape of digital dating.

Subscription Models in Dating Apps

Dating apps employ subscription models as a primary monetization strategy, offering users enhanced features and experiences in exchange for recurring payments. Here's a detailed explanation of how subscription models work in dating apps:

Premium Features

Dating apps often entice users to subscribe by offering a range of premium features that enhance the user experience beyond what's available in the free version:

1. **Unlimited Swipes:** Free users may be limited in the number of profiles they can swipe through daily. Subscribers typically enjoy unlimited swipes, allowing them to explore more profiles and increase their chances of finding matches.
2. **Advanced Search Filters:** Subscribers often gain access to advanced search filters that enable them to narrow down their potential matches based on specific criteria such as location, interests, education, or relationship preferences.
3. **Ad-Free Experience:** Ads can interrupt the user experience and detract from engagement. Subscribers enjoy an ad-free environment, which enhances usability and reduces distractions while navigating the app.
4. **Rewind and Undo Actions:** Some apps offer a "rewind" feature that allows subscribers to undo accidental swipes or revisit profiles they've passed on, giving them more control over their interactions.
5. **Boosts and Visibility:** Subscribers may receive periodic boosts that increase their profile visibility for a certain duration, making them more likely to be seen and matched with other users.
6. **Messaging and Communication:** Enhanced messaging features such as the ability to see read receipts, send unlimited messages, or access to special emojis and gifs can be exclusive to subscribers.

Subscription Plans

Dating apps typically offer various subscription plans to cater to different user preferences and budgets:

1. **Monthly Plans:** Users can subscribe on a month-to-month basis, paying a fixed amount each month for access to premium features. This plan offers flexibility for users who may not want a long-term commitment.
2. **Quarterly Plans:** Quarterly subscriptions extend the commitment period to three months, often at a slightly discounted rate compared to monthly plans. This encourages users to commit to the platform for a longer duration.
3. **Annual Plans:** Annual subscriptions provide the most significant discounts compared to monthly and quarterly plans. Users pay upfront for a year of access to premium features, offering the best value for money and promoting long-term user retention.

Discounts and Promotions

To incentivize longer commitments and increase retention, dating apps frequently offer discounts and promotions:

- **Introductory Offers:** New users may receive discounted rates or free trials for the first subscription period, encouraging them to explore premium features before committing fully.

- **Renewal Incentives:** Apps may offer discounts or bonuses for users who renew their subscriptions before they expire, rewarding loyalty and reducing churn.
- **Bundle Offers:** Some apps bundle subscriptions with other services or features, providing added value and attracting users looking for comprehensive dating experiences.

User Benefits and App Revenue

Subscription models not only enhance user experience by offering valuable features but also provide a steady revenue stream for dating apps:

- **Predictable Revenue:** Recurring subscriptions provide predictable income, allowing apps to forecast finances and allocate resources effectively.
- **Enhanced User Engagement:** Premium features incentivize users to stay active and engaged on the app, increasing overall retention rates and user satisfaction.
- **Balancing Free and Paid Features:** Apps often maintain a balance between free and premium features to attract a wide user base while monetizing through subscriptions.

Conclusion

Subscription models play a crucial role in the monetization strategy of dating apps, offering users enhanced features and experiences in exchange for regular payments. By providing valuable benefits such as unlimited swipes, advanced filters, ad-free browsing, and exclusive communication tools, apps incentivize users to subscribe and contribute to sustainable growth and profitability in the competitive online dating market.

In-App Purchases in Dating Apps

In addition to subscription models, many dating apps leverage in-app purchases (IAPs) as another monetization strategy. These purchases typically involve virtual currencies, tokens, or gifts that users can buy to enhance their experience or interactions within the app. Here's a detailed look at how in-app purchases work in dating apps:

Virtual Currency and Tokens

1. **Purpose:** Virtual currencies or tokens serve as a form of digital currency within the app, allowing users to unlock additional features or perform specific actions that enhance their profile visibility or interaction capabilities.

2. **Acquisition:** Users acquire virtual currency or tokens through real-money transactions within the app. This can be done via credit card, PayPal, or other digital payment methods integrated into the platform.

3. **Usage Examples:**

○ **Boosts:** Users can purchase boosts that temporarily increase their profile's visibility in search results or on the app's homepage, making them more likely to be seen by other users.

○ **Super Likes:** Some apps offer a premium feature where users can send "super likes" or equivalent gestures to indicate high interest in another user's profile.

○ **Profile Enhancements:** Virtual currency may also be used to purchase profile enhancements such as additional photo slots, customization options, or badges that denote premium status.

4. **Economy Management:** Apps manage the virtual currency economy by setting prices for tokens and creating incentives for users to purchase them. This includes offering discounts for bulk purchases or periodic promotions to stimulate buying behavior.

Gifts and Boosts

1. **Purpose:** In-app purchases often include virtual gifts or boosts that users can send to other users, enhancing their visibility or expressing interest without direct messaging.
2. **Gifts:** Users can purchase and send virtual gifts, such as virtual flowers, drinks, or other digital tokens of affection, to other users as a way to initiate or enhance communication.
3. **Boosts:** Similar to profile boosts mentioned earlier, users may buy boosts that temporarily increase the visibility or prominence of another user's profile, providing a form of digital endorsement or attention.

Revenue Generation and User Engagement

1. **Revenue Streams:** In-app purchases generate revenue beyond subscription models by monetizing specific actions or enhancements that appeal to users seeking additional visibility or interaction advantages.
2. **User Engagement:** By offering virtual currency, tokens, gifts, and boosts, apps encourage increased user engagement and interaction within the platform. This can lead to higher user retention rates and overall satisfaction with the app experience.
3. **Monetization Strategy:** Dating apps carefully balance free and paid features to provide value to both paying and non-paying users. Virtual currency systems help apps maximize revenue while maintaining a

user-friendly experience.

Considerations for Users

1. **Cost and Value:** Users should consider the cost versus value of virtual purchases and how they align with their dating goals and budget.
2. **Privacy and Security:** Secure payment methods and clear policies regarding virtual purchases ensure user confidence in financial transactions within the app.

Conclusion

In-app purchases, including virtual currency, tokens, gifts, and boosts, represent a significant revenue stream for dating apps. By offering users enhanced visibility, communication tools, and interactive features through these purchases, apps can deepen user engagement and monetize user interactions beyond subscription fees. Effective management of virtual economies and user incentives helps apps sustain growth while providing a compelling and competitive online dating experience.

Advertising Revenue in Dating Apps

Dating apps utilize advertising as a key revenue stream, leveraging targeted ads and sponsored content to monetize their platforms. Here's a detailed exploration of how advertising revenue works in dating apps:

Display Ads

1. Targeting and Placement:

○ **Targeted Ads:** Dating apps collect user data such as demographics, location, interests, and behaviors to deliver targeted advertisements. These ads appear within the app interface, often integrated into user profiles, search results, or in between swiping sessions.

○ **Contextual Relevance:** Ads are tailored to match user interests and dating preferences, enhancing relevance and engagement.

2. Revenue Generation:

○ **Cost-per-Impression (CPM):** Advertisers pay dating apps based on the number of impressions (views) their ads receive. CPM rates vary depending on ad placement and targeting criteria.

○ **Click-through Rates (CTR):** Apps may also earn revenue based on clicks generated by users interacting with ads.

3. Ad Formats:

○ **Banner Ads:** Traditional display ads appear as banners within the app interface, promoting products, services, or other apps relevant to users' interests.

○ **Interstitial Ads:** Full-screen ads that appear between swipes or during transitions within the app, ensuring high visibility and engagement.

Sponsored Content

1. Collaborations and Partnerships:

○ **Branded Partnerships:** Dating apps collaborate with brands for sponsored content, integrating promotional campaigns that resonate with their user base.

○ **Native Advertising:** Sponsored posts or articles within the app blend seamlessly with regular content, offering informative or entertaining content while subtly promoting brands or products.

2. Revenue Impact:

○ **Fixed Fees or Performance-Based:** Brands may pay dating apps a fixed fee for sponsored content or engage in performance-based models where payment is linked to user actions such as app downloads or purchases.

○ **Long-term Partnerships:** Apps benefit from ongoing sponsorships and collaborations that provide predictable revenue streams and enhance user engagement through relevant content.

User Experience Considerations

1. **Balancing User Experience:** Apps strive to maintain a balance between monetization through ads and preserving a positive user experience.

○ **Ad Relevance:** Relevant ads enhance user engagement by aligning with user interests without disrupting the dating experience.

○ **Ad Frequency:** Managing ad frequency ensures ads do not overwhelm users, maintaining a seamless and enjoyable browsing experience.

2. **Data Privacy and Consent:**

○ **User Consent:** Apps prioritize user privacy and data protection, obtaining consent for personalized advertising and ensuring compliance with data privacy regulations.

○ **Transparency:** Clear policies and opt-out options empower users to control their ad preferences and data usage within the app.

Conclusion

Advertising revenue is integral to the financial sustainability of dating apps, particularly for free-to-use platforms. By leveraging targeted display ads and sponsored content, apps monetize user engagement while providing brands with effective channels to reach their target audiences. Strategic partnerships and innovative ad formats enhance revenue opportunities while enhancing the overall app experience, fostering a thriving ecosystem for users and advertisers alike.

Freemium Model in Dating Apps

Dating apps frequently employ a freemium model to monetize their platforms, providing basic features at no cost while offering premium upgrades for a fee. Here's a detailed exploration of how the freemium model works in dating apps:

Basic vs. Premium Features

1. **Basic Features:**

   ○ **Free Access:** Users can access essential functionalities such as creating a profile, browsing matches, and sending basic messages without charge.

   ○ **Limited Usage:** Basic users may encounter restrictions on the number of daily swipes, access to detailed profiles, or advanced search filters.

2. **Premium Features:**

   ○ **Enhanced Functionality:** Premium users unlock additional features designed to enhance their dating experience and increase their chances of finding compatible matches.

   ○ **Examples of Premium Features:**

   ▪ **Unlimited Swipes:** Removing restrictions on the number of profiles users can swipe through daily.

   ▪ **Advanced Filters:** Access to filters based on specific criteria such as location, interests, education, and relationship preferences.

   ▪ **Ad-Free Experience:** Eliminating advertisements from the app interface for uninterrupted browsing.

   ▪ **Boosts and Visibility:** Enhancing profile visibility to increase the likelihood of being seen by potential matches.

   ▪ **Message Read Receipts:** Notifying users when their messages have been read by recipients, enhancing communication transparency.

   ▪ **Rewind and Super Likes:** Features allowing users to undo swipes or express heightened interest in specific profiles.

Revenue Generation

1. **Subscription Plans:**

   ○ **Monthly, Quarterly, Annual:** Apps typically offer subscription plans spanning different durations (e.g., monthly, quarterly, annual). Longer commitments often come with discounts or incentives to encourage user retention.

○ **Tiered Pricing:** Apps may offer multiple subscription tiers with varying levels of access to premium features, catering to different user preferences and budgets.

2. **In-App Purchases:**

○ **Virtual Currency:** Some apps use virtual currencies or tokens that users can purchase to unlock specific premium features or enhance their profile visibility.

○ **Boosts and Gifts:** Users may buy boosts or virtual gifts that increase their visibility or send tokens of appreciation to other users, generating additional revenue for the app.

User Engagement and Retention Strategies

1. Feature Segmentation:

○ **Trial Periods:** Offering free trials or limited-time promotions for premium features to entice users to upgrade.

○ **Feature Bundling:** Bundling complementary premium features to create value-added packages that appeal to different user segments.

○ **Personalization:** Using user data and behavior analytics to personalize offers and recommendations, encouraging upgrades based on individual preferences and usage patterns.

2. Communication and Feedback:

○ **User Education:** Providing transparent information about premium features and their benefits to educate users on upgrading options.

○ **Feedback Mechanisms:** Soliciting user feedback to continuously refine and enhance premium offerings based on user preferences and satisfaction.

Conclusion

The freemium model enables dating apps to attract a broad user base with free basic features while monetizing through subscriptions and in-app purchases for enhanced functionalities. By offering a mix of free and premium features, apps cater to diverse user needs and preferences while maximizing revenue opportunities. Effective user engagement strategies and continuous improvement of premium offerings are key to sustaining user satisfaction and retention in the competitive dating app market.

Partnerships and Affiliations in Dating Apps

Dating apps often explore partnerships and affiliations as additional revenue streams, leveraging their user base and brand visibility. Here's a detailed explanation of how partnerships and affiliate marketing work within dating apps:

Affiliate Marketing

1. **Definition and Purpose:**

   ○ **Affiliate Programs:** Dating apps participate in affiliate marketing programs where they promote third-party products or services relevant to their users.

   ○ **Commission-Based:** Apps earn commissions or referral fees for driving traffic or sales to partner websites offering products like matchmaking services, relationship counseling, or lifestyle products.

   2. **Implementation and Strategy:**

   ○ **Targeted Promotion:** Apps strategically select affiliate partners whose offerings align with their user demographics and interests.

   ○ **Promotional Channels:** Affiliates may be promoted through in-app advertisements, email newsletters, or featured placements within the app interface.

   ○ **Tracking and Attribution:** Utilizing affiliate tracking links or codes to monitor user engagement and measure the effectiveness of affiliate campaigns.

   3. **Examples of Affiliate Partnerships:**

   ○ **Matchmaking Services:** Collaborating with professional matchmaking agencies or platforms offering personalized dating services.

   ○ **Relationship Counseling:** Partnering with therapists or counseling services specializing in relationship advice or mental health support.

   ○ **Lifestyle Products:** Promoting lifestyle brands or products that appeal to the dating app user base, such as fashion, wellness, or travel services.

Benefits and Considerations

1. **Revenue Diversification:**

   ○ **Additional Income:** Affiliate marketing provides dating apps with an additional revenue stream beyond subscriptions and in-app purchases.

   ○ **Monetization Potential:** Apps can monetize user engagement through targeted promotions without directly selling products or services.

2. **Enhanced User Experience:**

○ **Value-Added Services:** Partnering with reputable affiliates enhances the app's value proposition by offering users access to trusted services that complement their dating experience.

○ **Personalization:** Tailoring affiliate recommendations based on user preferences and behavior enhances relevancy and user satisfaction.

3. **Challenges and Management:**

○ **User Trust:** Maintaining transparency about affiliate partnerships to build and retain user trust.

○ **Relevance and Alignment:** Ensuring affiliate offerings align with the app's brand ethos and user expectations to enhance engagement and conversion rates.

○ **Compliance:** Adhering to regulatory guidelines and ethical standards in affiliate marketing practices to protect user interests and privacy.

Conclusion

Affiliate marketing enables dating apps to diversify revenue streams and enhance user experience by partnering with relevant third-party services or products. By strategically selecting affiliates and promoting them effectively, apps can capitalize on their user base while providing valuable resources that support users in their dating and relationship journeys. Effective management of affiliate partnerships involves maintaining transparency, ensuring relevance, and prioritizing user trust to optimize revenue potential and foster long-term user loyalty.

Engagement Features in Dating Apps

Dating apps continuously evolve to enhance user engagement through interactive features and robust messaging tools. Here's a detailed exploration of how these elements contribute to user interaction and platform retention:

Interactive Features

1. **Purpose and Functionality:**

   ○ **Encouraging Interaction:** Interactive features such as quizzes, games, or icebreakers are designed to stimulate user engagement beyond traditional profile browsing and swiping.

   ○ **Building Connections:** Quizzes or compatibility tests help users learn more about potential matches' personalities and preferences, fostering meaningful connections based on shared interests.

   ○ **Icebreakers:** Pre-set conversation starters or prompts facilitate initial interactions, reducing awkwardness and encouraging users to initiate conversations.

2. **Implementation and Strategy:**

   ○ **Integration:** Interactive features are integrated into the app interface, accessible alongside profile browsing or matchmaking algorithms.

   ○ **User-Centric Design:** Features are user-friendly, intuitive, and tailored to enhance user experience without complicating the navigation or core functionalities of the app.

   ○ **Personalization:** Some apps personalize interactive content based on user profiles or previous interactions to ensure relevance and engagement.

3. **Benefits and Considerations:**

   ○ **Enhanced User Experience:** Interactive elements add variety and entertainment value, making the app more enjoyable and engaging for users.

   ○ **Extended Session Duration:** Users are likely to spend more time on the app when participating in quizzes or games, contributing to higher retention rates.

   ○ **Differentiation:** Apps differentiate themselves in a competitive market by offering unique, interactive features that cater to diverse user preferences and engagement styles.

Messaging Tools

1. **Key Features and Capabilities:**

   ○ **Multimedia Support:** Messaging tools allow users to exchange text, photos, videos, and GIFs, enhancing communication and expression.

○ **Voice Messaging:** Some apps incorporate voice messaging capabilities, providing an alternative to text-based communication for more personalized interactions.

○ **Real-Time Chat:** Instant messaging fosters immediate communication between matches, promoting continuous engagement and relationship development.

2. **Functionality and User Experience:**

○ **Accessibility:** Messaging tools are easily accessible within user profiles or match lists, facilitating seamless communication across the platform.

○ **Security and Privacy:** Apps prioritize security measures to protect user conversations and ensure privacy, including encryption and moderation of inappropriate content.

○ **Notification Systems:** Real-time notifications alert users to new messages, encouraging prompt responses and active participation in conversations.

3. **Impact on User Engagement:**

○ **Building Connections:** Effective messaging tools facilitate meaningful conversations and emotional connections between users, driving engagement and retention.

○ **User Satisfaction:** Enhanced communication features contribute to overall user satisfaction by providing versatile ways to interact and build relationships.

○ **Monetization Potential:** Messaging tools may also support monetization through premium features like unlimited messaging or enhanced media sharing options.

Conclusion

Engagement features such as interactive quizzes and robust messaging tools play a crucial role in enhancing user interaction and retention on dating apps. By offering diverse ways for users to connect, communicate, and engage with potential matches, apps can differentiate themselves in a competitive market while fostering meaningful relationships and satisfying user experiences. Strategic implementation of these features requires continuous innovation, user feedback integration, and a commitment to enhancing overall app usability and functionality.

Personalization and Algorithms in Dating Apps

Personalization and advanced algorithms are pivotal in modern dating apps, significantly impacting user experience, satisfaction, and overall platform effectiveness. Here's a detailed exploration of how these elements work and their implications:

Matching Algorithms

1. Functionality and Purpose:

- **Data Analysis:** Advanced matching algorithms utilize extensive user data, including profile information, preferences, behavior patterns, and interaction history.

- **Compatibility Assessment:** Algorithms assess compatibility by comparing user profiles against predefined criteria or compatibility metrics, such as interests, values, lifestyle choices, and relationship goals.

- **Machine Learning:** Some apps employ machine learning techniques to continuously refine algorithms based on user feedback and success metrics, improving match accuracy over time.

2. Implementation and Strategy:

- **Algorithm Types:** Various algorithms, such as collaborative filtering, similarity-based algorithms, or hybrid models, are employed to generate matches that align with user preferences and relationship objectives.

- **User Interface Integration:** Match suggestions are seamlessly integrated into the app interface, presented through match lists, notifications, or personalized recommendations.

- **Feedback Loop:** Apps may incorporate user feedback mechanisms to refine algorithms and enhance match quality, ensuring relevance and satisfaction.

3. Benefits and Considerations:

- **Enhanced User Experience:** Effective matching algorithms streamline the dating process by presenting users with highly compatible matches, reducing time spent searching and increasing the likelihood of meaningful connections.

- **Retention and Engagement:** Improved match quality enhances user satisfaction and retention rates, as users are more likely to remain active and engaged on the platform.

- **Differentiation:** Algorithms differentiate apps in a competitive market, attracting users seeking efficient, tailored matchmaking experiences that align with their specific preferences and relationship goals.

Personalized Recommendations

1. Customization and User Insights:

○ **Behavioral Analysis:** Apps analyze user behavior, such as swiping patterns, messaging history, and interaction frequency, to personalize recommendations.

○ **Contextual Relevance:** Recommendations consider contextual factors like location, age, interests, and previous matches to suggest profiles that resonate with user preferences.

○ **Dynamic Updates:** Recommendations may be dynamically updated based on real-time user activity and changes in profile information, ensuring relevance and responsiveness.

2. User Interface and Engagement:

○ **User-Centric Design:** Personalized recommendations are prominently featured within the app interface, encouraging users to explore and engage with suggested profiles.

○ **Notification Strategies:** Apps use notifications to alert users to new recommendations or updates, prompting them to revisit the app and explore potential matches.

○ **A/B Testing:** Continuous testing and optimization of recommendation algorithms enhance their effectiveness in delivering relevant and appealing profiles to users.

3. Impact on User Interaction:

○ **Increased Engagement:** Personalized recommendations stimulate user engagement by presenting profiles that align closely with individual preferences and interests.

○ **Conversion Rates:** Well-targeted recommendations may lead to higher conversion rates from browsing to interaction, as users are more likely to express interest in profiles that meet their criteria.

○ **User Satisfaction:** Enhanced personalization contributes to overall user satisfaction by facilitating connections that are more likely to result in meaningful relationships or positive dating experiences.

Conclusion

Personalization and sophisticated algorithms are integral to the success of dating apps, transforming user experiences by optimizing match quality and relevance. By leveraging extensive user data and behavioral insights, apps can deliver tailored matchmaking experiences that align closely with individual preferences and relationship objectives. Continuous refinement of algorithms and personalized recommendations not only enhances user satisfaction and engagement but also strengthens app retention and competitive positioning in the dynamic online dating landscape.

Safety and Security Measures in Dating Apps

Ensuring the safety and security of users is paramount for dating apps to maintain trust and foster a positive user experience. Here's a detailed exploration of key safety features and practices implemented by dating platforms:

Trust and Safety Features

1. Profile Verification:

○ **Purpose:** Verification processes, such as email verification or linking social media accounts, authenticate user identities and reduce the prevalence of fake profiles.

○ **Benefits:** Verified profiles inspire confidence among users, increasing trust in the authenticity of interactions and reducing the risk of catfishing or identity fraud.

2. Reporting Systems:

○ **Functionality:** Apps provide mechanisms for users to report inappropriate behavior, harassment, or suspicious activities.

○ **Response Mechanism:** Reported incidents trigger prompt investigation and appropriate action by moderators, such as warning, suspending, or banning offending accounts.

○ **User Empowerment:** Effective reporting systems empower users to contribute to community safety and discourage misconduct, fostering a respectful environment.

3. Data Encryption:

○ **Security Protocol:** End-to-end encryption safeguards user data, including personal information and communication exchanges, from unauthorized access or interception.

○ **Compliance Standards:** Adherence to data protection regulations, such as GDPR or CCPA, ensures user privacy and reinforces app credibility.

Moderation and Support

1. Content Moderation:

○ **Content Policies:** Clear guidelines and community standards prohibit offensive, explicit, or misleading content on profiles, photos, or messages.

○ **Automated Filters:** Automated systems and AI-driven algorithms detect and filter out prohibited content, minimizing exposure to inappropriate material.

2. User Support Services:

○ **Accessibility:** Accessible support channels, such as in-app help centers, FAQs, or direct contact options, provide timely assistance to users experiencing issues or concerns.

○ **Response Time:** Prompt response to user inquiries or complaints demonstrates commitment to user safety and satisfaction.

Continuous Improvement and Adaptation

1. **Feedback Integration:**

○ **User Feedback Loops:** Incorporating user feedback on safety features and concerns informs ongoing improvements and policy adjustments.

○ **Iterative Development:** Iterative updates and enhancements to safety protocols reflect evolving user needs and emerging security threats.

2. **Collaboration and Best Practices:**

○ **Industry Collaboration:** Collaboration with cybersecurity experts, industry associations, and law enforcement agencies enhances app security measures and response strategies.

○ **Benchmarking:** Benchmarking against industry best practices and standards ensures alignment with global safety standards and user expectations.

Conclusion

By prioritizing trust and safety through robust features such as profile verification, reporting systems, and data encryption, dating apps can cultivate a secure and respectful environment for users. Effective moderation of content and proactive user support services further contribute to maintaining a positive user experience. Continuous adaptation to emerging threats and integration of user feedback are essential for staying ahead in addressing safety challenges and reinforcing user trust in the platform.

Retention Campaigns in Dating Apps

Retention campaigns are crucial strategies employed by dating apps to maintain user engagement and encourage continued usage. Here's a detailed exploration of key retention tactics:

Push Notifications

1. **Purpose and Functionality:**

   ○ **Re-engagement:** Push notifications are used to notify users about new matches, messages from potential interests, or activity on their profiles.

   ○ **Reminder:** Notifications serve as reminders for users to revisit the app, encouraging them to check updates and engage with potential matches.

2. **Targeted Approach:**

   ○ **Personalization:** Notifications are personalized based on user preferences, activity history, and location to increase relevance and effectiveness.

   ○ **Segmentation:** Apps segment users into cohorts based on behavior (e.g., active users, lapsed users) to tailor notifications for specific retention goals.

3. **Frequency and Timing:**

   ○ **Optimization:** Timing and frequency of notifications are optimized to align with user preferences and peak usage times, minimizing intrusion while maximizing user response.

   ○ **A/B Testing:** Continuous testing of different notification formats and timings helps identify the most effective strategies for re-engagement.

Incentives and Rewards

1. **Types of Incentives:**

   ○ **Free Boosts:** Offering free boosts that increase profile visibility can incentivize users to interact more actively on the app.

   ○ **Premium Trials:** Providing temporary access to premium features or exclusive content encourages users to explore enhanced functionalities.

   ○ **Discounts and Promotions:** Discounts on subscription plans or special promotions incentivize users to upgrade their membership or extend their subscription period.

2. **Behavioral Triggers:**

   ○ **Trigger Events:** Incentives are often linked to specific user actions or milestones, such as completing a profile, reaching a certain number of matches, or participating in app events.

○ **Gamification:** Incorporating gamification elements, where users earn rewards for achieving goals or engaging with the app, enhances retention by making interactions more enjoyable and rewarding.

Effectiveness and Optimization

1. **Measurement and Analytics:**

○ **Performance Metrics:** Metrics such as click-through rates, conversion rates, and user retention rates are tracked to assess the effectiveness of retention campaigns.

○ **Data Analysis:** Insights from user behavior and campaign performance guide adjustments and optimizations to improve overall retention strategies.

2. **Continuous Iteration:**

○ **Feedback Loop:** Incorporating user feedback and monitoring user sentiment helps refine retention tactics and tailor strategies to meet evolving user preferences.

○ **Adaptation to Trends:** Adapting campaigns to seasonal trends, cultural events, or changes in user behavior ensures relevance and effectiveness over time.

Conclusion

Retention campaigns leveraging push notifications, incentives, and rewards play a pivotal role in sustaining user engagement and loyalty on dating apps. By employing personalized and targeted strategies, apps can effectively re-engage users, enhance their app experience through incentives, and continuously optimize retention efforts based on user feedback and data analytics. Successful retention campaigns not only drive user retention but also contribute to long-term app growth and profitability in the competitive dating app market.

Continuous Innovation in Dating Apps

In the competitive landscape of dating apps, continuous innovation is essential to maintain user engagement, attract new users, and stay ahead of competitors. Here's a detailed look at how dating apps achieve continuous innovation through feature updates and adaptation to trends:

Feature Updates

1. **User-Centric Enhancements:**

   ○ **Feedback Integration:** Regularly soliciting and incorporating user feedback helps prioritize feature updates that address user pain points or enhance user experience.

   ○ **Iterative Development:** Agile development methodologies enable apps to release incremental updates quickly, ensuring continuous improvement without disrupting user experience.

2. **Enhanced Functionality:**

   ○ **New Features:** Introducing new functionalities such as video profiles, voice messaging, or AI-powered matchmaking enhances user interaction and engagement.

   ○ **Advanced Filters:** Adding advanced search filters or compatibility assessments based on user preferences and behaviors improves the matchmaking process and user satisfaction.

3. **Technical Advancements:**

   ○ **Performance Optimization:** Improving app performance, speed, and reliability through backend upgrades or infrastructure enhancements ensures seamless user experiences.

   ○ **Security Updates:** Implementing robust data encryption, privacy protections, and cybersecurity measures to safeguard user data and maintain trust.

Adapting to Trends

1. **Monitoring Industry Trends:**

   ○ **Market Research:** Regularly conducting market research and trend analysis helps apps identify emerging behaviors, preferences, and technological advancements.

   ○ **Competitive Analysis:** Monitoring competitor strategies and industry benchmarks informs app strategies and ensures relevance in a rapidly evolving market.

2. **Cultural Relevance:**

   ○ **Global Insights:** Recognizing regional or cultural differences in dating preferences and societal norms informs localized feature adaptations and marketing strategies.

○ **Inclusivity Initiatives:** Promoting inclusivity by accommodating diverse relationship models, LGBTQ+ communities, or cultural sensitivities enhances app appeal and user retention.

3. **Social and Behavioral Shifts:**

○ **Social Awareness:** Addressing societal shifts such as changing attitudes towards online dating, hookup culture, or relationship expectations helps apps stay aligned with user values.

○ **Integration of Social Media:** Leveraging social media integrations or partnerships to amplify app visibility, user engagement, and community-building efforts.

Strategic Implementation

1. **Agile Development Practices:**

○ **Iterative Releases:** Agile methodologies enable frequent updates and rapid iteration based on real-time user feedback and market demands.

○ **Testing and Validation:** Conducting A/B testing, user trials, and pilot launches ensures feature efficacy and user acceptance before full-scale deployment.

2. **Long-term Vision:**

○ **Roadmap Planning:** Developing a long-term product roadmap aligned with business goals and user needs ensures sustained innovation and strategic growth.

○ **Flexibility and Adaptability:** Remaining adaptable to unforeseen challenges or opportunities allows apps to pivot strategies and capitalize on emerging trends proactively.

Conclusion

Continuous innovation in dating apps involves a dynamic cycle of feature updates, trend adaptation, and strategic implementation to enhance user experience, maintain competitiveness, and drive sustainable growth. By staying attuned to user feedback, technological advancements, and societal shifts, dating apps can foster user loyalty, expand their user base, and establish themselves as leaders in the evolving digital dating landscape.

Chapter 13: Gender Dynamics on Dating Apps

Dating apps have transformed the landscape of modern dating, reshaping traditional gender dynamics and introducing new challenges and opportunities for both men and women. Here's a detailed exploration of the experiences, challenges, power dynamics, and gender roles influenced by dating apps:

Experiences of Men and Women

1. **Women's Experiences:**

○ **Attention and Selection:** Women often receive a higher volume of messages and attention compared to men. This can lead to feeling overwhelmed or pressured to sift through numerous matches.

○ **Safety Concerns:** Women may face higher risks of harassment, unsolicited explicit messages, or safety concerns when meeting matches offline. Apps' safety features are crucial for mitigating these risks.

○ **Profile Presentation:** Women may feel pressure to present themselves in a way that balances attractiveness with safety and authenticity, navigating stereotypes about femininity and dating.

2. **Men's Experiences:**

○ **Initiation and Response Rates:** Men typically initiate conversations more frequently than women. However, response rates can vary widely based on factors like profile presentation, messaging approach, and attractiveness.

○ **Competition:** Men often perceive a competitive environment due to the perceived abundance of male users and the challenge of standing out among potential matches.

○ **Pressure for Success:** Men may feel pressure to conform to traditional ideals of masculinity, such as being assertive in pursuing matches or showcasing success and status through their profiles.

Power Dynamics

1. **Initiation and Control:**

○ **Women's Empowerment:** Dating apps have empowered women by allowing them to initiate conversations and exert more control over their dating interactions. This shifts traditional gender roles where men historically took the lead.

○ **Gendered Expectations:** Despite increased empowerment, societal expectations or stereotypes about gender roles can still influence interactions. Women initiating conversations, for example, may face backlash or surprise from matches who expect traditional gender dynamics.

2. **Selection and Preferences:**

○ **Perceived Choice:** Both men and women navigate through a pool of potential matches, making decisions based on attractiveness, shared interests, and compatibility. This can create dynamics where perceived choice impacts power dynamics within interactions.

○ **Preference Influences:** Apps' algorithms and user behaviors may reinforce or challenge traditional gender preferences in dating. Preferences for physical attractiveness or specific traits can influence match outcomes and perceived power dynamics.

Influence on Gender Roles in Dating

1. Reinforcing or Challenging Norms:

○ **Reinforcement:** Dating apps can reinforce traditional gender norms, such as men being more assertive or women focusing on physical attractiveness in profiles. This can perpetuate societal expectations within digital interactions.

○ **Challenging Norms:** Conversely, dating apps provide opportunities to challenge and redefine traditional gender roles. Platforms that encourage diverse relationship models, inclusivity, and respect for gender identity contribute to evolving dating norms.

2. Communication and Expression:

○ **Expression of Identity:** Users, regardless of gender, use dating apps to express their identity, interests, and relationship preferences. Apps that support diverse forms of self-expression can empower users to navigate beyond traditional gender stereotypes.

○ **Communication Styles:** Differences in communication styles between genders, such as directness or emotional expression, may impact interactions. Understanding and respecting these differences can foster more meaningful connections.

Conclusion

Dating apps play a pivotal role in shaping contemporary dating dynamics and gender roles. They provide platforms where men and women navigate complex interactions, challenges, and opportunities influenced by societal norms, technological features, and individual preferences. By fostering empowerment, safety, and inclusivity, dating apps have the potential to promote more equitable and fulfilling dating experiences for users of all genders. Understanding these dynamics is essential for app developers, users, and society at large to navigate the evolving landscape of digital dating responsibly and inclusively.

Experiences of Men and Women

Women's Experiences on Dating Apps

Attention and Selection

1. **Volume of Messages:** Women frequently receive a higher volume of messages and attention compared to men on dating apps. This can be both flattering and overwhelming, as it requires them to sift through numerous matches to find those they are genuinely interested in.
2. **Pressure to Respond:** The influx of messages can create pressure on women to respond promptly or manage expectations effectively. This can be challenging, especially when trying to navigate conversations that may not align with their preferences or intentions.

Safety Concerns

1. **Harassment and Explicit Messages:** Women often face higher risks of harassment, receiving unsolicited explicit messages, or encountering disrespectful behavior on dating apps. This behavior can range from persistent messaging to more serious forms of harassment.
2. **Offline Safety:** Meeting matches offline introduces safety concerns for women, including the risk of physical harm or assault. Apps' safety features, such as reporting tools, blocking options, and verified profiles, are crucial for mitigating these risks and promoting a safer dating environment.

Profile Presentation

1. **Balancing Attractiveness and Authenticity:** Women may feel pressure to present themselves in a way that balances attractiveness with authenticity. This can involve selecting flattering photos, crafting engaging bios, and highlighting their personality traits while maintaining safety and privacy.
2. **Navigating Stereotypes:** There's often a societal expectation for women to conform to certain stereotypes of femininity or attractiveness. This pressure can influence how women choose to present themselves on dating apps, navigating between societal norms and their personal preferences.
3. **Authenticity vs. Safety:** Finding a balance between presenting an authentic self and ensuring personal safety is crucial. Women may opt to withhold certain personal details or interests to avoid unwanted attention or judgment.

Conclusion

Women's experiences on dating apps are shaped by a complex interplay of attention, safety concerns, and societal expectations. While these platforms offer opportunities to connect and explore relationships, they also present challenges that require thoughtful management of interactions and personal presentation. Enhancing safety features, promoting respectful behavior, and empowering women to assert their preferences are essential steps toward creating a more inclusive and supportive digital dating environment.

Men's Experiences on Dating Apps

Initiation and Response Rates

1. **Initiation Frequency:** Men tend to initiate conversations more frequently than women on dating apps. This behavior stems from traditional dating norms where men are expected to take the lead in starting interactions.
2. **Response Variability:** Response rates can vary widely for men based on factors such as their profile presentation, messaging approach, and perceived attractiveness. A compelling profile and respectful messaging style are crucial in influencing whether a woman responds positively.

Competition

1. **Perceived Abundance:** Men often perceive a competitive environment on dating apps, where the ratio of male to female users can skew towards more men. This abundance can create a sense of competition among men to stand out and attract the attention of potential matches.
2. **Standing Out:** Given the perceived competition, men may feel pressure to differentiate themselves from other users. This could involve crafting unique profiles, showcasing interesting hobbies or achievements, or using humor and creativity in their messages to capture interest.

Pressure for Success

1. **Traditional Masculine Ideals:** Men may feel pressure to conform to traditional ideals of masculinity on dating apps. This includes traits like assertiveness in pursuing matches, confidence in presenting themselves, and demonstrating success or status through their profiles.
2. **Expectations of Success:** There's often an expectation for men to initiate and lead conversations, plan dates, and demonstrate their ability to provide for potential partners. This societal expectation can influence how men portray themselves on dating apps and the strategies they employ to attract matches.

Conclusion

Men's experiences on dating apps are influenced by initiation patterns, competition for attention, and societal pressures to adhere to traditional masculine roles. Navigating these dynamics involves balancing assertiveness with respect, presenting an authentic self while standing out among competitors, and managing expectations of success in forming meaningful connections. Building empathy and understanding of diverse perspectives can contribute to creating a more inclusive and supportive digital dating environment for all users.

Power Dynamics

Women's Empowerment on Dating Apps

Initiation and Control

1. **Empowerment through Initiation:** Dating apps have empowered women by enabling them to initiate conversations with matches. This shift marks a departure from traditional dating norms where men typically took the lead in initiating contact. This empowerment allows women to take more active roles in their dating lives and pursue connections based on their own preferences and interests.
2. **Exerting Control:** Beyond initiating conversations, women also exert more control over their interactions on dating apps. They can choose whom to engage with, decide the pace of communication, and set boundaries that align with their comfort levels. This control contributes to a sense of agency in navigating the digital dating landscape.

Gendered Expectations

1. **Societal Influences:** Despite the empowerment afforded by dating apps, societal expectations and stereotypes about gender roles can still influence interactions. For instance, there may be lingering expectations that men should initiate conversations or take the lead in relationship progression. Women who defy these norms by initiating conversations may encounter surprise or even resistance from matches who hold onto traditional gender dynamics.
2. **Backlash or Surprises:** Women who initiate conversations on dating apps might experience reactions ranging from appreciation to confusion or even negative responses. Some matches may perceive this behavior as assertive or forward, especially if they adhere to more traditional views on dating dynamics. This can create challenges in navigating initial interactions and managing expectations on both sides.

Conclusion

Dating apps have significantly empowered women by allowing them to initiate conversations and exert more control over their dating interactions. This empowerment challenges traditional gender roles and provides women with greater agency in pursuing relationships. However, navigating gendered expectations and societal norms remains a nuanced aspect of digital dating, requiring awareness of individual preferences and respectful communication to foster meaningful connections.

Selection and Preferences in Dating Apps

Perceived Choice

1. **Navigating Potential Matches:** Both men and women engage with dating apps to explore a pool of potential matches, each evaluating profiles based on criteria such as attractiveness, shared interests, and perceived compatibility. This process introduces dynamics where the perceived abundance of choices can influence power dynamics within interactions.

2. **Impact on Power Dynamics:** The availability of multiple potential matches can affect how individuals approach their interactions on dating apps. For instance, individuals who perceive themselves as having many options may feel empowered to be more selective or assertive in their communication style. Conversely, those who perceive fewer options may approach interactions with a greater sense of caution or eagerness to connect.

Preference Influences

1. **Algorithmic Influence:** Dating apps often employ algorithms that suggest matches based on user preferences and behaviors. These algorithms can reinforce or challenge traditional gender preferences in dating. For example, preferences for physical attractiveness or specific personality traits may be prioritized in match recommendations, shaping users' perceptions of ideal partners and influencing their interaction choices.
2. **User Behavior:** User behaviors on dating apps, such as swiping patterns and messaging preferences, also contribute to the reinforcement of gender preferences. If certain traits or characteristics consistently receive more attention or engagement, it can perpetuate stereotypes or biases related to attractiveness, social status, or traditional gender roles.

Conclusion

Dating apps facilitate a complex interplay of selection and preference dynamics among users. The perceived abundance of choices influences power dynamics within interactions, where individuals navigate their preferences and evaluate potential matches based on various criteria. Algorithms and user behaviors further shape these dynamics by reinforcing or challenging traditional gender preferences in dating, highlighting the evolving landscape of digital interactions and relationship formation.

Influence on Gender Roles in Dating

Reinforcing or Challenging Norms in Dating Apps

Reinforcement of Traditional Gender Norms

1. **Behavioral Expectations:** Dating apps can reinforce traditional gender norms by shaping user behaviors and interactions. For example, men may be encouraged to initiate conversations more frequently, while women may feel pressure to present themselves in ways that emphasize physical attractiveness or conform to societal expectations of femininity.
2. **Profile Presentation:** The design and features of dating apps may inadvertently reinforce traditional gender roles. For instance, profile options or prompts that emphasize physical appearance or certain interests may steer users towards conforming to stereotypical gender norms in their profiles.
3. **Social Expectations:** Interactions on dating apps can reflect broader social expectations regarding gender roles. This includes assumptions about who should make the first move, how assertive or passive individuals should be in communication, and what characteristics are valued in potential partners.

Challenging Norms and Promoting Diversity

1. **Diverse Relationship Models:** Some dating apps actively challenge traditional norms by accommodating diverse relationship models, such as polyamory, open relationships, and LGBTQ+ partnerships. By providing platforms that embrace different relationship preferences, these apps contribute to redefining what constitutes a normative relationship.
2. **Inclusivity and Respect:** Platforms that prioritize inclusivity and respect for gender identity play a crucial role in challenging and reshaping dating norms. By promoting acceptance of diverse gender expressions and identities, these apps foster environments where users can authentically express themselves without conforming to traditional stereotypes.
3. **Educational Initiatives:** Dating apps can also challenge norms through educational initiatives that promote understanding and awareness of diverse relationship dynamics and identities. By providing resources and information on non-traditional relationships, apps empower users to explore and embrace relationship models beyond conventional norms.

Conclusion

Dating apps wield significant influence in either reinforcing or challenging traditional gender norms within digital dating environments. While some platforms inadvertently reinforce stereotypes through design and user interactions, others actively promote inclusivity and diversity, thereby contributing to the evolution of dating norms. By fostering environments that encourage authenticity, respect, and acceptance of diverse identities, these apps play a pivotal role in reshaping societal expectations surrounding gender roles and relationship dynamics.

Communication and Expression on Dating Apps

Expression of Identity

1. **Diverse Self-Expression:** Dating apps serve as platforms where users can express various aspects of their identity, including gender identity, sexual orientation, interests, and relationship preferences. Apps that provide flexibility in profile customization, such as options for gender identity beyond binary categories or prompts for diverse interests, empower users to authentically represent themselves.
2. **Challenging Stereotypes:** By allowing users to express their identity beyond traditional gender stereotypes, dating apps contribute to challenging societal norms. For instance, platforms that offer inclusive profile options or encourage users to share non-traditional relationship preferences help break away from conventional expectations about gender roles and relationships.
3. **Supporting Diversity:** Apps that prioritize inclusivity and respect for diverse identities foster environments where users feel validated and accepted. This inclusivity can extend to features like gender-neutral language in app interactions or algorithms that prioritize compatibility based on shared values rather than stereotypical gender roles.

Communication Styles

1. **Gender Differences:** Research suggests that men and women may exhibit different communication styles on dating apps. Men may tend towards more direct approaches or focus on initiating conversations, while women may prioritize emotional expression or nuanced communication.
2. **Understanding and Respect:** Effective communication on dating apps involves understanding and respecting these differences in communication styles. For example, acknowledging and responding to emotional cues or preferences for directness can enhance mutual understanding and rapport between users.
3. **Building Meaningful Connections:** Platforms that facilitate clear communication and respect for diverse communication styles can facilitate deeper connections. This may include features like multimedia messaging to convey emotions effectively or prompts that encourage thoughtful responses beyond superficial exchanges.

Conclusion

Dating apps play a pivotal role in allowing users to express their identity authentically and communicate effectively across diverse genders and identities. By supporting varied forms of self-expression and promoting understanding of different communication styles, these platforms empower users to navigate beyond traditional gender stereotypes and foster meaningful connections based on mutual respect and compatibility.

Chapter 14: Psychological Effects of Dating Apps

Dating apps have revolutionized how individuals meet and form relationships, but their impact on mental health warrants careful consideration. Understanding the psychological effects can help users navigate these platforms more effectively and mitigate potential negative consequences.

Introduction

Dating apps provide a convenient platform to meet potential partners, offering a wide array of profiles and communication tools that streamline the dating process. However, the pervasive use of these apps can influence users' mental health in various ways, affecting anxiety levels, contributing to feelings of depression, and influencing perceptions of loneliness.

Mental Health Impact

1. **Anxiety:** The process of swiping through profiles and initiating conversations can trigger anxiety. Users may experience fear of rejection, uncertainty about matches' intentions, or stress from comparing themselves to others' profiles. Over time, these anxieties can lead to heightened stress levels and apprehension about dating.
2. **Depression:** Continuous engagement with dating apps, especially without desired outcomes like meaningful connections or dates, can exacerbate feelings of sadness and hopelessness. Disappointment from failed matches or perceived lack of success may contribute to self-doubt and negative self-perception.
3. **Loneliness:** Despite their promise of connection, dating apps can paradoxically increase feelings of loneliness. Superficial interactions or a lack of genuine connections can leave users feeling isolated. Over-reliance on digital interactions may hinder efforts to cultivate meaningful relationships offline.

Coping Mechanisms

1. **Setting Boundaries:** Establishing clear boundaries around app usage, such as limiting daily screen time or specific times for engagement, can prevent over-engagement and help maintain a healthy balance with offline activities.
2. **Mindful Engagement:** Practicing mindfulness while using dating apps involves being aware of emotional responses and thought patterns. Mindfulness can help users navigate triggers like rejection or comparison with greater resilience and self-awareness.
3. **Seeking Support:** Talking openly with trusted friends, family members, or mental health professionals about dating app experiences can provide emotional validation and support. Sharing concerns and frustrations can reduce feelings of isolation and normalize common challenges.
4. **Focus on Quality Connections:** Prioritizing quality over quantity in interactions can alleviate pressure and anxiety associated with app use. Emphasizing genuine connections based on shared values and interests promotes more fulfilling relationships.
5. **Digital Detox:** Taking breaks from dating apps periodically can refresh mental well-being. Engaging in offline activities, hobbies, or socializing face-to-face can provide perspective and reduce reliance on digital validation.

Conclusion

While dating apps offer unprecedented opportunities to meet potential partners, they also pose risks to mental health through increased anxiety, depression, and feelings of loneliness. By implementing coping strategies such as setting boundaries, practicing mindfulness, seeking support, prioritizing genuine connections, and taking digital detoxes, users can navigate these platforms more effectively and safeguard their mental well-being. Balancing digital interactions with offline connections is essential for maintaining overall mental health in the modern dating landscape.

Mental Health Impact-Anxiety on Dating Apps: Causes and Effects

Dating apps have transformed how people approach relationships, but they also introduce unique challenges that can exacerbate anxiety among users. Understanding the causes and effects of anxiety on dating apps is crucial for users to navigate these platforms with greater awareness and resilience.

Causes of Anxiety

1. **Fear of Rejection:** Users often experience anxiety related to the possibility of rejection when initiating conversations or being unmatched. The fear of not receiving a response or being ignored can lead to self-doubt and reluctance to engage further.
2. **Uncertainty about Intentions:** Misinterpreting matches' intentions can heighten anxiety. Users may question whether matches are genuinely interested in them or merely seeking casual interactions, creating feelings of insecurity and hesitation in communication.
3. **Comparison with Others:** Constant exposure to curated profiles and seemingly idealized images on dating apps can trigger comparison anxiety. Users may feel inadequate or less attractive compared to others, impacting their self-esteem and confidence.

Effects of Anxiety

1. **Heightened Stress Levels:** Persistent anxiety on dating apps can lead to elevated stress levels. Constantly evaluating potential matches, overanalyzing interactions, and worrying about outcomes can contribute to chronic stress and emotional exhaustion.
2. **Apprehension about Dating:** Anxiety can create a cycle of avoidance or apprehension about dating. Users may hesitate to initiate conversations or set up dates, fearing negative outcomes or repeating past disappointments.
3. **Impact on Self-Esteem:** Repeated experiences of rejection or perceived lack of success can diminish self-esteem. Users may internalize negative experiences, questioning their attractiveness or worthiness of meaningful connections.

Coping Strategies

1. **Mindful Engagement:** Practicing mindfulness involves being present and aware of emotional responses while using dating apps. Mindfulness techniques can help users recognize and manage anxious thoughts, reducing the intensity of emotional reactions.
2. **Setting Boundaries:** Establishing clear boundaries around app usage can mitigate anxiety. Limiting screen time, taking breaks, or avoiding late-night browsing can prevent overstimulation and promote a healthier relationship with dating apps.
3. **Seeking Support:** Talking openly about dating app experiences with friends, family, or a therapist can provide validation and support. Discussing anxieties and receiving perspective from others can alleviate feelings of isolation and normalize common challenges.
4. **Focus on Personal Growth:** Redirecting focus from external validation to personal growth can alleviate anxiety. Engaging in hobbies, self-care activities, or pursuing personal goals outside of dating apps can foster self-confidence and reduce dependence on external validation.

5. **Therapeutic Approaches:** Cognitive-behavioral techniques or therapy can help users address underlying anxiety related to dating. Therapists can provide strategies to challenge negative thought patterns, build resilience, and improve coping mechanisms.

Conclusion

Anxiety on dating apps is a common experience due to factors like fear of rejection, uncertainty about intentions, and comparison with others. Recognizing these triggers and implementing coping strategies such as mindfulness, setting boundaries, seeking support, focusing on personal growth, and exploring therapeutic options can empower users to manage anxiety effectively. By fostering awareness and resilience, individuals can navigate dating apps with greater confidence and maintain their mental well-being in the process.

Mental Health Impact-Impact of Dating Apps on Depression

Dating apps, while designed to facilitate connections, can inadvertently exacerbate feelings of depression among users, particularly when desired outcomes are not achieved. Understanding the dynamics that contribute to this phenomenon is crucial for individuals navigating these platforms.

Causes of Depression

1. **Unmet Expectations:** Continuous engagement with dating apps without achieving desired outcomes, such as meaningful connections or dates, can lead to disappointment and frustration. Users may experience a sense of hopelessness or low self-worth if they perceive themselves as unsuccessful in their dating endeavors.
2. **Rejection and Disconnection:** Repeated experiences of rejection or lack of response from matches can contribute to feelings of sadness and isolation. Users may internalize these interactions, questioning their attractiveness or ability to form meaningful relationships.
3. **Comparison and Self-Esteem:** The culture of comparison inherent in dating apps can negatively impact self-esteem. Constantly viewing curated profiles and comparing oneself to others' perceived successes can intensify feelings of inadequacy or inferiority.

Effects of Depression

1. **Sadness and Low Mood:** Persistent disappointment and unmet expectations on dating apps can lead to prolonged feelings of sadness and low mood. Users may find it challenging to maintain enthusiasm or motivation for engaging with the platform.
2. **Self-Doubt and Negative Self-Perception:** Negative interactions or perceived lack of success can contribute to negative self-perception. Users may internalize rejections or lack of responses as personal failures, further reinforcing feelings of inadequacy or unworthiness.
3. **Withdrawal and Avoidance:** In response to negative emotions, some users may withdraw from dating apps or avoid initiating new interactions. This withdrawal can perpetuate a cycle of isolation and disengagement from social opportunities.

Coping Strategies

1. **Setting Realistic Expectations:** Adjusting expectations and recognizing that outcomes on dating apps may vary can alleviate pressure and disappointment. Focusing on the process of meeting new people rather than solely on outcomes can reduce the impact of setbacks.
2. **Limiting Exposure:** Monitoring and limiting time spent on dating apps can prevent overexposure and emotional exhaustion. Setting boundaries around usage, such as scheduling specific times for browsing profiles, can promote a healthier relationship with the platform.
3. **Seeking Social Support:** Talking openly about dating app experiences with friends, family, or a therapist can provide validation and perspective. Sharing feelings of disappointment or frustration can normalize these experiences and reduce feelings of isolation.
4. **Engaging in Self-Care:** Prioritizing activities that promote well-being, such as exercise, hobbies, or relaxation techniques, can improve mood and self-esteem. Investing in personal interests outside of dating apps can foster a sense of fulfillment and balance.

5. **Professional Help:** If feelings of depression persist or significantly impact daily life, seeking professional help from a therapist or counselor is advisable. Therapy can provide strategies to manage depression symptoms, challenge negative thought patterns, and build resilience.

Conclusion

Depression stemming from dating apps often arises from unmet expectations, rejection experiences, and negative self-perception. By recognizing these triggers and implementing coping strategies such as setting realistic expectations, limiting exposure, seeking social support, engaging in self-care, and considering professional help when needed, individuals can mitigate the impact of dating app usage on their mental health. Building resilience and maintaining a balanced perspective can help navigate the challenges of dating apps while preserving emotional well-being.

Mental Health Impact-Impact of Dating Apps on Loneliness

Dating apps, designed to facilitate connections and relationships, can inadvertently contribute to feelings of loneliness among users. Understanding the dynamics that lead to this paradoxical outcome is crucial for individuals navigating these platforms.

Causes of Loneliness

1. **Superficial Interactions:** Dating apps often prioritize initial attraction and brief interactions over meaningful connections. Superficial conversations or a focus on physical appearance can leave users feeling disconnected and unfulfilled emotionally.
2. **Lack of Genuine Connections:** Despite the potential for meeting new people, users may struggle to establish genuine connections on dating apps. Conversations may remain superficial, lacking depth or emotional intimacy necessary for combating loneliness.
3. **Digital Over-reliance:** Continuous engagement with dating apps can lead to over-reliance on digital interactions for social fulfillment. This reliance may detract from efforts to build meaningful relationships offline, contributing to a cycle of social isolation.

Effects of Loneliness

1. **Emotional Distress:** Persistent feelings of loneliness can lead to emotional distress, including sadness, anxiety, or low self-esteem. Users may experience a sense of emptiness or dissatisfaction despite engaging with dating apps regularly.
2. **Social Withdrawal:** In response to feelings of loneliness, some users may withdraw from dating apps or avoid initiating new interactions. This withdrawal can perpetuate feelings of isolation and reduce opportunities for meaningful social connections.
3. **Negative Self-Perception:** The inability to form meaningful connections on dating apps may lead users to question their social skills or attractiveness. Negative self-perception can further contribute to feelings of loneliness and hinder confidence in social interactions.

Contributing Factors

1. **Culture of Instant Gratification:** Dating apps promote a culture of instant gratification where users expect quick results and immediate connection. When these expectations are not met, users may experience disappointment and increased loneliness.
2. **Comparison and Insecurity:** Constant exposure to curated profiles and successful matches on dating apps can fuel feelings of inadequacy or comparison. Users may perceive others as more socially successful or attractive, exacerbating feelings of loneliness.

Coping Strategies

1. **Balance Online and Offline Interactions:** Striking a balance between digital interactions on dating apps and offline social activities is essential. Engaging in face-to-face interactions with friends, joining clubs or activities, and attending social events can combat feelings of loneliness.

2. **Seeking Meaningful Connections:** Prioritizing quality over quantity in interactions on dating apps can foster genuine connections. Investing time in conversations that delve deeper into shared interests, values, and emotions can reduce feelings of loneliness.

3. **Mindful App Usage:** Setting boundaries around dating app usage, such as limiting screen time or taking breaks from the platform, can prevent over-reliance on digital interactions. Practicing mindfulness and self-awareness can enhance emotional well-being and reduce loneliness.

4. **Professional Support:** If feelings of loneliness persist or significantly impact daily life, seeking support from a therapist or counselor can be beneficial. Therapy can provide strategies to address underlying issues contributing to loneliness and improve social skills.

Conclusion

Despite their intended purpose of facilitating connections, dating apps can increase feelings of loneliness through superficial interactions, lack of genuine connections, and over-reliance on digital communication. By understanding the causes and effects of loneliness associated with dating apps and implementing coping strategies such as balancing online and offline interactions, seeking meaningful connections, practicing mindful app usage, and seeking professional support when needed, individuals can mitigate loneliness and enhance their emotional well-being. Building resilience and fostering meaningful connections both online and offline are essential for navigating the challenges of dating apps while combating feelings of loneliness.

Coping Mechanisms-Setting Boundaries in Dating App Usage

Establishing clear boundaries around the use of dating apps is essential for maintaining a healthy balance between digital interactions and offline activities. These boundaries can help mitigate potential negative impacts on mental health and overall well-being.

Importance of Boundaries

1. **Preventing Over-Engagement:** Dating apps are designed to be engaging, with features that encourage frequent interaction. Without boundaries, users may find themselves spending excessive time swiping through profiles or messaging matches, which can lead to neglecting other aspects of life.
2. **Maintaining Offline Relationships:** Over-reliance on dating apps can detract from real-life relationships with friends, family, and colleagues. Setting boundaries ensures that users prioritize face-to-face interactions and maintain meaningful connections outside of the digital sphere.
3. **Protecting Mental Health:** Constant engagement with dating apps can contribute to anxiety, stress, and feelings of inadequacy. Setting limits on app usage promotes mindfulness and reduces the negative impact of comparison and rejection that can occur within the app environment.

Strategies for Setting Boundaries

1. **Limiting Screen Time:** Establishing a daily or weekly limit on the amount of time spent on dating apps helps prevent over-engagement. Users can use features on their devices or apps themselves to track and limit screen time effectively.
2. **Designating Specific Times:** Allocating specific times of the day or week for app usage helps create a routine and prevents compulsive checking. For example, setting aside 30 minutes in the evening for browsing profiles or responding to messages can help maintain balance.
3. **Creating Offline Time:** Designating periods where dating apps are completely avoided, such as during meals, social gatherings, or leisure activities, fosters a healthier balance between online and offline life. This practice encourages users to fully engage in present activities and relationships.
4. **Establishing Communication Boundaries:** Setting boundaries around messaging frequency and response times can manage expectations and reduce the pressure to always be available. Clearly communicating availability and response expectations with matches can promote healthy communication patterns.

Implementing Boundaries Effectively

1. **Self-Awareness:** Understanding personal triggers and habits related to dating app usage is crucial for establishing effective boundaries. Reflecting on how app interactions affect mood, productivity, and relationships can guide boundary-setting decisions.
2. **Consistency:** Consistently enforcing boundaries is key to their effectiveness. Users should prioritize their established limits even when faced with the temptation to exceed them due to curiosity or social pressure.
3. **Flexibility and Adjustment:** Periodically reassessing boundaries based on evolving needs and circumstances ensures they remain relevant and supportive of overall well-being. Adjustments may be necessary to accommodate changes in lifestyle or personal goals.

Benefits of Setting Boundaries

1. **Improved Well-being:** Establishing and adhering to boundaries promotes a healthier relationship with dating apps, reducing stress and anxiety associated with over-engagement. Users can experience enhanced mental clarity and overall well-being.
2. **Enhanced Productivity:** By limiting distractions from dating apps, individuals can focus more effectively on work, hobbies, and personal development goals. This increased productivity contributes to a more balanced and fulfilling lifestyle.
3. **Stronger Relationships:** Prioritizing offline interactions nurtures meaningful relationships with friends, family, and romantic partners. Users can invest more time and energy in building connections that offer emotional support and fulfillment beyond digital interactions.

Conclusion

Setting boundaries around dating app usage is essential for maintaining a healthy balance between online and offline life, protecting mental health, and fostering meaningful relationships. By implementing strategies such as limiting screen time, designating specific app usage times, creating offline periods, and establishing communication boundaries, individuals can cultivate a positive and mindful approach to using dating apps. Consistently prioritizing personal well-being and relationship building outside the digital realm contributes to a fulfilling and balanced lifestyle.

Coping Mechanisms-Mindful Engagement with Dating Apps

Mindful engagement with dating apps involves consciously approaching interactions with awareness of one's emotions, thought patterns, and reactions. This practice fosters resilience, self-awareness, and a healthier relationship with digital dating platforms.

Understanding Mindful Engagement

1. **Awareness of Emotional Responses:**

   ○ **Recognizing Triggers:** Mindfulness encourages users to identify triggers that evoke emotional responses while using dating apps. These triggers may include rejection from matches, feelings of inadequacy when comparing oneself to others' profiles, or frustration from lack of responses.

   ○ **Acknowledging Emotions:** Instead of reacting impulsively to emotions like disappointment or insecurity, mindfulness promotes observing these feelings without judgment. Users can acknowledge their emotions and understand that they are temporary reactions to specific situations.

2. **Monitoring Thought Patterns:**

   ○ **Challenging Negative Thoughts:** Mindful engagement involves questioning and reframing negative thought patterns that arise during app usage. For example, instead of internalizing rejection as a personal failure, users can practice self-compassion and recognize that compatibility is multifaceted.

   ○ **Staying Present:** Mindfulness encourages staying present in the moment rather than dwelling on past interactions or worrying about future outcomes. This helps users maintain perspective and approach each new interaction with openness and authenticity.

3. **Practicing Self-Reflection:**

   ○ **Reflecting on Intentions:** Mindful users reflect on their intentions for using dating apps. Whether seeking companionship, exploring relationships, or simply socializing, understanding these motivations fosters clarity and alignment with personal goals.

   ○ **Evaluating Impact:** Regular self-reflection allows users to assess how app usage affects their overall well-being, relationships, and daily life. This awareness helps in adjusting behaviors or setting boundaries to ensure a positive experience.

Strategies for Mindful Engagement

1. **Setting Intentions:**

   ○ **Clarifying Goals:** Before logging into a dating app, users can set intentions such as maintaining curiosity, practicing openness, or focusing on meaningful connections rather than superficial impressions.

   ○ **Grounding Exercises:** Starting app sessions with brief mindfulness exercises, such as deep breathing or body scans, helps users center themselves and approach interactions with presence and clarity.

2. Managing Expectations:

○ **Embracing Uncertainty:** Mindful engagement encourages users to embrace uncertainty inherent in dating app interactions. This mindset reduces anxiety about outcomes and allows for genuine curiosity and exploration.

○ **Avoiding Comparisons:** Users can minimize comparing themselves to others' profiles by appreciating uniqueness and valuing authenticity over idealized representations.

3. Balancing Engagement:

○ **Monitoring Usage:** Mindfulness involves monitoring the frequency and duration of app usage to prevent over-engagement. Setting time limits or designated app-free periods supports a balanced approach to digital interactions.

○ **Prioritizing Offline Connections:** Mindful users prioritize cultivating meaningful relationships offline, recognizing that digital interactions complement rather than replace face-to-face connections.

Benefits of Mindful Engagement

1. **Enhanced Emotional Resilience:** Practicing mindfulness builds emotional resilience, enabling users to navigate setbacks and rejections with greater ease and self-compassion.
2. **Improved Self-Awareness:** Mindful engagement fosters self-awareness of personal preferences, boundaries, and emotional needs within dating interactions.
3. **Authentic Connections:** By approaching app interactions with authenticity and presence, users increase the likelihood of forming genuine connections based on mutual understanding and compatibility.

Conclusion

Mindful engagement with dating apps involves cultivating awareness of emotional responses, monitoring thought patterns, and practicing self-reflection to foster resilience and authenticity in digital dating interactions. By setting intentions, managing expectations, and balancing app usage with offline connections, users can enhance their well-being and cultivate meaningful relationships within the digital realm and beyond. Mindfulness transforms the experience of using dating apps into an opportunity for personal growth, connection, and self-discovery.

Coping Mechanisms-Seeking Support

Seeking support while navigating dating app experiences is crucial for maintaining emotional well-being and gaining perspective on the challenges encountered. This process involves reaching out to trusted individuals or professionals who can offer empathy, guidance, and validation.

Importance of Seeking Support

Emotional Validation and Understanding

1. **Normalization of Experiences:**

   ○ **Validation of Feelings:** Discussing dating app experiences with friends or family members can normalize feelings of frustration, disappointment, or uncertainty. Knowing that others share similar challenges can alleviate feelings of isolation and reassure individuals that their experiences are valid.

2. **Perspective and Insight:**

   ○ **Gaining Outside Perspective:** Trusted confidants or mental health professionals can provide objective viewpoints and insights into dating dynamics and personal interactions on apps. This outside perspective can help users reframe situations, identify patterns, and make informed decisions.

Building Resilience and Coping Strategies

1. **Emotional Support:**

   ○ **Encouragement and Reassurance:** Supportive conversations offer encouragement and reassurance during moments of doubt or rejection. Friends and family members can remind individuals of their worth beyond dating app interactions, boosting self-esteem and resilience.

2. **Coping Strategies:**

   ○ **Developing Coping Skills:** Professionals can teach effective coping strategies for managing stress, anxiety, or disappointment related to dating apps. These strategies may include mindfulness techniques, cognitive reframing, or setting realistic expectations.

Practical Guidance and Safety Measures

1. **Navigating Challenges:**

   ○ **Problem-Solving Together:** Collaborative discussions with trusted individuals can involve brainstorming solutions to common dating app challenges, such as improving profile presentation, managing communication, or setting boundaries.

2. **Safety Concerns:**

   ○ **Addressing Safety Issues:** Open conversations can also address safety concerns related to online interactions, such as recognizing red flags, setting up safe meeting protocols, or using app features for reporting harassment or suspicious behavior.

Strategies for Effective Support

1. Choosing Supportive Relationships:

○ **Trust and Confidentiality:** Seek support from individuals who respect privacy, maintain confidentiality, and offer non-judgmental support. This ensures a safe space for discussing sensitive dating experiences.

2. Professional Guidance:

○ **Mental Health Professionals:** When challenges become overwhelming or impact mental health, consulting with therapists, counselors, or psychologists trained in relationship dynamics and digital interactions can provide specialized support.

3. Group Support:

○ **Community or Support Groups:** Joining online or local support groups focused on dating app experiences can connect individuals with peers facing similar challenges. These groups offer solidarity, shared insights, and practical advice.

Benefits of Seeking Support

1. **Emotional Resilience:** Regular support fosters emotional resilience, enabling individuals to navigate dating setbacks with greater confidence and self-awareness.
2. **Validation and Empathy:** Feeling heard and understood validates experiences and reduces feelings of isolation, promoting mental well-being.
3. **Skill Development:** Professional guidance equips individuals with coping skills, communication strategies, and safety measures essential for navigating digital dating landscapes effectively.

Conclusion

Seeking support while using dating apps is instrumental in maintaining emotional health, gaining perspective, and developing resilience. Open conversations with trusted individuals or professionals provide validation, practical guidance, and reassurance, enhancing overall well-being and empowering individuals to navigate digital dating experiences with confidence and clarity.

Coping Mechanisms-Focusing On Quality Connections

Focusing on quality connections rather than quantity when using dating apps can significantly enhance the overall experience and alleviate some of the pressures and anxieties commonly associated with online dating. Here's a detailed exploration of how prioritizing quality interactions can lead to more fulfilling relationships:

Benefits of Prioritizing Quality Connections

1. Reduced Pressure and Anxiety

- **Purposeful Engagement:** By focusing on quality, users can approach interactions with a more purposeful mindset, reducing the pressure to constantly swipe or engage with multiple matches.

- **Less Superficiality:** Prioritizing deeper connections minimizes the emphasis on superficial traits like physical appearance or initial attraction, which can alleviate anxiety related to image-consciousness or fear of judgment.

2. Emphasis on Compatibility and Values

- **Shared Interests and Values:** Quality connections are often built on shared interests, values, and life goals rather than solely on physical attraction. This focus encourages users to seek compatibility beyond surface-level attributes.

- **Meaningful Conversations:** Emphasizing quality encourages meaningful conversations that delve into topics of substance, fostering emotional connection and intellectual engagement.

3. Enhanced Relationship Satisfaction

- **Long-Term Compatibility:** Quality interactions tend to lay the foundation for more compatible relationships over the long term. Users are more likely to find satisfaction in relationships built on mutual respect, understanding, and shared interests.

- **Deeper Emotional Bonds:** Quality connections facilitate the development of deeper emotional bonds, contributing to greater relationship satisfaction and fulfillment.

Strategies for Prioritizing Quality Connections

1. Selective Matching

- **Selective Swiping:** Rather than swiping right on every profile, users can take time to review profiles thoroughly and match with individuals who align with their relationship preferences and values.

- **Compatibility Filters:** Utilizing app features such as compatibility assessments or detailed profiles can help filter potential matches based on shared interests and values.

2. Authentic Communication

- **Honest Profile Presentation:** Presenting oneself authentically in profiles can attract like-minded individuals who appreciate honesty and transparency.

- **Meaningful Conversations:** Engaging in meaningful conversations that go beyond small talk can reveal compatibility and shared values early in the interaction process.

3. Setting Boundaries

- **Personal Time Management:** Setting boundaries around app usage, such as limiting daily screen time or designating specific times for interaction, helps prevent burnout and maintains a healthy balance between online and offline life.

- **Clear Communication:** Communicating personal boundaries and expectations early in interactions can establish mutual respect and understanding, fostering a healthy dynamic from the outset.

Psychological Benefits

● **Reduced Stress:** Focusing on quality over quantity reduces the stress associated with maintaining multiple conversations or managing numerous matches simultaneously.

● **Increased Confidence:** Successful quality interactions can boost self-esteem and confidence, reinforcing the belief in one's ability to form meaningful connections.

Conclusion

Prioritizing quality connections on dating apps shifts the focus from volume to value, encouraging users to engage more meaningfully and authentically with potential matches. By emphasizing compatibility, shared values, and genuine communication, individuals can cultivate relationships that are more fulfilling and satisfying, ultimately enhancing their overall dating experience and emotional well-being.

Coping Mechanisms-Digital Detox

Taking a digital detox from dating apps involves consciously stepping away from these platforms for a period to prioritize offline activities and mental well-being. Here's a detailed exploration of why and how a digital detox can be beneficial:

Reasons for a Digital Detox from Dating Apps

1. Mental and Emotional Refreshment
- **Reduced Overstimulation:** Constant exposure to dating apps can lead to sensory overload and cognitive fatigue, impacting overall mental clarity and well-being.
- **Emotional Resilience:** Detoxing allows individuals to recalibrate emotionally, reducing feelings of anxiety, stress, or pressure associated with online dating.

2. Perspective and Self-Reflection
- **Offline Presence:** Stepping away from dating apps encourages individuals to be more present in offline activities, fostering deeper connections with oneself and others.
- **Self-Discovery:** Detox periods provide opportunities for self-reflection and introspection, helping users clarify personal values, goals, and relationship expectations.

3. Reduced Dependency on Digital Validation
- **Validation Balance:** Taking breaks helps individuals regain a healthier balance between seeking validation from digital interactions and validating oneself through personal growth and real-life achievements.
- **Authentic Connections:** Detoxing can enhance appreciation for face-to-face interactions and genuine connections, prioritizing quality over quantity in relationships.

Strategies for a Successful Digital Detox

1. Establishing Boundaries
- **Define Detox Periods:** Set clear timeframes for the detox period, whether it's a few days, weeks, or longer, based on personal needs and goals.
- **Communication:** Inform matches or connections about the detox to manage expectations and maintain open communication.

2. Engaging in Offline Activities
- **Explore Hobbies:** Dedicate time to hobbies, interests, or activities that bring joy and fulfillment outside of digital spaces.
- **Social Interaction:** Foster face-to-face social connections with friends, family, or new acquaintances, enhancing interpersonal skills and emotional well-being.

3. Mindful Reevaluation
- **Reflective Practice:** Use the detox period for self-assessment and goal setting, considering what aspects of online dating are beneficial and what might need adjustment.
- **Evaluate Experiences:** Reflect on past dating app experiences, learning from successes and challenges to approach future interactions with greater clarity and intention.

Benefits of a Digital Detox

● **Improved Mental Health:** Detoxing promotes mental clarity, reduces stress levels, and enhances overall emotional resilience.

● **Enhanced Well-Being:** Balancing digital interactions with offline activities supports a holistic approach to well-being, fostering a sense of fulfillment and contentment.

● **Renewed Perspective:** Returning to dating apps after a detox can bring renewed energy and a refreshed perspective, enabling users to engage more intentionally and authentically.

Conclusion

A digital detox from dating apps offers an opportunity for individuals to prioritize mental well-being, regain perspective, and foster meaningful connections offline. By establishing boundaries, engaging in offline activities, and reflecting on personal growth, users can navigate digital dating more mindfully and effectively, ultimately enhancing their overall happiness and satisfaction in relationships.

Chapter 15: Alternatives to Dating Apps

Introduction

In the realm of dating and social interactions, traditional methods and modern alternatives to dating apps offer distinct avenues for meeting potential partners and fostering connections. Each approach brings its own set of advantages and nuances that cater to different preferences and relationship goals.

Traditional Dating Methods

Traditional dating methods center around personal, face-to-face interactions and often involve established social circles or introductions through mutual connections:

1. **Personal Interaction**: Direct engagement allows individuals to assess chemistry and compatibility through non-verbal cues, body language, and the subtleties of conversation that digital communication may not fully capture.
2. **Contextual Understanding**: Meeting in shared social environments such as parties or community gatherings provides a deeper context for understanding someone's personality, interests, and values. This setting fosters a more holistic view compared to digital profiles.
3. **Established Connections**: Introductions facilitated by friends or family come with inherent trust and compatibility screening, potentially leading to more meaningful connections grounded in mutual acquaintanceship.
4. **Serendipity and Romance**: Traditional dating often involves spontaneous encounters or romantic gestures that contribute to an element of surprise and serendipity, enhancing the romantic experience.

Modern Alternatives

In contrast to dating apps, modern alternatives offer opportunities for social connections outside the digital realm:

1. **Meet-up Groups**: Organized gatherings centered around specific interests or activities bring together like-minded individuals in a casual, group setting conducive to forming friendships or romantic connections.
2. **Social Clubs**: Clubs focused on hobbies, sports, or cultural interests provide regular opportunities for socializing and meeting new people in an environment where shared passions can facilitate natural connections.
3. **Networking Events**: Professional networking events not only serve career-building purposes but also offer avenues for forging personal relationships based on shared professional interests, blending social and professional interactions.
4. **Speed Dating and Singles Events**: Structured events like speed dating allow participants to engage face-to-face with multiple potential matches in a short period, encouraging real-time connections and immediate feedback.

Conclusion

While dating apps offer convenience and broad access to a diverse pool of potential matches, traditional and modern alternatives provide avenues for more personalized, context-rich interactions. Choosing between them often hinges on individual preferences, comfort levels with technology, and desired relationship outcomes. Integrating a mix of these approaches can enrich one's social life, enhance interpersonal skills, and increase the likelihood of finding compatible connections that align with personal values and interests.

Traditional Dating Methods

Personal Interaction in Dating

Personal interaction refers to direct face-to-face engagement between individuals, which plays a crucial role in assessing chemistry, compatibility, and building relationships. Here are key aspects of how personal interaction facilitates these processes:

1. **Non-verbal Cues**: Non-verbal communication, such as facial expressions, gestures, eye contact, and posture, provides nuanced signals about a person's emotions, intentions, and level of interest. These cues can convey aspects of personality and emotional state that may not be fully apparent through text or photos on dating apps.
2. **Body Language**: Body language encompasses a wide range of signals, including proximity, touch, and physical demeanor. For example, leaning in during a conversation, mirroring gestures, or subtle movements can indicate comfort and rapport between individuals.
3. **Subtleties of Conversation**: In face-to-face interactions, conversations often flow naturally and allow for spontaneous responses, humor, and deeper exploration of topics. This depth can reveal shared interests, values, and perspectives that contribute to assessing compatibility beyond surface-level attributes.
4. **Instant Feedback**: Personal interaction provides immediate feedback based on real-time interactions. This allows individuals to gauge mutual interest and adjust their approach accordingly, fostering a sense of connection that goes beyond the initial impression.
5. **Building Trust**: Direct engagement allows for the gradual building of trust through shared experiences, active listening, and mutual vulnerability. This trust forms a foundation for deeper emotional connections and potential romantic relationships.

Benefits Compared to Digital Communication

While dating apps offer convenience and accessibility, personal interaction offers several unique advantages:

- **Authenticity**: Face-to-face interaction promotes authenticity as individuals can express themselves more fully and transparently, fostering genuine connections based on real-time interaction and mutual understanding.
- **Emotional Depth**: The richness of personal interaction allows for emotional depth and intimacy that can be challenging to achieve through digital platforms, where communication may be more controlled or curated.
- **Immediate Connection**: Physical presence enhances the immediacy of connection and allows for spontaneous expressions of attraction, affection, and shared interests, contributing to a more dynamic and engaging interaction.

Conclusion

In the realm of dating and relationship-building, personal interaction plays a vital role in assessing chemistry, compatibility, and fostering meaningful connections. While digital communication through dating apps offers convenience and initial access to potential matches, face-to-face interaction provides essential elements such as non-verbal cues, emotional depth, and instant feedback that contribute to building authentic and fulfilling relationships. Integrating both digital and personal interactions can enhance the dating experience by combining convenience with the richness of personal connection.

Contextual Understanding in Dating

Contextual understanding refers to gaining insights into someone's personality, interests, and values through shared social environments and activities. Meeting in settings like parties, community gatherings, or social events provides a richer context compared to digital profiles on dating apps. Here's how this setting fosters a more holistic view:

1. **Observing Behavior**: In social environments, individuals can observe how someone interacts with others, responds to different situations, and engages in conversations. These observations provide clues about their communication style, social skills, and emotional intelligence, which contribute to a more comprehensive understanding of their personality.
2. **Shared Interests and Activities**: Participating in activities or events together allows individuals to discover shared interests, hobbies, and passions organically. Whether it's discussing mutual hobbies, enjoying cultural events, or participating in group activities, these shared experiences deepen connections and reveal common values.
3. **Cultural Context**: Social gatherings often reflect cultural norms, values, and traditions, providing insights into someone's background and upbringing. Understanding these cultural aspects can influence interpersonal dynamics and compatibility, fostering mutual understanding and respect.
4. **Real-Time Interaction**: Unlike digital profiles that can be curated or edited, real-time interaction in social settings offers authentic glimpses into someone's personality and demeanor. This authenticity enhances trust and rapport, facilitating more meaningful connections.
5. **Depth of Conversation**: Face-to-face conversations in social environments allow for deeper and more spontaneous discussions compared to text-based exchanges on dating apps. Topics can range from casual banter to more profound discussions about life goals, beliefs, and personal experiences, providing a deeper understanding of each other's values and perspectives.

Benefits Compared to Digital Profiles

Meeting in shared social environments offers several advantages over digital profiles on dating apps:

- **Authenticity and Transparency**: Social settings promote authenticity as individuals can interact naturally and express themselves more fully. This transparency fosters genuine connections based on real-time interactions and mutual understanding.
- **Contextual Insights**: Observing someone in various social situations provides contextual insights into their behavior, attitudes, and interpersonal skills that may not be fully conveyed through digital profiles.
- **Cultural Compatibility**: Social environments facilitate exploration of cultural compatibility, allowing individuals to appreciate and respect each other's cultural backgrounds and traditions.

Conclusion

Contextual understanding through shared social environments enhances the dating experience by providing a deeper, more nuanced perspective on someone's personality, interests, and values. While dating apps offer convenience and initial access to potential matches, meeting in real-life settings fosters authenticity, cultural awareness, and meaningful connections. Integrating both digital and social interactions can enrich the dating journey by combining convenience with the depth and richness of personal context.

Established Connections in Dating

Established connections refer to introductions made through mutual acquaintances, friends, or family members in the context of dating. These introductions come with inherent trust and compatibility screening, which can lead to more meaningful connections. Here's how this process works and its benefits:

1. **Mutual Trust and Endorsement**: Introductions made by friends or family members carry a level of trust and endorsement. When someone recommends a potential match, they often do so based on their knowledge of both individuals' personalities, values, and relationship goals. This mutual trust reduces uncertainty and initial apprehension about the person being introduced.
2. **Compatibility Screening**: Friends and family members who facilitate introductions typically consider compatibility factors such as shared interests, values, and lifestyle preferences. This screening process increases the likelihood of compatibility between the individuals being introduced, laying a solid foundation for a potential relationship.
3. **Common Ground and Shared Circles**: Being introduced through mutual acquaintances establishes common ground and shared social circles. This shared network can foster a sense of community and support, providing a backdrop of familiarity and comfort that enhances the dating experience.
4. **Facilitating Natural Interactions**: Introductions in social settings often facilitate natural interactions where individuals can engage in meaningful conversations and activities. This natural environment allows for a more relaxed and genuine exchange, compared to the structured interactions typical of dating apps.
5. **Building Rapport and Trust**: Meeting through mutual connections allows individuals to build rapport and trust gradually. This process of getting to know each other within a familiar social context encourages openness and authenticity, contributing to the development of deeper connections.

Benefits Compared to Dating Apps

Introductions facilitated by friends or family offer several advantages over connections made through dating apps:

- **Personal Endorsement**: Recommendations from trusted sources carry a personal endorsement that can instill confidence and reassurance in both parties.
- **Shared Values and Interests**: Mutual acquaintances often facilitate introductions based on shared values and interests, enhancing the potential for compatibility.
- **Natural Progression**: Relationships initiated through mutual connections tend to progress more organically, allowing individuals to build trust and rapport over time.
- **Community Support**: Being introduced through friends or family integrates individuals into a supportive community, fostering a sense of belonging and shared social support.

Conclusion

Established connections through introductions by friends or family members offer a personalized and trusted approach to dating. They leverage mutual trust, compatibility screening, and shared social circles to facilitate meaningful connections grounded in familiarity and community support. While dating apps provide broad access and convenience, introductions through established connections enhance the dating experience by promoting authenticity, mutual understanding, and the potential for long-lasting relationships. Integrating both approaches—traditional introductions and digital platforms—can enrich the dating journey by combining personal endorsement with the convenience of online access to potential matches.

Serendipity and Romance in Traditional Dating

Serendipity and romance are intrinsic elements of traditional dating that stem from spontaneous encounters, chance meetings, and romantic gestures. Here's a deeper look into how these aspects contribute to a unique and memorable dating experience:

1. **Spontaneous Encounters**: Traditional dating often unfolds through unplanned encounters in everyday settings such as social gatherings, community events, or even chance meetings in public places. These spontaneous interactions allow individuals to meet unexpectedly, creating a sense of excitement and spontaneity.
2. **Unexpected Connections**: Serendipity in dating refers to the unexpected discovery of someone special through unplanned circumstances. It involves being in the right place at the right time and encountering someone who sparks a genuine connection or attraction. These chance encounters can lead to meaningful relationships that evolve naturally.
3. **Romantic Gestures**: Traditional dating embraces romantic gestures such as flowers, handwritten notes, surprise dates, or thoughtful gifts. These gestures are often spontaneous and heartfelt, demonstrating care, affection, and the desire to impress or delight a potential partner.
4. **Element of Surprise**: Unlike dating apps where matches are predetermined based on algorithms and preferences, traditional dating allows for surprises and unpredictability. Discovering mutual interests, shared values, or unexpected chemistry during face-to-face interactions adds an element of surprise that enhances the romantic experience.
5. **Building Emotional Connections**: Serendipitous encounters and romantic gestures play a crucial role in building emotional connections between individuals. These experiences create memorable moments and deepen the bond between partners, fostering intimacy and emotional closeness.

Benefits of Serendipity and Romance

● **Memorable Experiences**: Serendipitous encounters and romantic gestures create memorable experiences that individuals cherish and reminisce about in their relationships.

● **Enhanced Emotional Connection**: Spontaneous interactions and romantic gestures contribute to building a strong emotional connection based on shared experiences and meaningful moments.

● **Fostering Romance**: The element of surprise and spontaneity inherent in traditional dating fosters romance, making the dating journey more exciting and fulfilling.

● **Natural Progression**: Relationships that begin with serendipitous encounters or romantic gestures often progress naturally, as the initial attraction and emotional connection lay a foundation for deeper involvement.

Conclusion

Serendipity and romance in traditional dating add depth, excitement, and emotional connection to the dating experience. They involve spontaneous encounters, unexpected connections, and romantic gestures that contribute to memorable moments and foster genuine relationships. While dating apps offer convenience and access to potential matches, traditional dating methods allow individuals to embrace the unpredictability and magic of serendipitous moments, enhancing the romantic journey and creating lasting memories. Integrating both traditional and modern approaches to dating can provide a balanced and enriching experience that combines the best of both worlds.

moments, enhancing the romantic journey and creating lasting memories. Integrating both traditional and modern approaches to dating can provide a balanced and enriching experience that combines the best of both worlds.

Modern Alternatives

Meet-up Groups: Facilitating Connections Through Shared Interests

Meet-up groups are organized gatherings designed to bring together individuals who share common interests, hobbies, or activities. These groups serve as informal social platforms where people can meet in a relaxed and comfortable environment. Here's a deeper look into how meet-up groups function and their benefits in fostering connections:

1. **Purpose and Organization**: Meet-up groups are organized around specific themes such as hiking, book clubs, cooking, photography, gaming, or professional networking. They are typically initiated by individuals or organizations passionate about a particular interest, who create events and invite others to participate.
2. **Inclusivity and Diversity**: These groups attract a diverse range of participants who share a genuine enthusiasm for the activity or subject matter. Attendees come from varied backgrounds, ages, and experiences, contributing to a rich and dynamic social environment.
3. **Casual and Relaxed Atmosphere**: Unlike structured dating environments, meet-up groups offer a laid-back setting where individuals can engage in conversations, share experiences, and enjoy activities together without the pressure of formal dating expectations.
4. **Facilitating Connections**: The primary goal of meet-up groups is to facilitate connections. Participants have the opportunity to meet new people who share their passions, fostering friendships, professional connections, and potentially romantic relationships based on common interests.
5. **Building Community**: Over time, regular participation in meet-up groups can lead to the formation of supportive communities. Members develop a sense of belonging and camaraderie through shared experiences and mutual interests, enhancing their social lives and overall well-being.

Benefits of Meet-up Groups

- **Shared Interests**: Meet-up groups provide a platform for individuals to connect with others who share their specific interests and passions, leading to meaningful conversations and interactions.
- **Social Engagement**: These gatherings encourage social interaction and networking in a casual and non-intimidating setting, promoting friendship and relationship building.
- **Exploration and Learning**: Participants have the opportunity to explore new interests, learn from others, and engage in activities that contribute to personal growth and enrichment.
- **Low-Pressure Environment**: Unlike traditional dating scenarios, meet-up groups offer a low-pressure environment where individuals can socialize naturally and authentically, without the expectation of immediate romantic involvement.

Conclusion

Meet-up groups play a vital role in modern dating alternatives by providing opportunities for individuals to connect based on shared interests and activities. They foster inclusivity, social engagement, and community building, making them ideal for those seeking meaningful connections outside the realm of dating apps. Whether participants are looking for friendships, professional contacts, or romantic relationships, meet-up groups offer a supportive environment where genuine connections can flourish. Integrating participation in meet-up groups with other dating strategies can enhance one's social life and increase the likelihood of forming lasting relationships grounded in shared passions and mutual interests.

Social Clubs: Facilitating Social Connections Through Shared Interests

Social clubs are organized groups centered around specific hobbies, sports, cultural activities, or professional interests. These clubs provide regular opportunities for individuals to socialize, network, and form connections with others who share similar passions. Here's a deeper look into how social clubs function and their benefits in fostering social connections:

1. **Diverse Range of Interests**: Social clubs cater to a wide range of interests and activities, such as hiking, wine tasting, book clubs, dance classes, photography, chess, or professional networking. Each club focuses on a particular interest or hobby that serves as a common ground for its members.
2. **Structured Gatherings**: Clubs typically organize regular meetings, events, or outings related to their specific interest. These gatherings may include discussions, workshops, competitions, outings, or social events designed to engage members and foster interaction.
3. **Shared Passion and Engagement**: Members of social clubs are united by a genuine enthusiasm for the club's focus area. This shared passion serves as a catalyst for meaningful conversations, collaborations, and friendships among participants.
4. **Networking Opportunities**: Beyond socializing, social clubs offer valuable networking opportunities. Members can connect with others who share their professional interests or career goals, potentially leading to professional collaborations, mentorship, or career advancement.
5. **Community and Support**: Joining a social club provides a sense of community and belonging. Members often develop supportive relationships, share experiences, and celebrate achievements related to their shared interests.

Benefits of Social Clubs

- **Natural Connections**: Social clubs create a conducive environment for making connections based on shared interests and activities. Members can bond over their mutual passion, facilitating natural and authentic interactions.
- **Skill Development**: Many social clubs offer opportunities for skill development, knowledge sharing, and learning from experts or experienced members. This contributes to personal growth and enrichment.
- **Inclusivity and Diversity**: Clubs attract individuals from diverse backgrounds, ages, and professions who share a common interest. This diversity enriches interactions and broadens perspectives within the club community.
- **Social Engagement**: Participating in club activities promotes social interaction, reducing feelings of isolation and fostering a sense of camaraderie among members.

Conclusion

Social clubs play a significant role as modern alternatives to dating apps by providing structured opportunities for socializing and meeting new people based on shared interests and passions. Whether individuals are seeking friendships, romantic connections, or professional relationships, social clubs offer a supportive environment where genuine connections can flourish. By actively participating in club activities and engaging with like-minded individuals, members can expand their social circles, enhance their personal interests, and enrich their overall social and emotional well-being. Integrating involvement in social clubs with other dating strategies can diversify social interactions and increase the likelihood of forming meaningful and lasting connections.

Networking Events: Bridging Professional and Personal Connections

Networking events are organized gatherings designed primarily for professionals to connect, exchange ideas, and explore career opportunities within their industry or field. However, beyond their professional benefits, these events also serve as platforms for individuals to form personal relationships based on shared professional interests. Here's an in-depth look at how networking events function and their role in fostering both social and professional connections:

1. **Purpose and Structure**: Networking events are typically structured to facilitate introductions, conversations, and interactions among attendees. They may include formal elements such as keynote speeches, panel discussions, or workshops focused on industry trends, skills development, or career insights.
2. **Professional Focus**: These events attract professionals from diverse backgrounds, including executives, entrepreneurs, industry experts, and aspiring professionals. Attendees often seek opportunities to expand their professional network, seek mentorship, or explore career advancement possibilities.
3. **Informal Networking**: In addition to structured sessions, networking events often include informal networking opportunities such as coffee breaks, cocktail receptions, or networking lounges. These informal settings encourage more relaxed and spontaneous interactions among participants.
4. **Shared Interests and Goals**: Networking events unite attendees around shared professional interests, goals, or challenges within their industry. This common ground serves as a foundation for meaningful conversations and relationship building.
5. **Personal Connections**: Beyond professional interests, networking events provide occasions for individuals to discover commonalities beyond the workplace. Conversations can naturally segue into personal interests, hobbies, or shared experiences, fostering deeper, more personal connections.

Benefits of Networking Events

● **Career Advancement**: Networking events offer opportunities to connect with industry leaders, potential employers, or mentors who can provide guidance, career advice, or professional referrals.

● **Knowledge Sharing**: Attendees can gain insights into industry trends, best practices, and innovative ideas through interactions with peers and experts.

● **Social Engagement**: Networking events promote social interaction and relationship building, enhancing attendees' social and emotional well-being by expanding their professional and personal networks.

● **Mutual Support and Collaboration**: Building relationships at networking events can lead to collaborations, partnerships, or joint projects that benefit both personal and professional growth.

Blending Professional and Personal Interests

Networking events uniquely blend professional and personal interests, allowing individuals to engage authentically with others who share similar career aspirations or industry passions. This dual focus not only supports career advancement but also facilitates the development of genuine friendships and social connections beyond the workplace. By participating actively in networking events and nurturing relationships over time, attendees can cultivate a robust network of contacts that enriches both their professional endeavors and personal lives.

Conclusion

Networking events serve as dynamic alternatives to dating apps by offering structured environments where individuals can meet and connect based on shared professional interests and goals. These events provide a fertile ground for forging meaningful relationships, whether for career advancement, personal development, or social engagement. By embracing the opportunities offered by networking events, individuals can expand their social circles, enhance their professional network, and enrich their overall personal and professional experiences.

Speed Dating and Singles Events: Facilitating Real-Time Connections

Speed dating and singles events are structured gatherings designed to facilitate face-to-face interactions between individuals seeking romantic connections. These events offer participants a unique opportunity to meet multiple potential matches in a short timeframe, fostering real-time connections and immediate feedback. Here's an in-depth look at how speed dating and singles events function and their role in facilitating romantic interactions:

1. **Format and Structure**: Speed dating events typically involve participants rotating through a series of brief, timed interactions with potential matches. Each interaction lasts a few minutes, providing enough time for participants to introduce themselves, engage in conversation, and assess compatibility.
2. **Facilitation and Moderation**: Events are often facilitated by hosts or organizers who coordinate the logistics, manage timing, and ensure smooth transitions between interactions. Moderators may also provide prompts or icebreakers to facilitate conversation and ease initial nerves.
3. **Face-to-Face Engagement**: Unlike digital interactions on dating apps, speed dating emphasizes direct, in-person engagement. Participants can gauge chemistry, assess physical attraction, and observe non-verbal cues such as body language and facial expressions, which are integral to forming initial impressions and connections.
4. **Immediate Feedback**: After each interaction, participants typically provide feedback or indicate interest in potential matches through a structured system managed by event organizers. This immediate feedback loop allows individuals to receive timely responses and gauge mutual interest.
5. **Structured Environment**: The structured environment of speed dating events creates a focused atmosphere conducive to meeting new people and exploring romantic possibilities. This format eliminates the pressure of extended one-on-one interactions while encouraging participants to be open-minded and responsive to new connections.

Benefits of Speed Dating and Singles Events

● **Efficiency**: Speed dating events offer a streamlined approach to meeting potential matches, allowing participants to interact with multiple individuals in a single session. This efficiency maximizes exposure to diverse dating prospects in a short period.

    ● **Real-Time Connections**: Face-to-face interactions in real-time enable participants to establish immediate rapport, evaluate compatibility, and determine chemistry based on direct observations and interactions.

    ● **Low-Pressure Environment**: The structured nature of speed dating events creates a low-pressure environment conducive to casual conversation and genuine interactions. Participants can engage comfortably without the expectation of extended commitments.

    ● **Immediate Results**: Participants receive immediate feedback or matches shortly after the event, facilitating follow-up communication and further exploration of mutual interest.

Navigating Speed Dating and Singles Events

● **Preparation**: Participants can prepare for speed dating events by considering conversation starters, projecting confidence, and maintaining a positive attitude. Being open to new experiences and connections enhances the likelihood of meaningful interactions.

● **Follow-Up**: After the event, participants can follow up with individuals who expressed mutual interest or whom they found intriguing during the interactions. Prompt communication can solidify connections and facilitate ongoing dialogue.

Conclusion

Speed dating and singles events provide structured environments for individuals to engage face-to-face with multiple potential matches, fostering real-time connections and immediate feedback. These events offer a dynamic alternative to digital dating platforms by emphasizing direct interaction, physical presence, and personal rapport. By participating in speed dating and singles events, individuals can explore romantic possibilities, expand their social circles, and potentially meet someone special in a supportive and engaging environment.

Chapter 16: Reimagining Online Dating

Introduction

Online dating has revolutionized how people meet and connect in the digital age. Initially driven by algorithms and profile browsing, modern dating platforms are constantly evolving to offer more personalized, authentic, and engaging experiences. This evolution is not just about technology but also about understanding human dynamics and fostering meaningful connections in a digital landscape.

Reimagining Online Dating

Innovative Approaches

1. **AI and Machine Learning**: The integration of AI and machine learning algorithms can revolutionize matchmaking by analyzing vast amounts of user data. These technologies can learn from user behavior, preferences, and interactions to suggest highly compatible matches, improving the chances of meaningful connections.
2. **Virtual Reality (VR)**: VR technology offers the potential to create immersive dating experiences where users can interact in virtual environments. VR dates can simulate real-world scenarios, providing a more intimate and realistic interaction that goes beyond traditional text-based communication.
3. **Video Dating**: Moving beyond static profiles, video dating allows users to engage in real-time conversations and see each other's facial expressions and body language. This approach fosters a deeper initial connection and helps users gauge compatibility more effectively.
4. **Social Verification**: Implementing features that verify user identities through social networks or other credible sources enhances trust and safety. Verified profiles can reduce the risks of catfishing and create a more secure environment for building relationships.
5. **Event-Based Dating**: Hosting virtual or in-person events within dating platforms, such as themed parties or speed dating sessions, encourages natural interactions and community building among users with shared interests.
6. **Augmented Reality (AR)**: AR features can enhance offline dating experiences by providing information about nearby users or suggesting date-friendly venues based on user preferences. AR overlays can enrich interactions by blending digital and real-world elements.

Building Meaningful Connections

1. **Authentic Self-Presentation**: Encouraging users to showcase their genuine interests, values, and personalities in profiles attracts like-minded individuals. Emphasizing authenticity helps foster connections based on compatibility beyond superficial attributes.
2. **Quality Over Quantity**: Prioritizing meaningful interactions over a high volume of matches encourages users to invest time in getting to know each other deeply. Platforms can incentivize substantive conversations and mutual respect to promote genuine connections.
3. **Communication Skills**: Providing resources on effective communication, such as active listening and empathy, helps users navigate online interactions with authenticity and understanding. Strong communication skills are crucial for building trust and connection.

4. **Long-Term Compatibility**: Integrating compatibility assessments that consider factors like shared values, life goals, and communication styles supports users in forming lasting relationships rather than casual encounters. Platforms can focus on facilitating connections that align with users' relationship aspirations.

5. **Mindful Use of Technology**: Promoting mindful technology use encourages users to balance online interactions with offline activities and self-care. Setting boundaries around screen time and taking breaks from dating apps can enhance overall well-being and satisfaction.

6. **Community Engagement**: Building a supportive community within dating platforms through forums, support groups, or collaborative activities fosters camaraderie and mutual support among users. Community engagement enhances user retention by providing opportunities for shared experiences and emotional connection.

Conclusion

Reimagining online dating involves leveraging innovative technologies and strategies to enhance user experiences and facilitate meaningful connections. By embracing AI, VR, video dating, social verification, and event-based interactions, dating platforms can evolve to meet the diverse needs of users seeking genuine relationships in the digital age. Promoting authenticity, prioritizing quality interactions, and fostering community engagement are essential for creating fulfilling and enriching online dating experiences where meaningful connections thrive.

AI and Machine Learning

AI (Artificial Intelligence) and machine learning are transforming the landscape of online dating by leveraging advanced algorithms to enhance matchmaking processes. Here's a detailed explanation of how these technologies work and their impact on improving meaningful connections:

Understanding AI and Machine Learning in Online Dating

1. Data Analysis and Personalization
- **Data Processing**: AI algorithms are capable of processing vast quantities of data generated by users' interactions on dating platforms. This includes user profiles, preferences, messaging history, and behaviors.
- **Behavioral Analysis**: Machine learning algorithms analyze user behavior patterns such as swipe history, profile views, messaging frequency, and response rates. This analysis helps in understanding individual preferences and tendencies.

2. Predictive Modeling
- **Compatibility Prediction**: By learning from historical data, AI algorithms can predict the compatibility between users based on factors like interests, values, communication style, and relationship goals.
- **Recommendation Systems**: AI-powered recommendation systems suggest potential matches to users based on their preferences and behavioral data. These recommendations are tailored to increase the likelihood of users finding compatible partners.

3. Improving User Experience
- **Personalized Matches**: AI enhances the user experience by providing personalized match suggestions that align with individual preferences and compatibility factors. This reduces the time and effort spent by users in searching for suitable partners.
- **Real-Time Adjustments**: Machine learning algorithms continuously refine match suggestions based on real-time user interactions and feedback. This adaptive approach ensures that recommendations remain relevant and accurate over time.

4. Enhancing Quality of Matches
- **Focused Matching Criteria**: AI algorithms can incorporate complex matching criteria beyond superficial attributes, such as shared values, long-term goals, and personality traits. This focus on compatibility fosters more meaningful connections.
- **Reducing Bias**: Machine learning algorithms can mitigate biases that may influence manual matchmaking processes by focusing on objective data points rather than subjective judgments.

5. Challenges and Considerations
- **Privacy and Security**: Ensuring the responsible use of user data is crucial to maintaining trust. Dating platforms must implement robust data protection measures and transparency regarding how AI algorithms utilize personal information.
- **User Acceptance**: Educating users about the benefits of AI-driven matchmaking and addressing concerns about privacy and algorithmic decision-making are essential for fostering user acceptance and engagement.

Conclusion

AI and machine learning algorithms are revolutionizing online dating by offering more accurate, personalized, and efficient matchmaking experiences. By analyzing user data, predicting compatibility, and improving match quality, these technologies contribute to creating meaningful connections that align with users' preferences and relationship goals. As dating platforms continue to innovate with AI, the potential for fostering genuine relationships in the digital realm continues to expand, making online dating more effective and satisfying for users worldwide.

Virtual Reality (VR)

Virtual Reality (VR) technology represents a significant advancement in online dating, offering immersive experiences that transcend traditional digital interactions. Here's a detailed exploration of how VR can revolutionize the dating experience:

Understanding Virtual Reality in Online Dating

1. Immersive Environments

- **Simulated Realism**: VR technology creates virtual environments that mimic real-world settings, such as cafes, parks, or even exotic locations. Users can engage in activities like walking, talking, or sharing experiences within these immersive settings.

- **Enhanced Presence**: VR enhances the feeling of presence and immersion by allowing users to interact with virtual surroundings and avatars, providing a sense of physical proximity that is absent in traditional online communication.

2. Realistic Interactions

- **Body Language and Gestures**: VR enables users to convey non-verbal cues and gestures through avatars, such as hand movements, facial expressions, and body language. This enhances communication by adding layers of expression beyond text or emojis.

- **Voice Communication**: Real-time voice communication in VR enhances the authenticity of interactions, allowing users to hear tone of voice, nuances, and emotions, which are crucial for building rapport and understanding.

3. Customizable Experiences

- **Personalized Avatars**: Users can create customizable avatars that represent their physical appearance, style, and preferences. This allows for self-expression and identity presentation in a way that mirrors real-life self-representation.

- **Virtual Activities**: VR dating platforms can offer a variety of interactive activities, such as virtual games, collaborative tasks, or shared media experiences (like watching movies together), fostering shared moments and bonding.

4. Benefits in Dating

- **Enhanced Intimacy**: VR dates can create a sense of intimacy and connection that transcends traditional online messaging. Users can experience closeness through shared activities and meaningful conversations in a simulated environment.

- **Risk-Free Exploration**: VR allows users to explore relationships and interactions in a low-risk, controlled environment. This can be particularly beneficial for individuals who are shy, introverted, or apprehensive about face-to-face dating.

5. Challenges and Considerations

- **Technological Barriers**: VR technology requires specialized hardware (such as VR headsets) and a stable internet connection, which may limit accessibility for some users.

- **Privacy and Safety**: Ensuring privacy and security in virtual environments is critical to protect users from potential harassment or unwanted interactions. Platforms must implement robust moderation and safety measures.

- **User Adoption**: VR dating platforms may face initial challenges in user adoption due to the novelty of the technology and concerns about cost, comfort, and social acceptance.

Conclusion

Virtual Reality represents a transformative innovation in online dating, offering immersive experiences that enhance intimacy, realism, and interaction quality. By simulating real-world scenarios and fostering meaningful connections through personalized avatars and activities, VR has the potential to redefine how people meet and form relationships online. As technology advances and adoption grows, VR dating platforms may become more mainstream, providing users with new opportunities for genuine connections in the digital age.

Video Dating

Video dating represents a dynamic evolution in online matchmaking, leveraging real-time video technology to enhance the dating experience beyond traditional static profiles. Here's a detailed exploration of how video dating can foster deeper connections and improve compatibility assessment:

Understanding Video Dating

1. Real-Time Interaction

- **Dynamic Communication**: Video dating enables users to engage in face-to-face conversations in real-time. This allows for immediate interaction, where participants can observe each other's facial expressions, gestures, and vocal tones, enhancing communication richness.
- **Authenticity and Transparency**: Seeing and hearing potential matches in real-time promotes authenticity. Users can gauge sincerity, personality, and emotional responses, which are crucial for building trust and connection early in the interaction.

2. Enhanced Compatibility Assessment

- **Non-Verbal Cues**: Video calls provide access to non-verbal cues like eye contact, smiles, and body language, which play a significant role in understanding emotions and intentions. These cues help users assess compatibility and attraction more accurately than text-based communication.
- **Contextual Insights**: Conversations in video dating often unfold naturally, allowing participants to discuss interests, values, and experiences in a more fluid manner. This contextual understanding can reveal commonalities and shared perspectives that contribute to relationship compatibility.

3. Benefits in Dating

- **Personal Connection**: Video dating facilitates a sense of personal connection by bridging the gap between digital interactions and face-to-face encounters. This helps users establish rapport and build a foundation for deeper relationships.
- **Efficiency and Convenience**: Unlike traditional dating methods that require physical meetings, video dates offer convenience and flexibility. Users can connect from anywhere, reducing logistical barriers and saving time typically spent on commuting.

4. Practical Considerations

- **Technical Requirements**: Successful video dating relies on stable internet connections, compatible devices with cameras and microphones, and reliable video conferencing platforms or dating apps that support real-time video calls.
- **Privacy and Safety**: Ensuring privacy during video dates is essential. Platforms must prioritize secure communication channels and provide features like blurred backgrounds or video moderation to protect user identities and safety.

5. Cultural and Social Impacts

- **Normalization of Video Dating**: As video communication becomes more mainstream in daily life, the stigma associated with online dating may diminish. Video dating platforms can contribute to cultural acceptance and social normalization of virtual interactions.

Conclusion

Video dating represents a significant advancement in online matchmaking, offering users the opportunity to engage in real-time, face-to-face interactions that enhance authenticity, connection, and compatibility assessment. By enabling users to see and hear each other during conversations, video dating platforms foster meaningful relationships rooted in genuine communication and shared experiences. As technology continues to evolve and user preferences shift towards more interactive and personalized dating experiences, video dating is poised to play a pivotal role in shaping the future of digital romance.

Social Verification

Social Verification enhances the credibility and safety of user profiles on dating apps by validating identities through social networks or other reputable sources. Here's a detailed exploration of how this feature works and its benefits:

Understanding Social Verification

1. Enhancing Trust and Safety

- **Reducing Catfishing**: Catfishing, where individuals create fake identities, is a common concern in online dating. Social verification verifies users' identities against their social media profiles or other trusted sources, ensuring that the person behind the profile is genuine.

- **Building User Confidence**: Verified profiles instill confidence among users by assuring them that they are interacting with real individuals rather than fictitious personas. This transparency promotes a safer and more trustworthy environment for forming relationships.

2. Implementation Process

- **Linking to Social Networks**: Dating apps integrate with social media platforms like Facebook, Instagram, or LinkedIn to verify user identities. Users may opt to link their accounts, allowing the app to confirm their identity based on existing social media profiles.

- **Manual Verification**: Some platforms employ manual verification processes where users submit identification documents or undergo additional checks to verify their identity. This method adds an extra layer of security, especially for users who prefer not to link their social media accounts.

3. Benefits for Users

- **Enhanced Security**: Verified profiles reduce the likelihood of encountering fraudulent or deceptive individuals, enhancing overall user safety. This feature is particularly valuable for users concerned about online safety and privacy.

- **Improved Match Quality**: Users can filter and prioritize interactions with verified profiles, increasing the chances of meaningful connections based on verified identities and shared interests.

4. Challenges and Considerations

- **Privacy Concerns**: Users may be reluctant to link their social media accounts due to privacy concerns. Platforms must ensure robust privacy policies and secure handling of personal information to address these concerns.

- **Accessibility and Inclusivity**: Some users may not have active social media accounts or prefer not to disclose personal information online. Platforms should offer alternative verification methods to accommodate diverse user preferences and needs.

5. Cultural and Social Implications

- **Normalization of Verification**: Social verification contributes to the normalization of identity verification practices in online dating. As users become more accustomed to verified profiles, the stigma associated with verifying identities may diminish.

- **Trustworthiness of Platforms**: Dating apps that prioritize social verification demonstrate a commitment to user safety and integrity. This can enhance their reputation and attract users seeking a secure and trustworthy dating experience.

Conclusion

Social verification is a crucial feature in modern dating apps, offering users a reliable way to verify identities and build trust within the online dating community. By leveraging social networks or alternative verification methods, platforms can create a safer environment conducive to genuine connections and meaningful relationships. As technology and user expectations evolve, social verification continues to play a pivotal role in enhancing the authenticity and security of online dating experiences.

Event-Based Dating

Event-Based Dating introduces structured activities within dating platforms to foster natural interactions and community building among users. Here's a detailed exploration of this approach:

Understanding Event-Based Dating

1. Types of Events
   - **Virtual Events**: These events take place entirely online, utilizing video conferencing or chat rooms to facilitate interactions. Examples include virtual speed dating, themed discussion groups, or virtual parties where users can engage in real-time conversations and activities.
   - **In-Person Events**: Held at physical venues, these events bring users together for face-to-face interactions. Common examples include speed dating events, social mixers, or themed parties organized by the dating platform.
   2. Benefits and Advantages
   - **Facilitating Natural Interactions**: Events provide structured environments where users can engage in natural conversations and activities based on shared interests or themes. This setting encourages meaningful connections beyond typical profile-based interactions.
   - **Community Building**: By participating in events, users can connect with like-minded individuals within the dating platform's community. Shared experiences during events can strengthen social bonds and foster a sense of belonging among users.
   - **Enhanced Engagement**: Events enhance user engagement by offering interactive and varied experiences beyond swiping profiles. They provide opportunities for users to showcase their personalities and interests in real-time settings.
   3. Platform Integration
   - **Features and Tools**: Dating platforms integrate event management tools to facilitate event planning, registration, and participation. Features may include event calendars, RSVP functionalities, and notifications to inform users about upcoming events.
   - **Moderation and Safety**: Platforms implement moderation measures to ensure events adhere to community guidelines and maintain a safe environment for participants. This includes monitoring interactions during virtual events and ensuring security at in-person gatherings.
   4. User Experience
   - **Diverse Offerings**: Platforms offer a variety of event types to cater to diverse user preferences and demographics. Events may range from casual social gatherings to structured matchmaking sessions, appealing to different dating goals and interests.
   - **Feedback and Iteration**: Platforms gather user feedback to refine event offerings and improve the overall user experience. This iterative approach allows platforms to adapt events based on user preferences and emerging trends.
   5. Challenges and Considerations
   - **Logistical Challenges**: Organizing events, whether virtual or in-person, requires careful planning and coordination to ensure smooth execution and user satisfaction.
   - **Inclusivity and Accessibility**: Platforms must consider accessibility issues for users with disabilities or those in geographically remote areas who may face barriers to participating in events.
   6. Cultural and Social Implications
   - **Community Building**: Event-based dating fosters a sense of community among users, promoting social interaction and shared experiences that contribute to a positive platform culture.

● **Changing Norms**: Platforms that successfully integrate event-based dating may influence dating norms by emphasizing real-time interactions and shared activities over purely digital connections.

Conclusion

Event-based dating enriches the online dating experience by providing structured opportunities for users to engage in natural interactions and build community. Whether virtual or in-person, these events facilitate meaningful connections based on shared interests and experiences, enhancing overall user engagement and satisfaction within dating platforms. As platforms continue to innovate, event-based features play a pivotal role in fostering authentic relationships and supporting diverse dating preferences and goals.

Augmented Reality (AR)

Augmented Reality (AR) integrates digital information and virtual elements into real-world environments, potentially transforming offline dating experiences. Here's a detailed exploration of how AR can enhance dating:

Understanding Augmented Reality in Dating

1. Features and Functionality

- **Nearby User Information**: AR overlays can display real-time information about nearby users who match specified criteria, such as interests or compatibility scores. This feature allows users to identify potential matches in their vicinity, enhancing serendipitous encounters.

- **Venue Suggestions**: AR can suggest date-friendly venues based on user preferences, such as restaurants, cafes, or recreational spots. It provides real-time information about venue ratings, menus, availability, and reviews, facilitating decision-making for dates.

- **Interactive Enhancements**: AR overlays enrich interactions by overlaying digital content onto physical surroundings. For example, users can view shared interests, mutual connections, or personalized messages floating above a person or venue in real-time.

2. Benefits and Advantages

- **Enhanced User Experience**: AR enhances user engagement by providing immersive and interactive dating experiences. It blends digital information seamlessly with the real world, creating a dynamic and personalized dating environment.

- **Facilitates Planning and Decision-Making**: AR assists users in planning dates by offering venue suggestions and real-time information. It simplifies the process of selecting suitable locations and activities, improving the overall quality of dating experiences.

- **Promotes Serendipity**: By highlighting nearby users and shared interests, AR fosters serendipitous connections and spontaneous interactions in everyday settings. It encourages users to explore new places and engage with potential matches in their immediate surroundings.

3. Integration with Dating Platforms

- **App Integration**: Dating apps can integrate AR features directly into their platforms, allowing users to access AR functionalities through mobile devices. This integration enhances the app's usability and attractiveness to tech-savvy users seeking innovative dating experiences.

- **User Privacy and Safety**: Platforms must prioritize user privacy and safety when implementing AR features. Controls for sharing location data and personal information should be transparent and customizable to ensure user comfort and security.

4. Cultural and Social Implications

- **Changing Dating Norms**: AR in dating apps may influence norms by promoting real-time interactions and personalized experiences. It encourages users to engage with potential matches based on shared interests and physical proximity, potentially shifting traditional dating practices.

- **Community Building**: AR features that facilitate real-world interactions and venue suggestions contribute to building a sense of community among users. Shared experiences and interactions in augmented environments can foster social connections and platform loyalty.

5. Challenges and Considerations

- **Technological Limitations**: AR technology requires robust infrastructure and device capabilities to deliver seamless experiences. Compatibility issues with older devices or limited AR adoption among users may hinder widespread implementation.
- **Ethical and Legal Concerns**: Platforms must adhere to ethical guidelines and legal regulations concerning data privacy, augmented content accuracy, and user consent. Transparent policies and effective moderation are essential to mitigate misuse or abuse of AR features.

Conclusion

Augmented Reality presents an innovative approach to enhance offline dating experiences by integrating digital information and virtual elements into real-world environments. By offering real-time user information, venue suggestions, and interactive overlays, AR enriches interactions and facilitates meaningful connections based on shared interests and physical proximity. As dating platforms continue to evolve, AR features have the potential to redefine dating norms, promote community engagement, and elevate user experiences in the digital age.

Authentic Self-Presentation

Authentic Self-Presentation in online dating is crucial for establishing genuine connections based on shared interests, values, and personalities. Here's a detailed exploration of its significance:

Understanding Authentic Self-Presentation in Online Dating

1. Emphasis on Genuine Interests and Values

- **Showcasing Personality**: Authentic self-presentation encourages users to portray their true selves in profiles. This includes highlighting hobbies, passions, and personal beliefs that reflect their genuine interests and values. By presenting a comprehensive picture of who they are, users attract like-minded individuals who resonate with their authentic traits.

- **Building Trust**: Authenticity in profiles builds trust among potential matches. When users present themselves honestly, they establish a foundation of transparency and sincerity, which is essential for forming meaningful connections. Trustworthy profiles are more likely to attract individuals seeking genuine relationships rather than superficial interactions.

2. Beyond Superficial Attributes

- **Depth of Connection**: Profiles that emphasize authenticity facilitate connections based on deeper compatibility. Instead of focusing solely on physical appearance or superficial interests, authentic self-presentation invites conversations about shared values, life goals, and personal philosophies. This depth enhances the quality of interactions and increases the likelihood of forming lasting relationships.

- **Long-Term Compatibility**: Authenticity helps users filter potential matches based on compatibility beyond initial attraction. By showcasing genuine interests and values, individuals align with partners who share similar life perspectives and relationship expectations. This alignment lays the groundwork for sustainable and fulfilling relationships.

3. Strategies for Authentic Self-Presentation

- **Honest Profile Descriptions**: Users should accurately describe themselves in profile bios, highlighting passions, hobbies, and personal anecdotes that illustrate their identity. Avoiding exaggerations or misleading information ensures that profiles reflect true personalities.

- **Genuine Photos**: Authenticity extends to profile photos that accurately represent individuals. Choosing recent and candid photos, rather than overly edited or staged images, provides potential matches with a realistic portrayal of appearance and lifestyle.

- **Open Communication**: Encouraging open communication in initial conversations promotes authenticity. Honest discussions about values, interests, and life experiences allow individuals to gauge compatibility and build rapport based on shared authenticity.

4. Benefits of Authentic Self-Presentation

- **Enhanced Connection Quality**: Genuine self-presentation fosters deeper connections and emotional intimacy between individuals. When both parties present themselves authentically, conversations flow more naturally, and mutual understanding deepens.

- **Reduced Disappointment**: Authentic profiles reduce the likelihood of disappointment or mismatched expectations when meeting offline. By accurately representing themselves, users establish realistic expectations and increase the likelihood of positive dating experiences.

• **Personal Growth**: Embracing authenticity in online dating encourages self-discovery and personal growth. Users who confidently express their true selves in profiles and interactions cultivate self-awareness and attract partners who appreciate their genuine qualities.

Conclusion

Authentic self-presentation in online dating promotes meaningful connections by showcasing genuine interests, values, and personalities. By emphasizing honesty and transparency in profiles, individuals attract like-minded partners and establish relationships based on compatibility beyond superficial attributes. As dating platforms continue to evolve, prioritizing authenticity enhances the quality of interactions and contributes to fulfilling and lasting relationships in the digital age.

Quality Over Quantity in Online Dating

In the realm of online dating, prioritizing quality over quantity shifts the focus from accumulating a large number of matches to fostering meaningful connections and interactions. Here's a detailed exploration of this approach:

Understanding Quality Over Quantity

1. Investing in Meaningful Interactions

- **Depth of Connection**: Emphasizing quality encourages users to engage in conversations that delve beyond surface-level details. Instead of superficial interactions based on brief profiles or initial attraction, users are encouraged to invest time in meaningful conversations that explore shared interests, values, and life goals. This depth fosters emotional intimacy and establishes a stronger foundation for relationships.

- **Mutual Respect and Understanding**: Platforms promoting quality interactions prioritize mutual respect and understanding between users. Encouraging respectful communication and active listening allows individuals to appreciate each other's perspectives and experiences. This approach cultivates empathy and strengthens the bond between potential matches.

2. Incentivizing Substantive Conversations

- **Features and Algorithms**: Dating platforms can incorporate features and algorithms that incentivize substantive conversations. For example, algorithms can prioritize profiles that engage in longer conversations or exchange messages on diverse topics. This approach encourages users to invest effort in getting to know each other authentically, rather than focusing solely on quick judgments based on limited information.

- **Promoting Engagement**: Incentives such as badges or rewards for meaningful interactions can motivate users to prioritize quality over quantity. Recognizing users who initiate thoughtful conversations or receive positive feedback for respectful communication reinforces the value of substantive engagement within the community.

3. Strategies for Promoting Genuine Connections

- **Profile Emphasis**: Encouraging users to showcase their personalities, interests, and values authentically in profiles promotes genuine connections. Platforms can provide prompts or guidelines that prompt users to share meaningful aspects of themselves, rather than emphasizing attractiveness or popularity.

- **Communication Guidelines**: Establishing guidelines or tips for effective communication can guide users in fostering genuine connections. Suggestions for asking open-ended questions, actively listening, and sharing personal experiences facilitate meaningful exchanges and build rapport between matches.

4. Benefits of Quality Over Quantity

- **Long-Term Compatibility**: Prioritizing quality interactions increases the likelihood of finding compatible matches with shared values and relationship goals. Investing time in getting to know each other deeply allows individuals to assess compatibility beyond initial attraction, leading to more fulfilling and lasting relationships.

- **Enhanced User Satisfaction**: Users who prioritize quality over quantity report higher satisfaction with their dating experiences. Meaningful connections built on mutual respect and understanding contribute to positive emotional experiences and reduce feelings of frustration or disappointment.

- **Community Culture**: Platforms that foster a culture of quality interactions create a supportive and respectful community. Users feel valued for their personalities and contributions, which enhances overall user retention and satisfaction.

Conclusion

Prioritizing quality over quantity in online dating encourages users to invest in meaningful interactions that prioritize mutual respect, understanding, and emotional intimacy. By incentivizing substantive conversations and promoting genuine connections, dating platforms can enhance user satisfaction and facilitate the formation of fulfilling relationships. This approach not only benefits individuals seeking meaningful connections but also contributes to a positive and supportive online dating community.

Communication Skills in Online Dating

Effective communication skills are essential in online dating for fostering genuine connections and building trust. Here's a detailed exploration of how platforms can provide resources to enhance users' communication skills:

Importance of Communication Skills

1. Building Trust and Connection

- **Authentic Interactions**: Effective communication involves expressing oneself authentically while also actively listening to and understanding others. Platforms can educate users on the importance of authenticity in their profiles and interactions, encouraging genuine connections based on shared values and interests.

- **Establishing Trust**: Clear and respectful communication helps users establish trust with potential matches. Providing resources on active listening, empathy, and non-verbal cues can guide users in interpreting and responding to messages in a way that fosters mutual understanding and rapport.

2. Navigating Online Interactions

- **Digital Communication Tips**: Platforms can offer guidelines on effective digital communication, including tone, language choice, and response times. Tips on asking open-ended questions, sharing personal experiences, and validating others' perspectives can facilitate meaningful exchanges.

- **Managing Expectations**: Resources on managing expectations in online dating, such as understanding different communication styles and setting boundaries, help users navigate potential misunderstandings or conflicts constructively.

3. Empathy and Understanding

- **Educational Content**: Providing articles, videos, or workshops on empathy and understanding in online interactions can enhance users' ability to connect on a deeper emotional level. Learning to recognize and validate others' feelings and experiences contributes to building meaningful relationships.

- **Cultural Sensitivity**: Platforms can offer insights into cultural differences in communication styles and norms, promoting respect and inclusivity among users from diverse backgrounds.

4. Conflict Resolution

- **Handling Disagreements**: Resources on conflict resolution techniques, such as active listening, expressing feelings constructively, and seeking compromise, help users navigate disagreements or misunderstandings that may arise during online interactions.

- **Moderation and Support**: Platforms can provide moderation and support services to address inappropriate behavior or disputes promptly, maintaining a safe and respectful environment conducive to positive communication.

Benefits of Strong Communication Skills

- **Enhanced Connection**: Users with strong communication skills are better equipped to establish meaningful connections based on mutual respect and understanding. Effective communication fosters emotional intimacy and builds a foundation for trust and long-term compatibility.

- **Reduced Misunderstandings**: Clear and empathetic communication reduces the likelihood of misunderstandings or misinterpretations, leading to more satisfying interactions and relationships.

- **Positive User Experience**: Platforms that prioritize communication skills contribute to a positive user experience by promoting authentic connections and fostering a supportive community environment.

Conclusion

Providing resources on effective communication skills in online dating enhances users' ability to navigate interactions with authenticity, empathy, and respect. By promoting clear communication, active listening, and understanding, dating platforms can facilitate meaningful connections that lead to fulfilling relationships. Investing in communication education not only benefits individual users but also contributes to a culture of trust, respect, and inclusivity within the online dating community.

Long-Term Compatibility in Online Dating

Achieving long-term compatibility in online dating involves integrating comprehensive assessments and strategies that prioritize meaningful connections. Here's a detailed exploration of how platforms can enhance users' experiences towards forming lasting relationships:

Understanding Long-Term Compatibility

1. Factors Considered

- **Shared Values and Beliefs**: Compatibility assessments should delve into users' core values, beliefs, and life goals. Platforms can utilize questionnaires or algorithms that explore topics such as family values, spirituality, and personal ambitions to match individuals with aligned perspectives.

- **Communication Styles**: Assessing how individuals communicate, including preferences for openness, conflict resolution, and emotional expression, helps in pairing users who are likely to engage in constructive and effective communication over time.

- **Lifestyle Preferences**: Compatibility extends to lifestyle choices such as leisure activities, career aspirations, and living arrangements. Platforms can integrate preferences for lifestyle compatibility to support users in finding partners who share similar preferences and routines.

2. Facilitating Lasting Relationships

- **In-Depth Profiles**: Encouraging users to create detailed profiles that highlight their values, interests, and relationship expectations enables platforms to match individuals based on comprehensive criteria beyond superficial attributes.

- **Compatibility Algorithms**: Advanced algorithms can analyze user data to suggest matches that align with identified compatibility factors. Machine learning and AI technologies can refine recommendations based on user feedback and relationship outcomes, improving the accuracy of match suggestions over time.

- **Psychological Insights**: Platforms can provide educational content on relationship psychology, helping users understand the dynamics of long-term relationships, effective communication strategies, and conflict resolution techniques.

3. Supporting Relationship Aspirations

- **Tailored Matching**: Offering options for users to specify their relationship goals, such as seeking marriage, companionship, or casual dating, ensures that matches are aligned with their desired outcomes. Customizable preferences enhance user satisfaction by connecting them with partners who share similar relationship aspirations.

- **Feedback Mechanisms**: Implementing feedback loops where users can provide insights into their dating experiences and match quality enables platforms to continuously refine their matching algorithms and improve compatibility assessments.

Benefits of Long-Term Compatibility

- **Increased Relationship Satisfaction**: Users who find partners through platforms that prioritize long-term compatibility are more likely to experience relationship satisfaction and fulfillment. Shared values and life goals contribute to mutual understanding and support within relationships.

- **Reduced Relationship Dissolution**: Matching users based on compatibility factors reduces the likelihood of mismatches and relationship breakdowns. Platforms that facilitate genuine connections aligned with long-term compatibility foster relationships that are resilient to challenges and changes over time.

• **Enhanced User Retention**: Positive experiences with forming lasting relationships encourage user loyalty and retention. Platforms that successfully support users in finding compatible partners enhance their reputation and attract a loyal user base.

Conclusion

Integrating compatibility assessments focused on shared values, communication styles, and lifestyle preferences is crucial for facilitating long-term relationships in online dating. By prioritizing meaningful connections and supporting users' relationship aspirations, platforms contribute to fostering relationships that are grounded in mutual understanding, respect, and compatibility. Investing in comprehensive matching algorithms, user education, and feedback mechanisms enhances the overall user experience and promotes sustainable relationship outcomes in the digital dating landscape.

Mindful Use of Technology in Online Dating

In the fast-paced world of online dating, promoting mindful technology use is crucial for maintaining well-being and fostering positive experiences. Here's a detailed exploration of how individuals can practice mindfulness while engaging with dating apps:

Understanding Mindful Technology Use

1. Balancing Online and Offline Interactions

- **Setting Boundaries**: Establishing clear boundaries around app usage helps users maintain a healthy balance between online interactions and offline activities. This may include limiting daily screen time, designating specific times for app usage, or taking periodic breaks to focus on other aspects of life.
- **Prioritizing Self-Care**: Encouraging users to prioritize self-care and well-being involves recognizing when app usage starts to impact mental or emotional health negatively. Mindful technology use includes being aware of triggers such as anxiety from rejection or stress from constant engagement.

2. Enhancing Overall Well-Being

- **Engaging in Offline Activities**: Mindful use encourages individuals to participate in offline activities that promote mental and physical well-being, such as hobbies, exercise, or spending time with friends and family. This balance reduces dependency on digital interactions for validation and social connection.
- **Self-Reflection and Awareness**: Practicing mindfulness involves self-reflection on how app usage affects mood, self-esteem, and interpersonal relationships. Awareness of emotional responses to online interactions helps users make informed decisions about their dating experiences.

Strategies for Mindful Technology Use

1. Establishing Healthy Habits

- **Scheduled Breaks**: Taking regular breaks from dating apps allows users to recharge and maintain perspective. These breaks can prevent burnout and reduce feelings of overwhelm associated with constant engagement.
- **Offline Engagement**: Actively participating in offline social activities fosters genuine connections and reduces reliance on digital interactions for social validation. It promotes a balanced lifestyle that supports overall well-being.

2. Setting Boundaries

- **Screen Time Limits**: Setting limits on daily or weekly screen time helps prevent excessive use of dating apps and encourages users to allocate time for other personal interests and responsibilities.
- **Tech-Free Zones**: Designating specific areas or times as tech-free zones promotes mindfulness by encouraging focused attention on present activities and interactions without digital distractions.

Benefits of Mindful Technology Use

- **Improved Mental Health**: Mindful use of dating apps reduces stress, anxiety, and feelings of loneliness associated with online interactions. Users who practice mindfulness report greater emotional resilience and overall well-being.
- **Enhanced Relationship Satisfaction**: Balancing online dating with offline activities allows individuals to approach relationships with a healthier mindset. Mindful users are more likely to engage authentically and build meaningful connections based on shared values and interests.

● **Long-Term Well-Being**: By prioritizing self-care and setting boundaries, individuals foster habits that support long-term emotional and psychological health. Mindful technology use contributes to a balanced lifestyle that enhances overall satisfaction and fulfillment.

Conclusion

Promoting mindful technology use in online dating encourages users to approach app interactions with awareness, intentionality, and self-care. By setting boundaries, engaging in offline activities, and reflecting on emotional responses, individuals can cultivate a positive and balanced relationship with digital dating platforms. Mindful practices enhance well-being, support meaningful connections, and contribute to a fulfilling dating experience in the digital age.

Community Engagement in Dating Platforms

Building a supportive community within dating platforms is pivotal for enhancing user experience and fostering long-term engagement. Here's an in-depth exploration of how community engagement can enrich the dating app experience:

Understanding Community Engagement

1. Creating a Supportive Environment

- **Forums and Discussion Groups**: Dating platforms can integrate forums or discussion groups where users can share experiences, seek advice, and discuss relevant topics such as dating tips, relationship advice, or personal growth. These spaces provide a supportive environment for users to connect on shared interests and challenges.

- **Support Groups**: Specialized support groups within dating apps cater to specific demographics or relationship preferences, such as single parents, LGBTQ+ communities, or individuals navigating long-distance relationships. These groups offer a safe space for users to seek support, share resources, and build relationships based on shared experiences.

2. Collaborative Activities

- **Virtual Events and Meet-ups**: Hosting virtual events, meet-ups, or workshops within the app encourages real-time interactions and community building. These activities can include themed parties, speed dating sessions, or skill-building workshops related to dating and relationships.

- **Group Challenges or Activities**: Introducing collaborative activities or challenges promotes engagement and fosters a sense of belonging among users. For example, users could participate in relationship-building challenges, cultural exchanges, or community-driven projects that encourage meaningful interactions.

Benefits of Community Engagement

1. Enhanced User Retention

- **Emotional Connection**: Community engagement fosters emotional connections among users by providing opportunities for empathy, shared experiences, and mutual support. Users who feel connected to a community are more likely to remain active and invested in the platform over time.

- **Sense of Belonging**: Building a community within the dating app creates a sense of belonging and inclusivity. Users feel valued and understood within their community, which strengthens their attachment to the platform and encourages ongoing participation.

2. Support and Resources

- **Peer Support**: Forums and support groups offer peer support where users can receive advice, share stories, and offer encouragement to one another. This support network is particularly beneficial during challenging dating experiences or personal growth journeys.

- **Access to Information**: Community engagement provides access to valuable information, resources, and expert advice related to dating, relationships, and personal development. Users can learn from others' experiences and gain insights that enhance their own dating strategies and interpersonal skills.

Strategies for Building Community Engagement

1. Facilitate Meaningful Interactions

- **Moderated Discussions**: Ensuring discussions are moderated to maintain a respectful and supportive environment encourages constructive dialogue and discourages negative interactions.
- **Encourage Participation**: Promoting active participation through prompts, discussion topics, or user-generated content encourages users to contribute to community engagement initiatives.

2. Promote Diversity and Inclusivity

- **Diverse Representation**: Ensure community groups and activities represent diverse demographics, interests, and relationship preferences. Celebrating diversity fosters inclusivity and enriches the collective experience of users.
- **Cultural Sensitivity**: Respect cultural differences and sensitivities within the community to create a welcoming environment where all users feel valued and respected.

Conclusion

Community engagement plays a pivotal role in enhancing user retention, fostering emotional connections, and providing valuable support within dating platforms. By building a supportive community through forums, support groups, collaborative activities, and inclusive initiatives, dating apps can create a more fulfilling and meaningful experience for users. Community-driven interactions not only strengthen user engagement but also contribute to a positive and supportive ecosystem where individuals can navigate dating and relationships with confidence and support.

Conclusion

As we conclude this exploration of how dating apps are reshaping the landscape of modern relationships, it's clear that these platforms have both revolutionized and complicated the way we find and connect with partners. While they offer unprecedented convenience and access to potential matches, they also introduce new challenges and dynamics that can undermine the depth and authenticity of our connections.

Throughout this book, we've delved into the multifaceted impact of dating apps on our lives. We've examined the psychological toll of constant swiping, the societal shifts in how we perceive relationships, and the ethical considerations surrounding data privacy and algorithmic biases. We've also explored the benefits and pitfalls of traditional and modern alternatives to digital dating, offering a balanced perspective on how to navigate the complexities of finding love in the digital age.

Key Takeaways

1. **Awareness and Mindfulness:** It's crucial to approach dating apps with a heightened sense of awareness and mindfulness. Understanding the potential psychological impacts and being conscious of how these platforms shape our behaviors and expectations can help mitigate negative effects.
2. **Balancing Digital and Real-life Interactions:** While dating apps provide a valuable tool for meeting new people, they should complement, not replace, real-life interactions. Engaging in offline activities, social clubs, and traditional dating methods can provide richer, more holistic experiences.
3. **Prioritizing Quality Over Quantity:** In a culture that often values the number of matches over the quality of connections, it's essential to focus on building meaningful relationships. Prioritizing compatibility, shared values, and genuine interactions can lead to more fulfilling partnerships.
4. **Ethical Responsibility:** As users, we must be aware of the ethical implications of dating app usage. Advocating for transparency, data privacy, and responsible algorithmic practices can help create a safer and more equitable digital dating environment.
5. **Embracing Change:** The dating landscape will continue to evolve with technological advancements. Embracing change with a critical yet open mindset allows us to adapt and find innovative ways to connect meaningfully in an increasingly digital world.

Final Thoughts

The journey through the world of dating apps is one of complexity and contradiction. They offer both connection and isolation, opportunity and challenge. By navigating this landscape with informed caution, a willingness to adapt, and a commitment to authenticity, we can harness the benefits of technology while safeguarding the essence of genuine human connection.

As we move forward, it's essential to remember that the ultimate goal of dating—whether through apps or traditional means—is to build meaningful, lasting relationships. By integrating the insights and strategies discussed in this book, we can better navigate the digital dating world and foster connections that enrich our lives.

In the end, while dating apps have transformed the way we meet and interact, the core principles of love and connection remain timeless. Embracing these principles in our modern context will help us find not just partners, but true companions who share our journey through life.

Acknowledgments

I am deeply grateful to everyone who has supported me in the creation and publication of this book.

To my family, whose unwavering encouragement and belief in my work have been a constant source of inspiration, thank you for standing by me every step of the way.

I extend my heartfelt appreciation to my friends and colleagues who provided valuable insights, feedback, and moral support throughout the writing process. Your contributions have enriched this book beyond measure.

I am indebted to the experts and professionals who generously shared their knowledge and expertise, contributing to the depth and accuracy of the content presented in these pages.

Special thanks to kevin, whose guidance and encouragement have been instrumental in shaping the ideas and structure of this book.

I would also like to express my gratitude to the individuals who assisted with editing, formatting, and designing the book, ensuring its professional presentation.

Lastly, I dedicate this book to my readers. Your interest in exploring and understanding the complexities of relationships motivates me to continue sharing insights and knowledge.

Thank you all for being a part of this incredible journey of self-publishing.

Appendix: Additional Resources

Books on Modern Dating and Relationships

1. "Modern Romance" by Aziz Ansari and Eric Klinenberg

○ A humorous and insightful look at how dating has changed in the digital age, combining personal anecdotes with sociological research.

2. "The Paradox of Choice: Why More Is Less" by Barry Schwartz

○ This book explores how having too many choices can lead to decision paralysis and dissatisfaction, a concept highly relevant to dating app users.

3. "Attached: The New Science of Adult Attachment and How It Can Help You Find - and Keep - Love" by Amir Levine and Rachel Heller

○ A guide to understanding attachment styles and how they influence relationship dynamics.

Online Articles and Blogs

1. Psychology Today

○ Numerous articles on dating, relationships, and the psychological impacts of using dating apps.

○ Psychology Today - Relationships

2. The Atlantic - "The Pitfalls of Dating Apps"

○ An in-depth analysis of how dating apps impact human connection and relationship formation.

○ The Atlantic - Dating

3. Pew Research Center - "Online Dating in America"

○ Research reports and statistics on the trends and demographics of online dating in the United States.

○ Pew Research Center - Online Dating

Websites and Forums

1. Reddit - r/dating_advice

○ A community where users share experiences and advice about dating and relationships.

○ Reddit - Dating Advice[1]

2. Meetup.com

○ A platform for finding and joining local groups centered around various interests, including singles events and social gatherings.

○ Meetup[2]

3. PsychCentral - Relationships

○ Articles, tips, and advice on maintaining healthy relationships and navigating the dating scene.

○ PsychCentral - Relationships

Support and Counseling

1. American Association for Marriage and Family Therapy (AAMFT)

○ Resources and directories for finding professional relationship counselors.

○ AAMFT[3]

2. BetterHelp

○ An online platform for accessing licensed therapists and counselors who can provide guidance on relationship issues.

○ BetterHelp[4]

3. Relate

○ A UK-based organization offering relationship support, including counseling and workshops.

○ Relate[5]

Apps and Tools for Mindful Dating

1. Hinge

○ Designed to be deleted, Hinge focuses on fostering meaningful connections and serious relationships.

○ Hinge[6]

---

1. https://www.reddit.com/r/dating_advice/

2. https://www.meetup.com/

3. https://www.aamft.org/

4. https://wwww.betterhelp.com/

5. https://www.relate.org.uk/

6. https://hinge.co/

2. MeetMindful

    ○ A dating app for those interested in mindful living and deeper connections.

    ○ MeetMindful[7]

3. Couple

    ○ An app for couples to strengthen their relationship through shared activities and communication tools.

    ○ Couple[8]

Podcasts and Videos

1. "Where Should We Begin?" with Esther Perel

    ○ A podcast offering a unique glimpse into couples' therapy sessions with renowned therapist Esther Perel.

    ○ Esther Perel - Podcast

2. TED Talks on Relationships

    ○ A collection of TED Talks that explore various aspects of relationships, love, and human connection.

    ○ TED Talks - Relationships

3. "Modern Love" Podcast

    ○ Stories of love, loss, and redemption, based on the popular New York Times column.

    ○ Modern Love - Podcast[9]

Conclusion

This appendix provides a starting point for further exploration into the themes discussed in this book. By utilizing these resources, readers can gain deeper insights and practical advice for navigating the complexities of modern dating and relationships.

---

7. https://www.meetmindful.com/

8. https://couple.me/

9. https://www.nytimes.com/column/modern-love-podcast